PARTY TIME

PARTY TIME

TIME

WHO RUNS CHINA AND HOW

ROWAN CALLICK

Black Inc.

Published by Black Inc.
an imprint of Schwartz Media Pty Ltd
37–39 Langridge Street
Collingwood VIC 3066 Australia
email: enquiries@blackincbooks.com
http://www.blackincbooks.com

National Library of Australia Cataloguing-in-Publication entry

Callick, Rowan.

Party time : who runs China and how / Rowan Callick.

9781863955911 (pbk.)

Includes bibliographical references and index.

Communist parties--China.
China--Politics and government.

320.951

Index by Geraldine Suter
Book design by Peter Long
Typeset by Duncan Blachford and Peter Long

Printed in Australia by Griffin Press an Accredited ISO AS/ NZS 14001:2004 Environmental Management System printer.

CONTENTS

This book is dedicated to Jan, Rose, Christian and Paul, and to Enlang.

INTRODUCTION

A **METICULOUSLY CHOREOGRAPHED BUSINESS BANQUET –** tensions simmering beneath the countless courteous toasts – was under way in a private room off the marble-clad main dining room at the grand Beijing Hotel. The hotel, immediately to the east of Tiananmen Square, was built in 1900 as China stood on the verge of a century of wars and tyranny. It is magnificently located but has seen better times. Businesspeople prefer to stay in the city's myriad 21st-century hotels. They don't need to be near the tourist sites or the grand buildings of state.

After the usual exchange of name-cards, the head of the small foreign business delegation naturally paid especially close attention to the executive chairman of the state-owned corporation with which he hoped to clinch a deal – communicating through an interpreter employed by the Chinese hosts – and to the English-speaking general manager.

The foreign business leader did not pay any attention to another figure at the table, a quiet and earnest-looking man in his early forties – the only person who neither wore a tie nor offered a name-card, and who appeared somewhat distracted.

Half way through the banquet, which had become increasingly relaxed and rambunctious as the toasts showed no sign of slowing, this puzzling outsider suddenly spoke. In refined, Oxbridge-accented English, he intervened to make a robust point. The other Chinese fell silent, waiting for him to finish. The foreign chief executive realised he had lost the first round.

The new speaker, it dawned on him, was the person who would make any meaningful decision about the deal on the table. It would take considerable diplomatic acumen to recover from this initial faux pas, which was born of a presumption that anyone without a name-card must have no real standing, and almost certainly spoke no English.

The mystery man was a representative of the ruling Chinese Communist Party (CCP). It was he who would make the call whether to pursue the proposed foreign connection. They were eating at the Beijing Hotel in part because it is state-owned, and in part because party members sometimes like to put foreign concepts of fashionability in their place. Party officials will go some way towards the Western way of doing business, but never all the way. No senior leader, for instance, will ever be seen playing golf. Anywhere. Even miniature golf.

Many foreigners, including businesspeople, misread China. This is not a new phenomenon. Others have misread the country in the past, for instance during the Cultural Revolution when visitors were ushered through Chinese versions of "Potemkin villages" – those Soviet-era model communities constructed specially to impress foreign visitors. They returned to their countries singing the praises of the new, altruistic society that Mao Zedong had built, with its barefoot doctors and warm-hearted, open-minded intellectuals learning from peasants. They failed to see, or to uncover, the truth about what was to become China's lost decade, disfigured by anarchy and cruelty and costing untold numbers of lives every week.

Today's most common misreading is to praise China's economic development while claiming such material success as a victory for capitalism or for Western technology. Sometimes, it's true, the role of the party is subtly concealed, as at the business banquet. But even when it is emblazoned in public, many outsiders don't want to believe what they are seeing. Entering the Forbidden City from Tiananmen Square, visitors may gaze up at the massive portrait of Mao that hangs over the outer gate, but discount it as a quaint nod to a communist past, as though Mao were an emperor from a long-ago dynasty. What, they wonder, can that era of bicycles and safari suits have to do with the futuristic skyline of 21st-century Beijing?

But perceptions can of course be misleading. They can even be designed to that effect. *Trompe l'oeil* was not unique to the French gardeners who devised the term. Virtually every Chinese garden features the clever device called *zhang jing* – "blocked view" or "screened scenery" – by which, even in a comparatively confined space, the stroller keeps encountering fresh, formerly hidden vistas. A visitor to Shanghai's famous 450-year-old Yu Yuan Garden, for instance, following the mazy paths between countless goldfish ponds, peony beds and airy pavilions, readily believes that it is far bigger than its modest five acres.

So it goes with China's biggest landscape, its national story. You catch a glimpse – perhaps beguiling, perhaps rocky and to the Western eye alienating – of where China seems to be heading, and then the outlook swiftly changes, you lose focus, a fresh view emerges, and truths either suddenly appear or are cunningly concealed.

No wonder many fail to take today's China at face value. They prefer to disregard the obvious because it does not conform with their belief that modernity automatically displaces communism, as a rock thrown into a pool displaces water.

In fact, if your eyes are open, almost everywhere you look in the 21st-century Chinese landscape – sometimes subtly concealed, sometimes in-your-face – the ruling party plays a dominant role. China's communist leaders are seen – and see themselves – as a chosen people entrusted with authority, through the means of a chosen state, to rule over a chosen civilisation that is entering a golden age of prosperity, known in China as a *shengshi*.

As China's own fortunes have soared, so have those of the Communist Party – which has now become the most powerful organisation in the world, even overtaking the Vatican, whose authority, focused by Pope John Paul II, helped destroy the Soviet Empire in the 1980s.

Yet the CCP's *modus operandi*, the way it runs the world's most populous country and increasingly drives the world economy, remains extraordinarily little understood, even by people who visit China frequently. This suits the party's leaders, who are no longer larger than life, charismatic figures like Mao or Deng Xiaoping, but committee-men who seek consensus and weed out those who are awkward or contrary. Hu Jintao, China's top leader for a decade until the end of 2012, remained an enigmatic figure about whom little is known even today. Not much more is known about his successor, Xi Jinping, despite his more open face and more ready grin; his wife, the singer and TV variety star Peng Liyuan, is considerably more famous in China than he is.

The Chinese Communist Party retains little of the dubious glamour of an evil empire, that macabre glamour that still lures collectors to hoard Cultural Revolution memorabilia. Instead, it rules today in a manner that is routine, impersonal, even somewhat boring to some of its own members, as we shall see – but also relentless and unapologetic.

★

In this book, we shall take a walk through this intriguing political landscape, meeting brave and articulate people – including members of the party and its critics – who explain how China works today, and how the party runs China.

We shall see how the party both moulds and responds to the extraordinary transitions that China is undergoing, and how new leaders – and a new leadership style – are emerging to guide this epoch of change. It is an organisation that has become brilliantly adaptive. It is no longer the party of revolution, but of sound management and stability, the party of the middle class and of the ruling families, the party – it likes to think – of China.

This era of change in China recalls the experience of the United States in the 1940s and 1950s, when millions began to live the American Dream, and when American know-how appeared to be conquering all barriers, including space. Like middle-class Americans in those post-war years, more and more Chinese people are planning ambitious material and educational achievements for their families with real hope of success.

The preamble to the constitution of the People's Republic of China starts boldly, trumpeting its "culture of grandeur." Today, people in China compare their 21st-century golden age with famous historical periods of Chinese pride – with the Tang Dynasty in the seventh and eighth centuries, when the Silk Road and the Grand Canal seemed to carry the whole world into its heartland, and with the High Qing in the seventeenth and eighteenth centuries, when China's borders reached their broadest bounds and great imperial cultural ambitions were realised.

What a glorious time to be a Chinese citizen – and even better, a member of the party that has ruled the country for longer than any other group has held power anywhere else in the world. People in China enjoy greater personal freedom than at any time in the country's history, except perhaps during the early decades of the Republic last century. They can travel almost anywhere, choose their workplace, marry anyone, and buy whatever they can afford, including property.

Living in Beijing is like living in ancient Rome, or in London at the height of the British Empire. You feel that you are at the centre of things, that the world is coming to you, that the future is now. You are living in the present tense. The shopping malls are bigger and more glittering, the subway (hugely extended for the Olympics) larger and cleaner, the vast modernist apartment complexes more avant-garde, the nightclubs glitzier, the food more sumptuous, the art zanier than you can find anywhere else. Architects from the old European centres – French, British, Dutch, German – are flocking here to help construct the new Beijing, creating dramatic buildings they could only dream of back home.

Among them is Albert Speer Junior, the son of Adolf Hitler's favourite architect. Speer Senior was a leading creator of the settings for the 1936 Olympics, which did so much to announce Germany's arrival as a power – and as a threat. His son has done substantial work in China. His design for the new Public Security Ministry projects a suitably monumental image, just to the east of Tiananmen Square, opposite the Beijing Hotel. He was commissioned to create a master plan for the whole Olympic zone to the north of the city, connecting it to the heart of the capital. He devised a broad, green boulevard along the ancient north–south axis of Beijing. He claimed that his plan was "bigger, much bigger" than what his father had in mind for Berlin.

Chinese people prefer not to consider such comparisons with the faded empires of Europe. Since their civilisation – the world's oldest – began, they have sensed that they are themselves a very special group. During modern times they have used the Chinese characters *Zhongguo* – "central kingdom" – to describe their country. A recent series of books focusing on China's uniqueness and centrality included a volume entitled *China Has No Role Models*. Influential ideological commentators denigrate the notion of "universal values" such as human rights, freedom and democracy, dismissing them as peculiarly Western. The core objective of Chinese modernity, they argue, should instead be to enhance the prosperity and capacity of the state.

If the Chinese are the chosen people, their leaders are similarly select. The ancient Chinese concept of the "mandate of heaven," which emerged during the Zhou Dynasty (1100 to 221 BC), has to a degree been inherited by the Communist Party. This mandate entitles those in power to maintain their authority as long as they rule justly – and provided they do not lose the trust of their subjects or of the supreme being. A succession of natural and man-made disasters has often been viewed as a sure sign that the mandate has been lost. (Mao Zedong died just a few weeks after a terrible earthquake in Tangshan, east of Beijing, cost more than 250,000 lives.)

The Beijing Olympics showed the world that the mandate of heaven surely now rested again on the party and its leaders. It amply demonstrated the strengths of the new China: its engineering skills, its organisational prowess, its single-mindedness, its capacity to train a corps of athletes to leap to the top of the global table.

Visitors to China routinely compare the stunning new structures built for the Games – the soaring iron and steel air terminals, the teeming freeways and super-clean subways, the visionary opera houses and TV studios – with the decaying public infrastructure of much of the "old world" of Europe and the USA. Their sense of awe – and, often, surprise – has mirrored that felt in earlier centuries by ambassadors, trade envoys and provincial officials who arrived inside the "Great Within" of Beijing's imperial centre, the Forbidden City. And in the aftermath of its bold Olympic step onto the world stage, China has kept powering, economically, through the global financial crisis, spending freely to maintain a growth rate at or near double digits.

The facts and figures that describe China's soaring economic fortunes are the pride and joy of the party, constantly paraded as the crucial legitimation of its continuing rule, and of China's claims to greater global authority.

China's population is one and a half times that of Europe including Russia and Turkey, and four times that of the USA. Its land area is about the same as Europe excluding Russia. As its economy catches up, it is natural that its overall influence is also building. This transformation began in 1978 with Deng Xiaoping's opening of the manufacturing sector to foreign investors. Factory owners shut up shop in Taiwan and Hong Kong and re-opened in China, building dormitories alongside their plants to accommodate the millions of workers who flooded from the countryside, where they had been underemployed. By the start of the twenty-first century, a large proportion of goods bought in any country in the world already carried the stamp *Made in China* and were priced unthinkably cheaply. No wonder *Time* magazine named "the Chinese worker" its runner-up person of the year in 2009.

Since China's "opening and reform" era began, hundreds of millions of people have been lifted from poverty. China's own official statistics claim that the poverty rate fell from 53 per cent in 1981 to 2.5 per cent in 2005 – although in 2009, 150 million people were still trying to survive on less than US$1.25 a day. Between 1978 and 2011, China's gross domestic product per person soared from US$378 to US$5184.

In the early days of this modernising era, the "new three" household goods that families coveted were televisions, refrigerators and washing machines. By 2011, almost every household had at least one of each. For every hundred households in the countryside there were, by 2011, eighty-nine colour televisions, twenty-two refrigerators and sixty-two mobile phones. For every hundred households in the cities there were 137 colour televisions, ninety-two refrigerators and 153 mobile phones. Half of the urban households and 15 per cent of rural households had a computer with internet access, and 15 per cent of all households had one or more cars. No wonder many in China feel that they have "never had it so good," to borrow the words of Harold Macmillan, the British Tory leader of the 1950s and '60s.

In recent decades, Westerners have tended to view such progress as entailing an inexorable shift towards liberal democracy. But in China's case, no. Although it is shape-shifting to meet its own local challenges, it is not taking any steps towards becoming a liberal democracy that might be recognisable as such in the West. The party is driven to adapt, but it is driven as much by fear as by vision or even opportunism. The party is more in command of institutions and events than ever but it is less certain, in the Internet Age, of what is going on in people's minds.

Even apparent opportunities to celebrate are viewed instead as times of heightened danger. During the Olympics, Beijing became something of a ghost town, its streets deserted. People were warned to stay indoors and view the events on TV – for safety's sake. The following year, when the party celebrated the sixtieth birthday of the People's Republic, the Chinese people were not invited. It was, instead, just the party's party. A massive military parade marched down the great east–west boulevard leading into Tiananmen Square, but residents with views of the spectacle were warned not to look out of their windows, nor to venture onto their balconies, lest they wind up in the sights of an army sniper. They were issued with special new identification documents and prohibited from having visitors during the celebrations – so no private parties, either. After sixty years, most people in China do not need telling twice to take such advice. On the great day, 1 October, only specially invited guests were allowed in the vicinity of Tiananmen Square.

Why such anxiety, such focus on control? Surely a strong single-party state, hugely successful by many of its own measures, the author of a glittering new age of prosperity, does not fear its own people?

Enter the dragon. In Chinese legend, this creature is the great imperial symbol and the bringer of prosperity. It is the harbinger of rain, which brings abundant harvests – but also arouses storms in its wake. The sound of distant thunder can be heard behind China's frequent national celebrations. Anxiety lurks in the minds of ordinary folk: what if we lose our jobs, or someone in the family becomes seriously ill, or inflation eats up our savings? And the rich and the ruling class also worry: where does our legitimacy come from in the absence of elections? What if our privileged access to wealth is proven corrupt?

China's top leaders hear that distant thunder. They remain unconvinced about their capacity to retain the unmixed admiration of their own citizens. And they fret about perceptions of the party's legitimacy, for all its recent economic glories. They will have noted – smugly, perhaps, but also nervously – the ignominious electoral downfall in 2009 of the Liberal Democratic Party in Japan after fifty-five years in power. And they may have wondered whether there might also be a lesson or two in the 2012 presidential and parliamentary victories in Taiwan of the Kuomintang, the party from which the CCP itself emerged in the 1920s. Having begun to embrace democracy in the late 1980s, the Kuomintang has received wide international praise as well as unquestionable legitimacy (through elections) from the citizens of Taiwan.

At home, the party takes care to associate itself with success of all kinds. This means, however, that it risks being implicated when things turns ugly. If it is all-powerful, then it must be responsible for what goes wrong as well as what goes right. And the internet has made it extremely difficult for the party to cover things up as once it could, despite its tens of thousands of "net police."

This change was underlined by a lurid melodrama that went viral in April 2012, first inside China and then around the world. Bo Xilai – a charismatic party leader on the verge of becoming one of the nine most powerful people in China – was stripped of all his party posts while his ultra-ambitious wife, characterised as a Chinese Lady Macbeth, was convicted of murdering an upper-class English businessman, Neil Heywood. This communist glamour-couple have a socialite son, educated at Harrow, Oxford and Harvard, with a penchant for fast cars. They epitomised both the glittering promise held out by this great new age of prosperity and the distant thunder that warns of troubles ahead.

After casting out Bo, the party leadership regrouped by reaffirming its core task of maintaining stability – *wen wei*. But even as it did so, some within its ranks were arguing that the best way to achieve this was by a fresh wave of reforms, while others insisted that it was time to return to the party's long-established policies, purging heretics to the right and left.

Wen Jiabao, seen by many Chinese as a kindly grandfatherly figure, said at the close of the National People's Congress in 2012, "As the economy has developed, it has caused unfair distribution, the loss of credibility, corruption and other issues. I know that to solve these problems it is necessary to enter not only into economic reform but also political reform, especially reform of the party and the state's leadership system. Reform has reached a critical stage. Without the success of political reforms, economic reforms cannot be carried out ... a historical tragedy like the Cultural Revolution may occur again. Each party member and cadre should feel a sense of urgency."

Many identify with such frank analysis, but few have answers as to how to resolve those pressing challenges. Every alternative seems likely to arouse antagonism from one or other of the key interest groups that comprise the party's core. The usual answer is thus to carry on much as before. One Chinese academic describes his ambivalent feelings about communist rule thus: "It's as if a group of people seized control of the plane called China sixty years ago, and they're still flying it around. We're not all happy about how we're being piloted, but no one else on board knows how to fly a plane, so we just carry on looking out the window."

Is the destination of that flight still a nirvana named communism? If the Age of Prosperity has already dawned, some in China ask, does the country still need the Communist Party? What dreams remain for it to fulfil? To date, the CCP has shown an impressive ability to adapt to changing circumstances. But is it now reaching the limits of this capacity? How much longer can it sustain its core, apparently contradictory strategies of globalisation and nationalism, using the languages both of modern technocratic capitalism and of Mao-inspired socialism?

After the demonstrations of 1989 against inflation and corruption, the party moved swiftly to ensure there would be no repeat. These protests had started to destabilise the structure Mao had established, just as it was starting for the first time to produce real economic benefits. In response, the state began shuffling wealth into the hands of China's elite, including the intellectual and entrepreneurial classes – with a result that the wealth gap has widened rapidly. The 700 million urban Chinese earn on average three times the income of the 600 million rural Chinese. China is far less egalitarian than Japan, the USA, or even Eastern Europe, according to Li Shi, an authority on income distribution trends at Beijing Normal University. Many in the West assumed that this growing middle class would demand greater liberalisation and democratisation, but that hasn't happened. Instead the middle class, as the prime beneficiary of the status quo, has become its staunchest supporter.

During and since the Olympic year, a new Chinese nationalism has burgeoned. Many middle-class supporters of the party, especially those too young to remember the Cultural Revolution, are avid followers of nationalist commentators such as Wang Xiaodong. An influential leader of the China Youth and Juvenile Research Centre (affiliated with the party's Youth League), Wang has become a widely published cheer-leader for this new nationalism. Brooding and intense, he has no time for small talk at our sombre meeting in his office-cum-flat-cum HQ. Wood-panelled and sparsely lit, it is furnished in austere, traditional style. He launches straight into his manifesto, his every word noted down by a young female acolyte.

The younger generation, he says, "has more contact with the West. They understand it better. They speak more fluent English, they have learned a stronger sense of individual rights from Westerners." This new generation, he says, rejects Mao's socialism but embraces his nationalism, while also tentatively re-adopting some traditional Chinese values. China's current leaders are essentially administrators – but when today's students succeed them, "China will globalise its national interests, and this will affect not just our close neighbours but the whole world. [China] must gain the capacity to protect those interests."

Crucially, Wang and his acolytes are insiders looking out, not outsiders with their noses pressed against the windowpanes of power. Their prospects, their influence, their access to media and to important Chinese forums, are secure. Tomorrow, they feel, assuredly belongs to them. They are impatient for China to assume global leadership and most cannot conceive of this happening without the party, the great constant in the China story today.

The party attracts growing support among young people. Most do not apply but are invited to join – like Rotarians or Freemasons – on the basis of their displaying signs of leadership or intellect or altruism, or even ambition, or because of who their parents are. Very few turn down the offer of membership, which chiefly involves attending regular meetings at which they are notionally consulted but allowed little say.

Are they really "communists" in the sense that still sends shudders through some in the West? Maybe not in the sense that Mao was, but they do not have any other way of describing themselves – although young party members increasingly add that they are, naturally, also Chinese nationalists. Today the party has zealously wrapped itself around the identity of the whole Han Chinese world, as the encapsulation of opportunity, prosperity and strength, claiming to personify China. Ultimately, as we shall see, the party has not succeeded, however, in displacing China itself. A culture, a very individualistic and resilient culture, survives every effort of the party to mould the country into its own image.

Although the constitution of the People's Republic stresses that "all power belongs to the people," the preamble states explicitly, if turgidly:

> Under the leadership of the Communist Party of China and the guidance of Marxism-Leninism, Mao Zedong Thought, Deng Xiaoping Theory and the important thought of Three Represents [introduced by Jiang Zemin], the Chinese people of all nationalities will continue to adhere to the people's democratic dictatorship and the socialist road, persevere in reform and opening to the outside world, steadily improve socialist institutions, develop the socialist

market economy, develop socialist democracy, improve the socialist legal system and work hard and self-reliantly to modernize the country's industry, agriculture, national defence and science and technology step by step and promote the coordinated development of the material, political and spiritual civilizations, to turn China into a socialist country that is prosperous, powerful, democratic and culturally advanced.

In practice, this means that every key institution in China is answerable to the party. For instance, the People's Liberation Army, the world's largest military force with about 2 million members, is "an army led by the party," as then President Hu Jintao reminded everyone on its eightieth birthday in 2007. It is not the army of the government, or of China more generally, but of the CCP. And the party intends to continue to dominate for a long time yet. As then Premier Wen Jiabao said in 2007, "We must adhere to the party's basic guidelines for the primary stage of socialism for one hundred years."

But what does it mean to be a communist state today? When Mao seized power from the Kuomintang, communist governments were appearing around the world, with the Soviet Union extending its empire through Eastern Europe. Today, the only other surviving communist countries are Cuba, Vietnam, Laos and, the black sheep of the family, North Korea.

The China of today may not much resemble the old Soviet Union – but beneath the modern veneer many of its institutions, little changed during its decades in power, retain their origins in Lenin's Russia. The state remains highly centralised, at least in theory, even if in practice people in the provinces constantly act on the premise that "the mountains are very high and the emperor is far away." They push the envelopes of provincial autonomy as far as they can stretch. But China remains the only country of its size that is not a federation – the USA, Brazil, Indonesia, Canada, Australia, India, even Russia, all now have federal structures.

Social controls also remain. A residency permit (or *hukou*) is still required to live in most cities, and without one many basic services are unavailable. But this system is under review, with a couple of pilot towns having been opened up to all comers. The *danwei*, or work unit, which has been the principle unit of official society since 1949, has been disintegrating as people change jobs more frequently and as employers – both government and private – have ceased to provide cradle-to-grave social support, including housing, schools and medical clinics. In its place, says Yu Keping, Director of the Centre for Chinese Government Innovations at Beijing University, civil organisations are becoming more important to help deliver government policy and programs. There are now 700,000 registered organisations, while a further 2.3 million operate informally.

Censorship is still pervasive, especially when it comes to Chinese history. The historian Xia Chuntao, vice director of the Deng Xiaoping Thought Research Centre, one of China's key ideological think tanks, stresses that "there is only one correct and accurate interpretation of history, and only one explanation that is closest to the truth. There is a pool of clear water, and there's no need to stir up this water. Doing so can only cause disturbance in people's minds." Like many practices that appear at first blush to be quintessentially communist, such censorship – along with *hukou*, party secrecy and the utter separation of its leaders from ordinary life – harks back to the imperial era.

One of the best analysts of China, Arthur Kroeber, the Beijing-based director of the economic research firm Dragonomics, has warned how attempts – even by the country's own government – to define China typically founder on misunderstandings. Thus, he says, "It is always possible to find some evidence in support of any generalization, no matter how outlandish."

He says that all of the following common contemporary definitions describe part of the truth, underlining the *zhang jing* experience: ever-changing scenery and purposely misleading perspectives lead people to believe they are seeing the true China – but when they turn a corner, they find a different vista.

China, he says, is at once:

An emerging global economic and political power and regional hub, like the USA and Germany in the late nineteenth century – and a vulnerable economy heavily dependent on foreign investment, technology and markets;

A despotic communist state run by a disciplined technocratic elite – and a despotic communist state run by a hopelessly corrupt elite increasingly unable to manage the social tensions created by economic growth;

A post-communist state whose government has embraced the most ruthless version of mid-nineteenth-century capitalism – and a post-communist state whose government has pursued sensible, pragmatic policies that have raised millions out of poverty;

A highly centralised state where the national government ultimately controls almost everything – and a decentralised state in which the central government is unable to enforce its writ on almost anything;

A civilisation with a long history in which traditional Confucian values are re-asserting themselves – and a society so unmoored from traditional values that its material success is matched by a spiritual vacuum.

A single constant remains: the party itself.

The party has made its central task not just economic development but perpetual adaptation. It seeks to identify and respond to social shifts before they have a chance to morph into demands for political reform and democratisation. Nicholas Bequelin, a senior researcher at Human Rights Watch, says, "By following this principle, the CCP has become what could be best described as the first Darwinian–Leninist Party in history, one that sees constant adaptation as the key to survival. This goes a long way towards explaining why the party has introduced wide ranging reforms."

The party has not developed an exit strategy, as the Kuomintang did in Taiwan. The only hint that the CCP might ever expect to bow out – or that it would have the capacity to withstand such an event – might be the immense assets that the most powerful party families have accumulated. Some state assets have passed into private hands, and many wealthy party families have prepared bolt-holes abroad, acquiring education and real estate in congenial overseas locations. But if these are preparations for change, they are rudimentary. Despite the frequent forecasts of its demise, the party is not heading out the door any time in the foreseeable future. It remains, in its own eyes and those of most others in China, the party of success.

The classic Maoist anthem "The East Is Red" could today be rewritten, observes the eminent Australian National University sinologist Geremie Barmé, as "The East Is Rich." China is contriving, somehow, to be both. That rousing song starts: *The east is red, the sun is rising. / China has brought forth a Mao Zedong.* Mao himself, despite presiding, embalmed, from his "Maosoleum" in the centre of Tiananmen Square, has now been consigned to the history books. But the final verse of "The East Is Red" remains more pertinent than ever: *The Communist Party is like the sun. / Wherever it shines, it is bright. / Sometimes it soothes, sometimes it scorches, but within China it is always present.*

The deal being negotiated at the Beijing Hotel was never finalised. But others, many others, are following. The party today feels confident that, as with the emissaries sent to the imperial court in the old Forbidden City, trembling as they entered each succeeding vast courtyard, there are many more beyond the Great Within waiting to be ushered inside. And the party likes to deal with other people, other companies, other countries, on its terms.

People approaching China can only hope to build useful relationships of any sort – doing business, conducting diplomacy, exchanging cultures, making friends – if they are alert to hidden meanings, to misreadings, and to the obvious as well. They should start by placing themselves in the shoes of the people who run China: the members of the party.

CHAPTER 1: JOINING THE PARTY

WHAT IS IT LIKE TO BE A MEMBER OF THE CHINESE Communist Party? How do you join? What do you do at meetings?

Answers are not freely available. The party holds its secrets as close to its chest as Freemasons used to do – but with much more at stake. This is now the most powerful organisation in the world, and one of the least understood.

In this chapter, we meet three ordinary party members and a party official, who talk with rare frankness about how the CCP operates at its most basic level: the local branch. Two of them, who are critical of the party of which they remain members, were nervous about letting their true names be used. But their accounts – which are strikingly apolitical, and whose critique includes the sheer boredom of being a 21st-century communist – are true ones.

From each of them, we learn fascinating details about the life of a grassroots party member in the world's last great communist power. Their views vary greatly because they are unique individuals, in a culture that – beneath its communist governance – remains hectically individualist. They respond differently to the demands of membership, but taken together, their accounts also reveal many common experiences – the selection of the best and brightest, the top-down flow of information and the constant self-criticism, designed to ensure a sense of vulnerability rather than of entitlement.

First, we meet Liu Meiling (not her real name), a smart, ambitious woman in her thirties who is working for a foreign–Chinese joint venture in

1

Wuhan, an ancient but dynamic city of 10 million people in central China. She is smart, petite, dressed in a black and white corporate suit. We meet in a hotel with a view down to the Yangtze River. She chooses a table in the coffee shop where we will not be overheard. I order jasmine tea; she opts for a cappuccino.

Every month, she tells me, she and about a third of the forty colleagues in her section of the firm file into a special party meeting room, either during their lunch hour or just after work. When their general manager enters the room he is wearing, metaphorically, a different hat – as general secretary of the firm's party branch.

The primary business of these meetings is to relay instructions from officials higher up the chain of command. At many, perhaps most, companies, the general manager is also the secretary of the department's party branch. "You have to be careful because he is also your boss. He is judging you related to your work performance. Everyone becomes careful and wants to say something to make the boss feel you are special. You part-plan what you are going to say even in the most casual-seeming conversations. It's not like at uni, where you might become careless. You become careful. If you talk too much about your good deeds at meetings, people will think you are proud. Modesty is very acceptable in China."

Most of the foreigners working at Liu's company are not aware that their firm has a party branch. They would be even more surprised to discover that someone as modern-minded, fluent in English and generally savvy as Liu is a member. Why is the party still so attractive to aspiring young Chinese that, now 80 million strong, it can turn away would-be members? How does it lure people like Liu, whose Western counterparts are unlikely to join any organisation except a gym?

The main attraction is success, at both individual and national levels. Joining the party means joining a success story that opens the door to almost unlimited career opportunities. The party has placed itself in such a central role in so many dimensions of Chinese life that it now appears irreplaceable. And, being a jealous party that brooks no rivals, it has no competitors. If you have ambitions in 21st-century China, you need to think very hard before passing up a chance to join the party. Being part of the select group, the chosen people who wield such extraordinary authority, is naturally attractive to ambitious young people.

Party patronage provides a crucial stepping stone towards prosperity in China. Smart young people head for jobs in the government or in state-owned enterprises these days, not so much with international firms, unless they are thinking of shifting overseas. Foreign firms may pay more, but they cannot compete with the state in offering access to assets – to flats, say, or to big new share issues.

The country's startling economic success has brought about a rejuvenation of the party, and an extension of its grip on China's burgeoning private sector. In 2011, on the party's ninetieth birthday, its membership reached 82.6 million, having grown from about fifty members at its birth to nearly 4.5 million when the People's Republic was founded in 1949. According to Wang Qinfeng, deputy head of the party's all-powerful Organisation Department, about 21.6 million people applied to join in 2010, but only 3.2 million were accepted, a net increase of 2.3 million. During the same year, a total of 32,000 people were expelled or withdrew from the party. Most of these were "forced out to ensure the advanced nature and purity of the CCP," Wang told me.

The two top sources of new members in 2010 were college students and "people at the frontline of production or work, such as industrial workers, farmers, herders, and migrant workers," according to Wang, each accounting for about 40 per cent of the total new members. Only 23.3 per cent of members were women in 2011, and 6.7 per cent were from China's fifty-five official ethnic minorities. A quarter were aged under thirty-five. Just 38.5 per cent were farmers or urban workers, reflecting the party's shift towards a technocratic caste. Its average members are now professional people; 39 per cent have degrees; they are the country's managers. It has become standard for the annual reports of Chinese companies to feature at or near the start the number of party members employed by the firm.

Party branches have now been established, Wang says, in "nearly all government agencies, state-owned and private enterprises, and social organisations. They have also been set up in 99.9 per cent of villages and urban communities and in all associations of lawyers and certified accountants." Migrant workers who move from rural areas to the towns and cities – about 3 million party members – can participate in branches in their new places of residence, "so that they can stay connected with the party."

Wang confirms that the party is actively recruiting talented young people. "Party members are the vanguard soldiers of communist consciousness," he says. "They diligently serve and work hard in a selfless way. They are role models in every undertaking." Would-be members who are not targeted for recruitment by party officials must be sponsored by a party member – so connections (*guanxi*) are important.

In 2006 Ouyang Song, then the deputy head of the Organisation Department and director of the party's education campaign, gave a rare press briefing. More than 85 per cent of China's private enterprises with three or more individual party members – the minimum to establish a party branch at a workplace – had set up branches, he announced, and the party would work towards opening branches in every firm in China. This would promote healthy and sound development of the private sector and had the support of private business owners and entrepreneurs. It was now important, he continued, "to educate party members about recent outcomes of the development of Marxism with Chinese characteristics" – in particular its "focus on the increasing capacity to get rich and get out of poverty." "History will prove once again," he concluded, "the Chinese Communist Party is glorious and great."

Tall young computer scientist Ren Jie, wearing a wispy beard, is a true believer in such glory and greatness. When I meet him, he is patiently queuing in the massive new vestibule at Beijing Normal University, edging towards a desk where party members who are soon to graduate are registering their next workplaces or universities, so that their membership can be transferred to the appropriate branch. He is about the only person in the queue not talking on a mobile phone or sending a text message. He is heading next to Beijing University, one of the country's top academies, to study for an MA. Ren's girlfriend is also a party member. Many young communists naturally find partners through their party involvement.

Ren joined the party in 2003, when he was at high school, one of four best friends who joined at the same time. His father, a factory worker who assembles bicycles, is also a member. But, Ren insists, "It's not easier for me because he is a member. The party doesn't judge you according to your family background, but on your personal behaviour, on character."

In high school, he says, party members met once every week and occasionally at weekends. Sometimes the branch officials – who were also teachers – showed the students a DVD, sometimes the teachers handed out speeches by top party officials.

"Joining the party leads us to do a lot of things," he says. "I needed to be excited, in study and in social activity, and becoming a member was a great stimulant. As young communists, we have to be always learning new things about social life, about the country and the world."

Once he was at university, Ren found that almost every dormitory – most Chinese students live in such dormitories – included a party member. That student's task was "to set a good example to others, not just in learning but in daily living. We provide social guidance to other classmates. Maybe some students don't understand us, but we should make them believe our good behaviour demonstrates how it is a glorious thing to be a party member. The motto of our own university branch is 'Advance together with the team.'"

The university branch met every fortnight. The meetings, held on campus in the evenings, might last four or five hours. Students pay only "a few mao [cents] a month" for their subscription. Once they start to work, they will have to pay a portion of their income.

Ren is not sure what career he will pursue after finishing his masters. "Maybe I'll go to a private company that specialises in IT. Or I will end up as a teacher in a uni. But I am concerned that a foreign or private company wouldn't give me as much time off to attend party meetings."

Liu Mei-ling, the smart young businesswoman from Wuhan, also became a party member in high school. Her parents were both already members. They had to be: her father worked in public security, and her mother, as a telephonist in pre-mobile days, had the opportunity to listen to important conversations. Both jobs could only be held by trusted party members. Liu's father still does not talk much about his job, amplifying her curiosity about it. Once a classmate had an item stolen, and to Liu's surprise her father turned up to investigate. Her grandfather, a war hero who died fighting for the People's Liberation Army against the Kuomintang, was also a member. Liu recalls that her mother often complained about having to attend monthly party meetings, viewing them as a waste of time when "they just needed your presence." She would have preferred to spend the time with her family.

In fifth grade, Liu read a newspaper article about the party holding an important meeting about reforming the countryside, which interested her because some relatives lived in tough rural communities. Her teacher encouraged her interest, commending party membership as the way to get into the best careers. When Liu entered junior middle school, she was told she could join the Young Pioneers. She was among the 90 per cent who did so. Their first step was to wear the red scarves celebrated in communist propaganda posters since the party's early days in power. Her parents encouraged her, saying it would improve her career prospects, as well as demonstrating that she was a good person there and then. "Three things were required to prove you were a good student," she says. "To study well, have a healthy mind and body, and be politically sound. The few in the class who were left out without Young Pioneer scarves didn't really belong to the group. They were isolated."

When she was thirteen or fourteen, Liu graduated to junior party membership, slightly younger than most. She was a precocious young communist. She applied by writing an essay explaining why she wanted to join. "You have to self-criticise," she recalls. "You have to state your shortcomings. One is enough. Usually people will say something modest, like 'I'm not seriously minded.' The answer the party leaders give is usually to spend more time with classmates or help people more." The party took a while to consider her application, but she was confident about the outcome and eventually received her membership card and certificate. Meetings were infrequent. "You were just expected to be good. Nothing much else. Most of my friends were also members."

Like the exemplar she was expected to be, she focused on her studies. Her academic performance was strong and she won a place at one of China's top universities, studying science. She was there for four years, mingling with especially bright people. "Wherever we had come from, about 50 to 60 per cent said they wanted to become party members, influenced either by their families, or by a wider vision of society. Some – fewer – were not interested at all. My family guided me and I applied to join formally, and it was approved."

Branch members get to vote on all new applications. The applicant writes an essay and the leader will read it aloud at a branch meeting. People who know the student will supply additional information and suggest areas for improvement. Then the members vote, almost always in favour – because if the candidate has come this far, she or he is overwhelmingly likely to be deemed acceptable by the authorities. After this, the members vote whether to require a formal trial period of one year.

If an application is rejected, the branch leaders will tell the applicant that she or he still has some problems and can improve in the following months. But they don't indicate what the problems are.

In the applicant's first year of membership, the party branch monitors his or her performance especially closely. New members must write regular self-criticisms to reveal what kind of a person they really are. Says Liu, "Young people are guided by this concept of self-criticism to be able to express nonsense from an early age. You learn how to make it up." Although most pass this first stage, ultimate approval nevertheless proves problematic for many applicants. Liu says that the party makes it look as if it is a competition, where the places are limited – although it also celebrates its growth in membership and places no obvious cap on numbers.

At both of Liu's universities, the branch secretaries were students, but a professor supervised meetings and would read news items or party documents and ask people to comment on them. "Nothing serious," she says. Meetings were held every month, in the office of a lecturer or professor or in a classroom. The party secretary of the department was always there. Usually the meetings were held in the evenings after class and lasted about an hour. Nobody asked questions. "We were all very passive," Liu says. Occasionally students would talk about politics. When officials read statements by party leaders, "We commented how wise they were. Always very wise. But they were very dull. No real business was conducted." Members were told which National People's Congress candidates they could vote for. "But it seemed meaningless to me," says Liu. "I never voted. They just gave us names, but I thought the process was ridiculous since we didn't know the candidates, and were given almost no information about them."

Wu Jing-fei (not her real name), a 34-year-old Shanghai woman, first became actively involved in the party at university. I meet Wu for lunch – Ningbo cuisine – at a busy restaurant near her office. She is dressed in blue jeans and a grey jacket. Although it is her lunch hour, when time is usually pressing, she is relaxed – relishing, she says, the chance to talk to an outsider about a topic she usually keeps very much to herself. The hub-bub around is too great for anyone else to be able to hear what she is saying, even by chance. She has come with her boyfriend, who has heard it all before, and who orders half a dozen dishes as Wu gets into her stride.

Wu comes from a family of party members, with the notable exception of her father, who regularly jokes, "I'm not sufficiently advanced as a human being." Her mother, grandfather and an uncle, a senior police-man, are all members, and all are or were working for the government. At home, says Wu, they have never talked much about the party. "But Mum thinks that being a member means being the most advanced per-son – as a student or as a worker – in your performance and in your thinking. That you should be a leader in every area of life. The party leaders stress this too."

Wu was a top student at university. Many members are recruited there, after being observed by communist teachers. Wu was taken to one side after a lecture and told by one of her professors, "We think you are qualified to join the senior party as a full member." First, she had to take a course to learn more about the party, the constitution and other essen-tials. Then she was given some tests and a professor who had examined her overall performance at the university – her behaviour as well as her academic work – produced a report for the branch committee, which approved her membership.

"I was happy when I was approached," says Wu. "That meant to me that I was moving up. I thought it would be a great advantage at job interviews and so on, especially for joining a state-owned enterprise. I did the test, the self-criticism, everything required. I fabricated some stuff for the self-criticism, everyone does." After joining, she says, "It was no big burden on my life at uni. But I was expected to work as a leader among other students, and to be more active in some areas than in others. Mum was happy. Almost all the members there were top stu-dents." As graduation approached, the most senior official in her branch started to discuss what career path she might take. The party, naturally, would help her along it.

Professor Wang Binglin, born in 1961, has a different view of how the party works. He is the deputy party secretary at Beijing Normal Uni-versity, where his office is next to those of the United Front Work

Department, which is responsible for the party's relations with non-party groups. He is relaxed, open in conversation, yet precise – an appropriate father-figure for the young party members in his care, who are almost all living away from home for the first time. He is keen to stress that his concept of the party goes beyond Deng Xiaoping's saying that "To get rich is glorious" and answers the needs of the rising genera-tion, which is seeking something more satisfying than money and material possessions.

A student who becomes a party member before graduation, says Wang, "Will find a comfortable and good job. But also, students want to have a belief, a faith in their life, something to go after. It is written in our constitution that religious belief is free in China, but we don't have a national religion. So by joining the party, the member illustrates that they have a faith in their life, and the party has abundant reasons for its leading role. To participate as a member is glorious. Many students want to join the party, it's true, and what we teach them is to combine their personal ambitions with their goals for society as a whole."

Members at the university spend an average of half a day every week on party matters, he says. "Such a strict demand helps provide members with a greater sense of discipline and organisation." He believes that as long as the economy is going well and society is maturing, the party will remain attractive to students. "Our understanding of communism is as a society where every individual has the freedom to develop his or her self, where everyone can enjoy the benefits from the economy – unlike the situation where some are rich, the rest are poor. But we still have a long way to go."

Wang's parents were not party members. "They were peasants, with-out much education." But his older brother is an army officer, and thus almost certainly a member. Wang himself became a member as a post-graduate student. "I felt when I joined that this was something very glorious. How could I have even gone to university without benefiting from the party's good policies?"

What becomes of these young party members when they enter the work-force? When Liu graduated from university, she started work for a state-run financial institution and later moved to the joint venture involving a foreign corporation. Her father helped her to obtain her first job. "I knew he could do that," she says. "I was aware he did it for other people, but I didn't want that. I didn't like it." She wanted to rely on herself and had told her mother, even when she was very young, that she would not use her parents' money. She says, "I read and re-read the novel *Jane Eyre*. Like her, I wanted to be myself."

By now, Liu's enthusiasm for the party had waned. At her first job, one of the company directors was a candidate for the National People's Congress. All staff were guided to vote for him. Usually, however, party members knew nothing about the candidates they were asked to vote for. There was a choice of different names, but only the candidates' job titles and hometowns were provided. "At the party meeting when candidates were listed, I sighed – apparently from the heat, but my ennui went deeper than that. I felt this was all removed from my everyday life. People separate this party involvement out from their understanding of the world. Their membership is like an altar with a Buddha on it. It looks good in its place, but for most people it doesn't penetrate into real life."

Fortunately, Liu's first boss judged her for her work, not for her involvement in the party. "She could see I was not interested." This boss was less focused on party rhetoric than on getting the job done. She was very good at developing the business, Liu recalled, but often needed to be reminded about party meetings. "She knew it was a waste of time." When Liu left this job, the party "asked me to transfer my membership to a similar unit of the district where I lived. I got the certificate to do so, but called the local organiser and asked if I could keep my membership in the financial institution until I was firmly settled in my new workplace." For Liu, this was a way to quietly disengage from party activities for a while. "I'm not sure if there is a formal procedure for resignation."

Now, in her new workplace, Liu is expected to write an essay every year about her understanding of the party, its policies and theories, and what she does for it. "We learn how to write this bullshit," she says. "But nobody will look at it seriously afterwards."

Meetings at Liu's *danwei* usually start at noon. Their lunch break starts at 11.30 and ends at 1, which circumscribes the length of meetings. Sometimes they will meet after work instead, if this is the only time the boss will be available. A roll is taken, and members must ask for permission in advance to be absent. There is little discussion of party policy. The topics for formal discussion are laid down by higher echelons of the organisation. "We learned about the good things the leaders had done.

Mao was almost never mentioned. We heard more of Deng. But we were trained to speak nonsense – that's one reason I didn't go to work for the government, where there would be even more of this." Members are expected to bring a notebook and pen to branch meetings, says Liu, but "Nobody knows what to do with them." Informally, just before or after meetings, there is naturally some discussion between members. Rumours of corruption are a favourite topic for gossip.

Whatever dirt might emerge about individual leaders, however, the first duty of members is to support the party and its theories. "Even if you don't care about your fellow members," Liu says, "you won't do something to hurt the party. You won't spread bad comments or gossip around. The secret is that it is actually well organised, even though that's not the adjective most people would ascribe to it, and even though it doesn't always feel that way when you're a grassroots member."

It may be well organised, but the party doesn't go out of its way to make membership fun. Occasionally branch officials arrange for members to visit a party museum or memorial, or to see a film together for education – never for entertainment. They might watch, for example, a new documentary about model workers. "You have to go," Liu says. "The members sit together and work out who is absent."

Most branch members no longer call each other *tongzhi*, the Chinese word for comrade. Originally introduced by Sun Yat-sen and adopted by Mao as an equivalent of the Soviet *tovarich*, in recent years *tongzhi* – which means "the same will" or "same inclination" – has been appropriated by China's gay and lesbian community. This prompts sometimes ill-concealed mirth when it is still used by po-faced party cadres on formal occasions.

The party has made some efforts to appear more participatory. At his 2006 press briefing, Ouyang Song described the introduction of "elections" for some local posts – although the party selected the candidates. This was a key step towards "intra-party democracy," he said. "We attach great importance to the quality and competence of members." He reported that a recent opinion poll of 6.03 million members and non-members registered a 97 per cent approval rating of the CCP's rule – reflecting, he said, the public's "rights of participation and choice and information." He said that the party had used US$300 million – mostly from the national budget – to build or refurbish 164,000 "activity centres" for its 3.5 million local branches, to reinforce its attractiveness and efficiency.

And the proportion of members in state-owned enterprises and joint ventures is high, especially at the management level. These managers are strategically important to the party, even in the provinces, where they run key parts of the modern economy including the finance, telecommunications, transport, media and logistics sectors.

Liu has noticed, however, that colleagues who didn't join the CCP at university seemed less willing to do so once they entered the workforce. "For staff who showed a potential in skills, knowledge and management, the boss would give a hint that they should write an application for the party," she says. "But the new generation is not so interested. I still remember how my first boss, who got the opportunity of an education after the Cultural Revolution, always told new staff that we must learn to sacrifice before we can celebrate. But today the newcomers, the Generation Y-ers, are not interested in all that, they just ask why they are not paid extra for overtime, and make other material demands that even my generation would never raise. They even sometimes sue the organisation. Something completely different."

Wu agrees. "Young people mainly join for promotion. It's a sacrifice of time that they make in order to gain a step up ... It's easier to get promoted if you're a member. And sometimes people who are promoted purely on talent are then invited to join the party, because it now also recognises their capabilities." For some young professionals, however, this sacrifice is no longer appealing. Wu tells me of one colleague who received such an invitation but declined to become a member. Why? He had a negative view of the party. "Although the party wants to absorb the top people in our company, perceptions of corruption and an unfair wealth gap and other issues are causing the party's image to decline with some people."

Both Ren and Wang see people's motives for joining the party very differently. Ren says that membership has enabled him to do good rather than just do well. "I discovered that making money was not my whole destiny," he says. "I think a person should do something more, though it's important for us to learn about the economy. Money is a measure, it helps us to live, but it's not everything, not something we care most about."

In Ren's view, the party's ideology remained relevant. "In my opinion, Marx is the basis and every party member should learn his basic theory … Marxism hasn't lost its glory. But a totally planned economy has been proved to be unsuitable for China." China has therefore opened many sectors of its economy up to reform and to private industry. But state-owned enterprises remain the core of the economy, Ren stresses. "Other types of business are there to add more liveliness and life to the economy. We have always been told if we are in control of the mainstream, through state-owned enterprises, the orientation will be correct." Should the party itself open up to competition, as China's economy has? Ren is not convinced. "We are providing room for even more reforms in the economy – but we think, at least for the present, a one-party system is more suitable for China politically."

Wang, as a party official, naturally agrees. "The party is paying much attention to education, telling the younger generation that power comes through hard struggle." Economic development was key to the party's legitimacy: by meeting the material needs of the people – for instance, by dividing land amongst the peasants in the past, and more recently by giving employment to workers – the party had won their hearts. "That is the greatest source of legitimacy of the party," he says. "Of course we have had zigzags and made mistakes. But we make corrections."

There are naturally big differences between members' experiences. Ren and Wang view their involvement in the party as considerably more important, and indeed interesting, than do Wu and Liu. Yet they all remain members. Leaving is not easy; for some it seems impossible. Wu Si, the editor of controversial party magazine Yanhuang Chunqiu (*History Review*), became a member in 1976. He became disenchanted in 1989 and refused to pay his subscription. When he left to start working at the magazine he refused to transfer his party membership to his new *danwei*. The branch officials told him that this would require him to quit his membership altogether, which would make trouble for them. They told him, he says, "'If you're not willing to pay your subscription, we'll pay it for you, just to make everything go smoothly.'" So he remains technically a member, one of the 80 million.

For Wu Jing-fei, party membership today holds little of the romance it still clearly carries for Ren. She too went on to work for a foreign – Chinese joint venture. Her workplace *danwei* has its own office in the building and members meet quarterly, after work or on Saturdays. Different departments within the company have separate meetings at different times. There are about ten people in Wu's departmental party group. She started off paying a much higher subscription than when she was at university – 25 yuan (about US$4) a year. Her branch makes few social forays – just an outing to the site of the first party congress, and another to the heroes' war memorial. Once they went to see the Peking Opera, which performed a dance originally choreographed by Jiang Qing, the fourth and final wife of Mao Zedong, a member of the infamous Gang of Four who killed herself after being convicted in a dramatic show trial following Mao's death. Usually, says Wu, members formed closer relationships with fellow members than with other colleagues. "You get to know them a little better."

At meetings, she says, the departmental leader, who is often a manager, "reads out documents. If time is limited, he or she reads some out and sends others to you online to study later. You can make comments about candidates who are being promoted to the next level, but it is not clear whether your remarks are sent on anywhere else. Someone writes the meeting notes. But only the group leader can see the minutes, which do not need to be agreed by the members." Typically the meetings last about ninety minutes. Members can raise issues, but mostly they are only expected to absorb what they are told. "We don't raise problems," says Wu. "It's all really boring for young people. You don't exactly feel you're at the centre of power making decisions for the country, or even for Shanghai."

Wu's chief complaint is that "the party's core leadership in Beijing hasn't a feeling for the grassroots. What they are thinking about doesn't touch people … People don't really feel spiritually committed to the party; it's more of a cosmetic connection. It's just a neutral presence for me, the party is just there – though Mum still has some emotional belief, and Grandad thought everything the party did was exactly right. My mother's commitment is a bit less intense. And now my generation's is cooler again."

The documents they are asked to consider at meetings are opaque. Most are written in the party's ornate rhetorical language, which dates back to the eras of Marx and Lenin. They don't offer figures or details or evidence, which makes it difficult for members to comment. For instance, Wu laments, a paper might conclude that "We have to improve everyday life ..." But how? And what should be changed? "It's hard to write much in response. Then I get home and turn on CCTV [China Central Television] news and just get more of the same."

Wang makes a case for this lack of internal debate. He applauds the way "the party has always taken care to construct its ideology so that members are not divided among themselves with different thoughts." Although foreign observers tend to divide the party into right and left wings, he says, "it doesn't see itself like this. There might be some different agendas during the process of discussion about new policies, but they are united by the central party and carried out. One group might pay more attention to tradition and another to Western ideas, but the policy will be one on which we will all be united in the end."

He admits that the Cultural Revolution – about which the party has mostly remained silent – was "an upsetting and chaotic time, a very serious mistake made by the party itself. We learned that we must improve the construction of a complete system, to avoid the dictatorship of any individual." The party also learned from the 1989 protests, he says, that it must fight against corruption and educate the new generation in the need to maintain social stability. "History has proven that to listen to the Soviet Union is not correct," he says. "The Chinese path must be explored by the Chinese. We are also good at learning from other peoples and countries and parties, including from Western countries – such as Australia."

As it extends its reach into the private sector, the party is certainly finding out how foreign business works. In recent years, the party has become more active within fully foreign-owned companies, as well as in state-owned corporations and joint ventures. One way it does this is though the Beijing Foreign Enterprise Human Resources Service Co. Ltd., or FESCO. According to its website, FESCO is "Your human resources total service provider in China," and "the primary HR strategic partner for multinational companies." It recruits local staff for foreign companies, taking a third of their wages as a service fee. If the recruit is a party member, the membership will be transferred to FESCO, which will also receive the member's subscription payments. At branch meetings within these foreign companies, members primarily discuss the business itself. They will still read and discuss party documents, Wu tells me, but are less likely to be expected to provide written responses than in state-owned enterprises or joint ventures. She says, "Members will aim to be well informed about what the company is doing – and through them, the party and the government will have good intelligence on foreign corporations." On rare occasions, Wu says, members receive modest payments for providing copies of exceptionally interesting and possibly confidential documents.

Liu's view of her membership now is chiefly pragmatic. "I always thought I worked hard. I was not so stupid. I wouldn't just flatter the boss. It was simple: if they didn't like me, I would leave. There are other options in a big city like mine. You don't have to rely on the party." But membership certainly helps. And she has not, in the end, quit the party.

Liu's parents regard her party membership as a useful tool for the future, "to make life easier for me." And they both still have deep feelings for the party, which come out when, for instance, they hear the old "red songs" they recall from their youth. Liu, however, cannot recall Mao's name ever being mentioned at a party meeting.

For Liu, party activities are now passionless and predictable. "I'm never surprised by anything that happens at the meetings, or by what anyone says," she says. The only time she felt any emotion while involved in party duties, she tells me, was when she performed her first public self-criticism on joining the workplace branch after leaving university. This was a difficult time for her in many ways, she explains. "My whole life was messy." Thus "my self-criticism was very genuine. I even cried. I just felt something was wrong, after more than ten years when my life should have been guided by the party. I wanted to tell the truth. My colleagues were very surprised. But by then I didn't care what they thought of me. No one put an arm around me; they just gave me some tissues. My boss was a bit embarrassed.

"That's the only time I tried to tell people something true at a meeting."

CHAPTER 2: CADRE SCHOOL

WHEN THE CHARISMATIC, TELEGENIC "PRINCELING" BO Xilai, party secretary of the vast municipality of Chonqing, was sacked in dramatic circumstances in 2012, and his wife, Gu Kailai, charged with murdering their British friend, business ally and alleged MI6 informer Nick Heywood, Chinese netizens and micro-bloggers were agog – and divided in their response.

Some condemned Bo a self-aggrandising throwback to an earlier era when unaccountable authority led to tyranny. But many others expressed outrage at the ousting of a bold, decisive hero. He had championed the resurrection of "red culture" in a form of retro-Maoism, including the mass public singing of songs (*changhong*, or "singing red") from the Cultural Revolution era, and dancing to Mao-era music in public parks. This had struck a chord with many people far beyond Chongqing, who look back not in anger but in nostalgia at what they now perceive as a more egalitarian era, for all its harshness.

Chongqing, a city with steep banks straddling the Yangtze, was the wartime capital of the Nationalist struggle against the Japanese, led by Chiang Kai-shek and his glamorous wife, Soong Mei-ling. It became known under Bo, who is fluent in English, for its modernistic dynamism. The city strove hard, during Bo's five convulsive years in office, to boost business growth by attracting foreign investors. But his campaigning administration also became widely known for its fierce nationalism, in the manner encouraged by the party – that is, with the party's own story, emblems and heroes linked inextricably with those of China itself – and for its championing of redistributive policies to reduce China's yawning wealth gap.

The melodrama that was Bo's Chongqing, with its mix of aims and methods, highlighted the apparent contradictions in the contemporary ethos of the Communist Party as a whole. The leadership in Beijing eventually pulled the plug on the top cadres running the Chongqing experiment – but it cannot so easily distance itself from the core elements behind that program.

For the party still stresses the need for China to keep modernising and globalising, engaging with the wider world – especially with countries that can offer the new technology, resources and ideas the country covets. At the same time, the party persists with the full panoply of communist lore, including how it saved China from its plight as a victim of rapacious foreigners, how Chairman Mao's "red sun" is still rising, and how its "socialism with Chinese characteristics" has framed its economic success.

Both are key features of the party's education programs – the need to strive for modernity through change, and the importance of learning to love and follow the examples thrown up by the party's history, especially its romantic wilderness years. The Bo Xilai affair illustrated how hard it is to hold onto both threads, like steering a cart pulled by two horses that want to head in different directions. But letting go of either, the party worries, will place its very existence in peril. It roots its legitimacy in doing both – holding out promises of a constantly improving future while justifying its *modus operandi* with reference to its glorious and successful past. Little effort is put into combining these two themes in a coherent way; they are simply expected to co-exist in current and future party members and leaders.

These leaders are shaped, as we shall see, in schools and universities, and above all in the 2000 party schools, which are today probably the best equipped educational institutions in the world, and which play a crucial role both in developing new thinking and policies, and in entrenching perennial party values. Such schools seldom open their doors to outsiders, but we shall take a good look inside, and discover what Chinese communists are learning today. Their tough assignment is clear: to keep the party on course, and to maintain its hold on China while equipping it to respond to future challenges.

★

The party's entrenchment in the minds of China's citizens starts early. Almost all children aged between seven and thirteen are enlisted as "Little Red Pioneers," after which they may graduate, if they apply and are accepted, into the Youth League of the party. Children used to have to compete to achieve Pioneer membership. But by the late 1990s it had become routine for virtually all young students to be inducted after their first year at school. Terry Woronov, an anthropology lecturer at the University of Sydney, writes that "rather than being an outdated relic of the nation's Maoist past, this provides insight into contemporary Chinese nationalism ... The goal of the Pioneers has long been to inculcate in children organisational and leadership skills, discipline, collectivism, obedience to party directives, and patriotism."

Most primary schools' Pioneer cells are linked to the Communist Youth organisation in their local school district, and each school assigns at least one teacher to supervise Pioneer activities and report regularly to district-level party authorities. These authorities determine which themes the teachers who run Pioneers should pursue, such as the anniversaries of important events in party history. The best essays are posted on bulletin boards lining the school hallways. Woronov was especially struck by essays about the annual National Day Parade on 1 October. She cites a typical example: "I saw our Liberation Army march along Tiananmen Square ... I especially liked seeing the weapons displayed. Seeing this makes me want to grow up to be a scientist, so that I can build better weapons to defend the Motherland."

During the annual International Children's Day celebrations on 1 June, Pioneer members carry and salute the national flag, take loyalty oaths to the party and perform patriotic plays or soliloquies. The climax of these performances is the ritual tying of a red scarf around the neck of each of the first-graders, to mark their entry into the Pioneers. "This red scarf," says Woronov, "is a sacred symbol that represents a corner of the national flag stained by the blood of the revolutionary martyrs; wearing it daily around their necks is supposed to symbolize a child's ties to the party and the nation, and their remembrance of those who died for the revolution."

At this initiation, children chant the pledge: "I am a Little Red Pioneer! Beneath the Pioneer flag I swear that I am determined to obey the teachings of the Chinese Communist Party, that I will study, work and labour diligently, and that I am prepared to dedicate all my efforts to the cause of communism."

The party also plays a dominant role at the other end of China's education system, in the universities. Antonia Finnane, a professor of history at the University of Melbourne who has been based for several years in Beijing, describes the "carefully cultivated signs of normalcy" posed in the pictures presented to the outside world of Chinese universities – they portray a hard-working society earnestly pursuing the goal of a higher education system based on universal values of learning.

However, Finnane says, "There is something missing from this picture, and it is the Chinese Communist Party, sometimes hard to see because of its ubiquity." Classes in Marxism-Leninism are compulsory. And while Western universities have chancellors who preside over graduations, universities in China have party secretaries who ensure that challenges to authority are not also challenges to the government – that is, to the party.

It is an organisation that believes absolutely in the power of planning, including planning its own continued success – a task in which education plays a crucial role. Just as the country as a whole retains its five-year plans – the twelfth runs from 2011 to 2015 – the party has its own five-year plans, which include training requirements for every member, including members of the national Politburo, provincial party chiefs and the heads of state-owned enterprises. They have to drop all their responsibilities and participate in live-in courses at party schools as required, sometimes for months – perplexing their foreign business partners, who believed they were dealing with conventional corporate types.

Such training classes are crucial for the evolution and implementation of party policy, for the renovation of management skills, and for the party's constant renewal. This process mostly takes place in China's 2000 party or administration schools, which are located in every province and major centre – about the same number as government-run tertiary institutions. Andrew Nathan, a leading China expert at Columbia University, says, "Today's Communist Party is a highly developed bureaucracy like IBM or General Motors. It's not the party of Mao's time." And just as the big corporations nowadays expect their leading managers to have MBAs from business schools, so does the party expect its top leaders to graduate from its ideological finishing schools.

The premier such institution is the Central Party School. Its mostly ultra-modern buildings are surrounded by spacious grounds – a good setting for contemplating how to run the world's biggest country, akin to the cloistered walks of mediaeval European monasteries, where many important matters were debated and decided a millennium ago. It is located next to the "new" Summer Palace, the "old" Summer Palace having been sacked by British and French troops in 1861. The CPS was founded in another time of turbulence, in 1933. Its presidents have included Mao Zedong and fellow party leaders Liu Shaoqi and Hua Guofeng. Xi Jinping, the new party leader, has been president since 2007. This is where important seminars and briefings are held before the party or the government introduces major new strategies – such as in June 1992, when Jiang Zemin, the then general secretary, gave a speech on the market economy, after which the party began opening its ranks to businesspeople at its fourteenth national congress. In February 2004, the then secretary general Hu Jintao spoke at the school about his new core aim of creating a harmonious society.

Ideas for new strategies also emerge from the Central Party School's staff. In 2011, a national bestseller titled *Why and How the Communist Party Works in China* was written by historians at the school to mark the party's ninetieth anniversary. The school was closed, like most of China's educational establishments, by the Cultural Revolution. Its re-opening was attended by Deng Xiaoping. An entire department of the school is dedicated to "party construction." Marxist theory remains a major item on the curriculum – but with "Chinese features."

One of the perennial questions under discussion in the corridors of power and in the shaded gardens of the CPS is whether China needs political as well as economic reform. The school's Professor Wei Zehuan replied unequivocally when I asked him back in 1997: "Economic change necessitates political change. This is the basis of Marxism." Fifteen years on, this remains a live and unresolved issue. In 2012, another CPS professor, Wang Changjiang, wrote an article in the party newspaper *Beijing Daily* aiming to set the scene for the October party congress, saying that democracy could develop within a one-party system, and that democratic development did not necessarily lead to multiple parties. If and when the time comes for the party to take the plunge into elective democracy, the CPS will be there to help "prove" that this naturally evolved out of Marxist and Dengist thoughts.

Another issue with which the party continues to grapple is that of state ownership – though these days this does not mean owning the means of production, but owning contemporary means of control, such as logistics and finance and communications. Originally, a third of the school's curriculum was devoted to Marx's "political economy," said Wei Zehuan, but *Das Kapital* had effectively disappeared from the curriculum. "We have diversified," said Wei. "We also have courses on the macro-economy, and on globalisation." And there on the reading list for eager young cadres, even back in 1997, were capitalist thinkers Adam Smith and Paul Samuelson. But, Wei stressed, the Chinese version of a market economy must involve public ownership. "If not, we don't call the economy socialist."

Wei added: "We are looking at how to keep the pace of reform up" – the signal being that party slackers and old-style central planners should get off, for the train was just starting to gather speed. The party schools continue to drive that requirement for constant self-examination and reform.

Shanghai, which boasts that it is the most modern and cosmopolitan city in China – it is certainly the largest – hosts an especially impressive new party school. It is one of four national-level institutions, which are only surpassed in influence and importance by the central school in Beijing. It is titled in English the China Executive Leadership Academy Pudong (CELAP). Its Chinese name explains more straightforwardly what it is: National Cadre School.

This Shanghai academy is especially globally minded – inevitable given its location in the thrusting satellite city of Pudong, which today teems with international corporate offices that have been created since 1990, across the Huangpu River from the Bund of old Shanghai. As recently as the 1980s, the area's chief features were rice paddies and a few run-down warehouses. Now, it provides the setting for three of the world's tallest buildings: the Jin Mao Tower, with eighty-eight floors, the Shanghai World Financial Centre with 101 floors, and – due for completion in 2014 – the Shanghai Tower, which will have 128 floors.

The party school is no less impressive, in an only slightly more subtle way. Its main building, designed by the French architect Anthony Bechu and completed in 2006, is a massive red-roofed structure from which an office tower juts. Its shape is intended to resemble a Ming Dynasty Chinese scholar's desk, with the tower like the brush-holder.

There are 870 rooms for students and guests on the campus, within five five-storey hotel-like blocks shaped to resemble folding books. The accommodation, including the meals, is administered by JinJiang, one of China's best-known hotel chains. Each student's window has a view over Shanghai's Huangpu River, or over a lake which has been created at the centre of the school's grounds. The whole site is bounded auspiciously by Prosperous Street and Future Expectations Street. Like the CPS in Beijing, and the other party schools, it is fenced around, and only people with appointments with staff are allowed inside the gates.

The school's library is massive and surprisingly diverse. Alexander McCall Smith, creator of *The Number One Ladies Detective Agency*, rubs shoulders on the shelves with *Angel Customers & Demon Customers: Discover Which Is Which*, and *Turbo-Charge Your Stock*.

The person who runs the school, vice president Jiang Haishan, is fluent in English, and highly articulate about what CELAP is doing. The titular head, the president, was in 2012 Li Yuanchao, the chief of the national party's Organisation Department, based in Beijing – a formidable patron and ally for any party institution.

Jiang spoke with me at length, over many cups of tea, one afternoon in a room at the centre of the main school building. He has spent almost two years studying in Australia, taking education courses at La Trobe University in Melbourne and at Queensland University, and has invited a number of Australian leaders, including former prime minister Bob Hawke, former foreign minister Alexander Downer, and Australia's former chief competition regulator Allan Fels, to speak at the academy.

He pointed out that Shanghai was doubly ideal as the centre for a party school. It was the birthplace of the Chinese Communist Party. And because the Yangtze delta had been at the fore of China's economic engagement in globalisation, it was the natural home for an institution that seeks to transfer the experiences and lessons of the dynamic era since the country opened to the world. "We want China to become more integrated into the international community," he said. The party's then general secretary Hu Jintao said he wanted the Pudong centre "to seek new paths, to apply leadership training in a practical way, to obtain concrete results." Thus every year, CELAP runs two fortnight-long programs for the bosses at state-owned enterprises on how to pursue the new national imperative to "go global" by investing aggressively around the world.

The CELAP model, Jiang says, is to focus the curriculum on problem-solving. "We hope the officials of today can really understand our context, our situation, and the world situation. So we have run many programs on the (post 2008) financial crisis." Every year CELAP has two or three courses with forty participants at the ministerial level, and recently most have focused on solving financial dilemmas. Lecturers have come from Citibank, Goldman Sachs and other big multinational companies.

Other recent courses, says Jiang, have been dominated by advice on how to transform China's central agencies or its regions or state-owned corporations into environmentally friendly and energy-saving entities. Emergency and risk management provide another prominent theme.

"Society is changing so swiftly," he says, "especially due to rapid urbanisation, that some imbalance is inevitable, and conflicts emerge that need to be addressed. Many challenges are thus related. Our job is to provide some advice as to how to manage them. We catalogue crises." Whether they are to do with public health, business, natural disasters, social crises that trigger demonstrations, or international issues, the school sends people to the relevant places to conduct investigations and gain first-hand material.

The school has at its heart a space like an especially large laboratory. Students who gather there divide into four groups and each focuses on one area of concern, to which they apply their solutions following dis-cussion. The technology for this "smart city" laboratory has been provided with the assistance of IBM. But the content has been developed by CELAP itself. That includes issues that have arisen in the challenging process of urbanisation in China. It also includes coping with financial crises, with extensive data made available from twenty-seven global stock markets so that students can be tested in real-life situations.

Media labs are another feature of CELAP. Before 2000, there was lit-tle or no training available in China for leaders in how to deal with media, says Jiang. "We have been pioneers. Already thousands of offi-cials have been through our media courses – which are especially important now that every level of government is being asked by Beijing to be more transparent, and press conferences have become not only common, but a requirement." This, he says, represents a strikingly new direction for China, which in the past never trained its leaders to talk in public. Confucius, for instance, advocated a low profile. But today, tech-nical skills alone are not enough for leadership, Jiang says.

A further innovation at CELAP is the introduction of more than 150 "field situation sites" in Shanghai and in adjacent Jiangsu and Zhejiang provinces. Thus the new Xintiandi ("new heaven and new earth") development in Shanghai's old French quarter, with its trendy cafes, bars, stores and houses, is visited by CELAP students not only as the birthplace of the Communist Party, whose first congress was held in the area, but also for the lessons it teaches about balancing heritage and commerce.

Jiang says that ten years ago, many smaller state-owned businesses were in the process of being privatised, chiefly by being sold to individuals. But "much corruption resulted," since there was insufficient transparency, and they were not large enough to be listed. Visiting such companies, examining their intellectual property issues and other challenges, is one of the most popular field study topics run by CELAP.

Agricultural development is another major theme. The party students take field trips to Huaxi Village of Jiangsu province, which is claimed as the wealthiest village in China, to fathom reasons for its success. Such visits, asking questions of the people who work in those situations, fill a third of most courses at CELAP, taking them out of the lecture rooms.

Jiang says that "traditional philosophy is also still very important in our training, in the area we call 'values education.' That emphasises loyalty, to your position, to the state, and to the people." This part of the program involves traditional Chinese philosophy as well as Maoist thought, capacity building and behaviour orientation. The students learn to make speeches, to organise press conferences, to "meet the people." Jiang says that "Marxism still dominates ideology in China, but we can't just copy it from books. We must learn to apply it in practice. We can't expect that Karl Marx of 150 years ago would have known exactly what would be happening today. He didn't know anything of motor vehicles or the internet." The CELAP courses routinely include teaching about "the new practice of Marxism," or "localized Marxism" – sometimes known as socialism with Chinese characteristics.

The traditional pure state ownership of companies is evolving, Jiang says. "Now we are creating multi-share structures, which are symbolic of new forms of socialism. We can't just copy these ideas from books. We have had to develop according to our changed situation. That is the Chinese way. Everything should move with the times." And, he asked, what is socialism anyway? "We are still on the way to understanding that," he responded frankly to his own question. According to classic

Marxism, he says, socialism should be based on well-developed capitalism. But 93 per cent of the Chinese population in the 1950s were farmers. Now less than half the population lives in the countryside. "So how to build socialism in that context? Some Westerners have said we are capitalists. We ask what that means too. We are at the stage of seeking."

Thus even in its elite party schools – or perhaps especially there – the CCP is struggling to balance its dual need to strive for modernity through change, and to honour the party's early history.

Jiang says that while Deng Xiaoping's version of pragmatism was to advise "crossing the river by feeling the stones," the water is now deeper, so China should be careful. The obvious reforms have been done already. The new challenges are being taken on by a younger generation, who will only have seen Mao on TV history shows, or on party DVDs. Most of the cadres who come to CELAP are aged in their forties. These are very senior officials, says Jiang.

"We can't say we are never affected by history – and China is such a large country, and under the imperial system before 1911 it was governed in a top-down, very centralised way." But he now believes that provincial governors should be elected at people's congresses, and that the party should devolve more democracy and responsibility to local people. "We learn from other nations, but we don't copy" their political structures, although he points out that the People's Republic did originally take ideas from the Soviet Union in many areas.

What are party members encouraged to think about the demise of the USSR, which naturally came as such a shock to Beijing in 1990, coming immediately after the Chinese party's own torrid time during the Tiananmen protests? This left China alone in the world as a major communist power. It has been vital for the party to ensure its members are all pointed in the "right direction" in responding to the Soviet Union's collapse – presenting it with a major educational challenge.

It took a long time for the CCP to think this through at the top level, and then to develop a plan for a mass education program. Finally, in 2006, all party members were required to watch a series of eight glossily produced DVDs titled *Think of danger while living in safety: the lessons from the collapse of the Soviet Union Communist Party*. They were marked never to be shown to the general public. Party members were required not only to view all eight shows, but to submit written responses. Some of these were posted on party units' websites.

26

The programs stated that despite severe disagreements between the Chinese and Soviet parties, "deep in the hearts of Chinese communists and the Chinese people, there remains a strong emotional link with Lenin and with the home of the October Revolution." When Joseph Stalin died in 1953, they stated, Mao Zedong wept loudly at the Soviet embassy in Beijing. "Through the passage of time, people realise more and more deeply that the mistakes of Stalin cannot negate his role as a great proletarian revolutionary and Marxist." The thinly coded message for Chinese party viewers: for Stalin, read Mao. Allow his exalted status to be undermined, and the party's prestige and authority will also be crucially damaged. Khruschev's era was denigrated in the Chinese DVDs because, crucially, it denied the role of Stalin and thus "denied the history of the Soviet Union, which in turn triggered severe problems." Thus the shows underlined the need for the Chinese party to retain its rigid insistence on the correct historical line being portrayed in essays, books, TV and films.

Enter the real villain. The programs placed most of the blame on Mikhail Gorbachev for "the extinction of the party, which must mean the extinction of the country" after seventy-four years in power. By extension, the same equation may be applied to China: the end of the party's rule would mean the fragmentation and collapse of the country itself. As the DVD put it: "Collaborating with nationalists, the so-called democrats within the party sped its split and that of the Soviet Union ... encouraged by concepts advocated by Gorbachev, including democratisation, openness and diversity of public opinion." On Christmas Day 1991, it said, "the flag with the hammer and sickle, deeply loved by generations of people in the Soviet Union and around the world, sunk in the cold winter wind."

Gorbachev, the programs said, "accepted the capitalist view of the world, which turned him into a complete traitor to socialism and communism," and his "so-called openness" – *glasnost* – opened the country to anti-communist forces, and to Lenin being branded "a hooligan." The Chinese shows were emphatic about the importance of keeping control of the media. They cited a post-Soviet Russian writer saying how the failed German invaders of 1941 lacked one weapon that eventually brought the country down fifty years later – "publications and TV stations armed with bacteria."

The core reason for the disaster was that the party turned its back on Marxism and Leninism. "When strong ideology that unites the hearts of the people and party members is thrown away, can that party survive?" Personal style was another factor. "Stalin always lived simply, and when he died, people found only four suits in his wardrobe, two civilian and two military." Gradually corruption prevailed, with "party internal democracy and supervision disappearing," starting with the allegedly self-regarding Khruschev and culminating in the demonic Gorbachev, "a two-faced person only good at playing tricks."

The Russian people, the series concluded, were now re-thinking what happened, and two-thirds surveyed regretted the fall of the Soviet Union. "When Vladimir Putin stepped in, he re-established pride in the country. The party history was published again by the education ministry, many books praising Stalin were released, and his statues were re-erected. Of course, the renaissance of Russia still has a long way to go. But we firmly believe that with its collapse as a rare negative lesson, human history must have a colourful new spring."

Generally, however, areas in which China sought to copy directly from the Soviets failed – as in the planning system, said CELAP chief Jiang. As a result of taking that Soviet route, by the 1980s China had more than 100 government ministers. In 2012 it had twenty-seven. Now, China is sending officials to learn about best administrative practice from countries all over the world – from the USA, Australia, Europe, Japan, South Korea. And CELAP has contacts with many overseas institutions. Such international contacts help to broaden horizons, Jiang says. "All governments in China used to be fixated on gross domestic product growth. It is up to us to change this attitude, with a focus also on public service and the environment and energy needs. If we can't tackle such issues ourselves, it will be disastrous, and our leaders need to understand that." CELAP is also encouraging local government leaders to learn from the opinions of netizens – China's massive population of online commentators.

Underlying the long list of problems with which CELAP seeks to grapple, Jiang says, is the awareness that the party must constantly be aware that it "comes from the people." The Soviet Union collapsed because its party lost that connection – "we have many studies on that. If people's living standards don't improve, how can we just sit there? That's the big story for us."

Jiang worked in the Shanghai municipal government in 2000, when "most government officials were feeling very important." Today, officials have to change such attitudes, or problems will result – for them as well as for the party, which Jiang describes as at the cutting edge of change. "We are telling people that if they don't change their mindset, their job has to change. If a leader can't understand this national strategy, it would be very difficult for them here." The CELAP students who fail to get on message during their courses at party schools are thus likely to find their paths to promotion blocked, and older officials will be sidelined.

New members are thus especially keen to demonstrate their eagerness to learn during their time at the schools. One of them, a staffer at the powerful State-owned Asset Supervision and Administration Commission of the State Council, revealingly posted online his notes on study sessions in which he participated in 2012. The notes were spotted by *China Digital Times*, based at the University of California's Berkeley campus.

The SASAC staffer said that the course for new members began at the party school at 8.30 in the morning. There were about 120 students. Most were young. "Surprisingly," he wrote, "some were already driving BMW 3 series cars. Most of the girls were carrying Louis Vuitton bags." Although SASAC itself is immaculately well resourced, the new member conceded that at the party school "the facilities really weren't bad at all … first class!"

A booklet titled *The Essentials of Joining the Party* was distributed. Then after a short and simple opening ceremony, they started the first session: "Development history of the party of the working class." The lecturer was even younger than the new member. She introduced the topic of the Soviet Communist Party, systematically explaining the reason for its downfall: chiefly, it had been rejected by its own working class. On the Chinese party's reform of the job-for-life cadre system, replacing it with strictly imposed retirement ages, the instructor gave the example of Jiang Zemin, who, after the age of seventy, needed to rest, the lecturer said, lacking the energy to participate in scheduled activities. "She asked: if we could imagine all the leaders in the party in such a state, would the country still have hope?"

The lecturer continued by criticising North Korea's cult of worship of the Kim family, connecting this with China's own ten years of Cultural Revolution chaos. She said an intellectual family member of hers had hanged himself from the rafters, in humiliation and grief, after being publicly criticised. After taking the body down, they discovered he had written, in brushstrokes on his forearm, "Long live Chairman Mao."

The critique then shifted to Japan's Liberal Democratic Party, and how powerful family politics had forfeited its future control. The lecturer's final comment was that the CCP is the political party of the working class, of which white-collar workers are today an important part.

Following this lecture they ate lunch, a crucial test for the credibility of any establishment in China. The party school passed. The new member wrote: "The school's cafeteria wasn't bad." Perhaps partly as a result, he noted, many dozed off during the afternoon class – which began with a lecture on motivation for entering the party, followed by small discussion groups.

The next instructor was a career naval officer, who – the new member presumed – must also be a political cadre. The officer said that if the rising generation gets old before fully understanding what communism is, "then we will be successful, because the objectives of the party will change as the era changes." He criticised those who are now joining in large numbers in order to be promoted or get a raise, and said that too many of the new members were college students.

The instructor discussed the self-criticisms that members are required to make, illustrating his slightly sceptical views with what the new member described as "half-jokes": "When you make a mistake and are immediately placed under review, you are an ordinary member. When you make a mistake and do your best to explain, you are a section head. When you make a mistake and don't make a sound, you are a department head. When you make a mistake and steadfastly deny it, you are a director."

After the first day of class, the new member wrote, "I felt that the political cadres weren't so pedantic or conservative. They hadn't lost touch. But the closer to the basic level you get, the lower the quality of leaders and cadres." The instructor had expressed the opinion that government decrees don't get far beyond Zhongnanhai, the national leaders' HQ compound, immediately to the west of the Forbidden City.

The next day, the course was given the impression by an instructor that there were now too many party members. "This isn't good news," the SASAC staffer thought to himself – because he feared it meant a likely rash of "fringe thinking." The instructor only mentioned the dangers of extreme leftists within the party – he didn't mention rightists.

Another lecturer gave him the impression that "it's almost impossible to get out of the party," even if people decided they wanted to leave.

The new members were told of a survey by the Organisation Department which found that some of the 3,170,000 party organisations had fallen into a state of partial paralysis or decline. For example, it cited a common phenomenon called 3860, meaning party branches composed entirely of women over sixty (8 March is Women's Day). The men in those communities had moved elsewhere to find work and rarely returned.

There was also discussion of democracy and supervision within the party. Realistically, the new member thought, "we will have to wait until after Princeling Xi (Xi Jinping) to realize the establishment of a democratic system within the party."

The new members all took a test at the end of the course. The SASAC staffer passed and received a training certificate the next morning. At the end of the final session, a party school director spoke. "Young people today understand far too little and sleep in class," he said in a dour tone. Some people had cheated in their tests and prepared answers in their smart-phones beforehand, the director lamented. The new member thought: "Man, how come they needed to cheat to answer such simple questions?" For those whose heads and hearts were actually somewhere else, the director said, it was best to drop their party membership right now. Finally, he wished them success at their jobs.

"It was over," the new member summed up. "While studying, I hit it off with a few new friends. This wasn't bad, I felt. Tomorrow I would take my certificate to the party committee so I could reimburse my training fee – 400 yuan (US$61)."

If such a conclusion appears a little limp and even mercantile, that may not be so disastrous for a party struggling to keep in tandem two apparently contradictory core aims – technocratic modernity, and party verities dating back to Mao. Its members may not be joining for the reasons the party most wishes, and their views may not be entirely in line with the leadership's. But they are still joining, in greater numbers than ever. They will respond, in a fashion, to party expectations and requests. They form a corps of 83 million, including many of the country's best and brightest – the insiders who run almost every institution in China.

CHAPTER 3:
HOW THE PARTY RULES

EVERY MARCH, AS BEIJING IS STILL SHIVERING IN THE freezing winds sweeping down from the Gobi Desert, the National People's Congress – China's parliament – meets for its annual fortnight-long session. The venue is the Soviet-style Great Hall of the People, to the west of Tiananmen Square, which stands at the centre of both the city and the nation.

For the opening session, the square is empty, fenced off by police. The 3000 delegates arrive by buses that have picked them up from their high-security hotels. They are shielded throughout their stay in the capital from the general public – the *laobaixing* – they represent, and especially from the bothersome petitioners who find their way in their thousands to Beijing from the provinces, as they have since the imperial era, seeking to catch the attention of the leaders to redress injustices they or their families have suffered.

The delegates are dressed overwhelmingly in business suits, except for the representatives of China's non-Han minorities, who are encouraged, perhaps required, to wear their traditional dress, accentuating their largely decorative role. The buses park on the empty square and the delegates file up the steps into the Great Hall. They warm up by taking tea and snacks and greeting old friends before filing in to fill the lower tier of the grandest room within the Great Hall.

Up on the stage, facing them, sit the members of the NPC's Standing Committee and other luminaries. At the very front of the stage sit the most senior elite, including the nine members of the Standing Committee of the Politburo of the Communist Party, the men who ultimately rule China. Young women in uniforms pour water and tea for them, take messages in and out and tactfully wake elderly party veterans who have nodded off.

In the centre of the front row sits China's paramount leader, Xi Jinping, general secretary of the party and chairman of the Central Military Commission. His only official position within the government (as opposed to the party) is the largely ceremonial role of president. As the opening of the People's Congress is the government's day in the sun (or, more often, the snow), the burden of the day falls on the premier, the leader of the government and number two in the party hierarchy – who from March 2013 will be Li Keqiang.

The Congress opens with a People's Liberation Army band playing the stirring national anthem, "The March of the Volunteers," which was originally written for a play in Shanghai in 1934. The event is covered live by China Central TV, with cameras almost everywhere. They pan to delegates chosen for their representativeness, or their colourful dress, as they sing the martial lyrics: *Arise, all those who don't want to be slaves! Let our flesh and blood forge our new Great Wall! As the Chinese people have arrived at their most perilous time, every person is forced to expel his very last cry. Arise! Arise! Arise! Our million hearts beating as one, brave the enemy's fire, march on!*

The premier then delivers his "work report," a state-of-the-nation address that comprises the Chinese government's chief annual policy statement. Economic conditions – watched with increasing anxiety by a wider world now dependent on China to set the pace for global growth – are sketched and new policies foreshadowed, usually in the broadest of brush strokes. Sinologists scrupulously count the number of references to Marx, Mao, Deng and other communist divines (the former two are by now usually missing altogether).

This address, which takes at least two hours to deliver, sets the tone and provides the agenda for the NPC meetings that follow. The delegates meet in rooms named for their province or region. There are thirty-three regional bodies in China: twenty-two provinces, four municipalities, five autonomous regions and two special administrative regions (Hong Kong and Macau). The Great Hall also includes a room named for the "province" of Taiwan, which is represented by delegates – none of whom come directly from the island itself, but claim other links. The People's Liberation Army and overseas Chinese have their own delegations too.

Delegates discuss the NPC's agenda and can raise concerns with top government leaders who are spread around the provincial meetings, one per room. Journalists are allowed to attend these meetings for limited periods. The delegates are chosen for five-year terms by a convoluted, pyramidical process involving provincial and other congresses. At the 2011 NPC, 21 per cent of delegates were women. Crucially, the great majority are party members – usually more than 80 per cent.

They mostly, though not always, approve all items on the agenda, including bills and executive appointments – although they first have an opportunity, in smaller sessions, to raise local questions or concerns. Most of the real work of the NPC is conducted by its Standing Committee of 150 people, which makes decisions between the annual meetings. At the end of the annual congress, the premier holds the only regular press conference – but the questions, and the questioners themselves, are pre-approved.

Immediately following the premier's address at the opening ceremony, the leaders file off the platform and into a tiny open square inside the Great Hall complex, where their black Audis await. They are driven, in strict order of party precedence (and in a brilliant display of logistics, given the tight space), the 300 metres back to the Zhongnanhai leadership compound just across the road. They sometimes drive there through a broad tunnel beneath the road, which enables the leaders to come and go freely without forcing the traffic to stop – and without attracting speculation as to the reason for their journey. Mao Zedong built a vast underground infrastructure in Beijing, to shelter the city from nuclear attack or conventional bombing, and these tunnels now provide handy thoroughfares for the leaders.

This great annual event, with its history and ritual, illustrates the extent to which China's government and the Communist Party are intertwined. It would be extremely difficult to extricate party and government structures – although not totally impossible, as illustrated by Taiwan's experience in the late 1980s.

The extent of this entanglement starts with Article 1 of China's constitution, which asserts: "The socialist system is the basic system of the People's Republic of China. Disruption of the socialist system by any organisation or individual is prohibited." This is not an historical curiosity. These words are to be taken seriously and at face value by anyone who has dealings with China. The party's top priority is control of every area of national life, which it uses not in lieu of legitimacy but as a source of it. The party takes immensely seriously its duty to rule China the way it believes China needs to be ruled and, it is increasingly explicitly argued, the way China has always been ruled, especially during its previous great ages of prosperity.

While China's physical landscape has been revolutionised in the twenty-first century, and while people's lifestyles, especially in the cities, continue to evolve rapidly, China's core institutions have remained almost unchanged since 1949. The five-yearly congresses are still crucial. The Politburo Standing Committee of seven men (no woman has yet become a member) remains the peak decision-making body. All government bodies – the ministries, the provincial governors, the mayors – are subordinate to the party policy makers. In official diagrams of the Chinese government, which can be found on office walls throughout the country – especially of foreign enterprises, as they puzzle over whom to approach for approvals – the structure of the government itself, with the State Council at its pinnacle, does not make it to the top half of the page. The upper branches are reserved for the Central Committee of the CCP and its general secretary, now Xi Jinping.

The party's seventeenth congress, in October 2007, opened under stunningly bright blue skies in a Beijing that had been more than usually shrouded in pollution. The driver of the taxi in which I headed as close as I could get to Tiananmen Square wound down the windows and turned up the radio as a symphonic version of "The East Is Red" came on air, thumping the steering wheel in time.

Inside the Great Hall, the band of the People's Liberation Army struck up "The March of the Volunteers" and the then general secretary, Hu Jintao, strode to the rostrum and started his speech against a massive hammer and sickle backdrop. "*Tongzhimen*," he said. "Today, socialist China is standing rock-firm in the East, oriented towards modernisation, the world and the future." All seemed right in the communist firmament.

Sun Xian-mei, the party secretary of a low-income residential compound in Yinchuan, the capital of the poor northern Ningxia region, was attending her first congress. As she stepped blinking into the sunlight afterwards, gazing across the empty Tiananmen Square, she told me that Hu's 2.5-hour speech had been "exciting and encouraging." She pledged, "I will practise what was said, and make a greater contribution to building a harmonious society."

Not everyone in the Great Hall seemed so caught up in the excitement, however. Hu's predecessor, Jiang Zemin, then aged eighty, was either meditating or napping during much of the speech. He was seated in the front row on the stage behind Hu, along with former premiers Li Peng and Zhu Rongji as well as Song Ping, who as minister for party organisation in the 1980s "talent spotted" Hu, then a provincial official, bringing him to the attention of Deng Xiaoping.

We shall examine in this chapter how China is administered and how the government exercises its remarkable capacity to micro-manage people's daily lives when it needs to, with remarkably few taking offence.

This is a vast country, in which the provinces naturally play an important role. Policies are set centrally, but tend to be implemented a little differently everywhere. The top party leaders are required to gain an understanding of provincial realities – they are almost always promoted to the most powerful central positions only after serving several terms as provincial chiefs. Mere national ministers are thus a rung down in authority to provincial party secretaries. And prospective new policies tend to be road-tested in one or two locations in regional China before being fine-tuned and adopted nationally.

However, despite the widespread attitude in regional China that the further from Beijing, the more room they have to do their own thing, the provinces are only given so much leeway. They are by no means akin to American or Australian states, for instance. If a provincial leader is perceived to have overstepped a mark or been disloyal to the central authorities, he is swiftly removed, as was Chen Liangyu in Shanghai in 2006, and Bo Xilai in Chongqing in 2012. Provincial governors are members of party committees, usually consisting of about twelve people; the governor is accountable to the local party secretary and is only one of a group of decision-makers.

There are two clear exceptions to this centralised model: Hong Kong and Macau, the former British and Portuguese territories that were returned to Chinese sovereignty at the end of the twentieth century. When Hong Kong returned on 1 July 1997, its Basic Law – in effect the constitution of Beijing's new "special administrative region" – provided for fifty years of independence for its courts, media, economic policy, religious institutions and businesses, and a degree of control over its borders. The extent of this concession was lost in the drama surrounding the "handover" of Hong Kong, one of the last big set-pieces marking the end of the Western colonial era. In the colour and movement of this event, it was the uniqueness, within China, of Hong Kong – and two years later Macau as well – as beneficiaries of the "one country, two systems" formula attributed to Deng Xiaoping, that was emphasised. Few made much of the rather more striking point, that the supposedly unusual concessions granted to Hong Kong and Macau in fact highlighted the uniqueness of China's own system. They point to the ways in which China itself differs from most of the world, and from its East Asian neighbours. China's system of government is today rare and strange in global terms.

Despite its massive structure of provincial and local officials, they remain in effect agents of the central authority. China is the only country of its size to be ruled in a unitary manner without devolving power. India, the USA, Canada, Brazil, Russia, Indonesia, Australia – all the other nations that might be compared in either their landmass or population to China are federations. Ürümqi, the capital of the region of Xinjiang in the north-west, is 2200 kilometres west of Beijing. But its schools, businesses and government offices have to operate on Beijing time, requiring them to start studying and working – in theory, at least, although many informally run their own timetables – when it is still pitch dark. There is only a single time zone throughout China.

This unified system is more stable, predictable and prosperous than it was under Mao, who set it up. The legal apparatus, the media (including the internet), business, the education system, the bureaucracy and, of course, the security forces, are operated – or at least directed – by the Communist Party. Despite a brief period of experimental, incremental detachment under the ill-fated premier Zhao Ziyang in the late 1980s, the party remains inseparable from the state it rules.

Ministries and other government agencies each contain, alongside the public servants who administer and implement policy, teams of elite party officials. The party secretary always takes precedence in decision-making over, for instance, a mayor or a governor. Typically, the party team takes special responsibility for human relations – making key appointments, determining promotions and organising training – while the public service team focuses on infrastructure. At its best, this structure strikes a balance between the party and the government, although the party must always be seen to get its way on big issues. In practice, the lines often blur. The governor or mayor, for instance, will also be a party member, and will sit on the core party committee, usually as deputy to the party secretary.

In recent years, the party has made a show of introducing a degree of "intra-party democracy," by which some less senior public positions are now open to competition, with party members choosing between preselected candidates. At the lowest levels, some town officials are now chosen through a "three-ticket" system. First, candidates compete for the popular vote. Then, they must perform well in an exam – a return to the old Confucian days of imperial civil service tests, one of the world's earliest forms of meritocracy. Third, they are considered by the local party committee.

One of the top experts on Chinese governance is Jean-Christophe Iseux, a loquacious, cosmopolitan Frenchman who has become a Canadian citizen – and, most unusually, a trusted insider in China. He is the director of the Institute of World Economy at the People's University in Beijing and has served as an adviser to the international department of the CCP's Central Committee. He believes that despite the underlying continuities, China's governance structures are starting to adjust, moving slowly towards broader participation.

He has himself been specially appointed – a rare event for a foreigner – a member of the Chinese People's Political Consultative Conference (CPPCC) in Changchun, the capital of Jilin province in the north-east. This CPPCC is a third body in China, alongside the party and the National People's Congress. Structured like a pyramid, with national, provincial and local levels, members of the CPPCC are chosen from a range of commercial, artistic, scientific, sporting and other fields, and are intended to represent the broader community.

Iseux views the CPPCC as the best example of democratic consultation in China today. Mao used it only once, in 1949, to enlist approval from beyond the party for the constitution of the new China. Deng initiated its routine use. "It was an inspired move," says Iseux, for it gave a voice to views not otherwise represented within the party. "But it's only a consultative house."

He gives as an example the decision by the Changchun CPPCC to oppose the opening up of coal processing to foreign firms. This was passed by 92 per cent of the representatives and then sent on to the local NPC, which passed it on to a subcommittee of the provincial NPC and then on to the provincial government. "It's one way to source laws and directives very differently from central government. There's starting to be more bottom-up consultation – providing a step towards constitutionalism," he says. The CPPCC delegates hold their meetings before the local and provincial NPC meetings draw up their legislative agendas. Thus, says Iseux, about a third of the bills passed at Changchun's NPC originated with the local CPPCC.

Each of these three structures – the party congress, the people's congress and the CPPCC – has members and meetings at a local level, who pass suggestions and delegate representatives up ever higher steps until reaching their national congresses. Iseux says that the congresses experience a large turnover by the time they reach the national level, with 30 to 50 per cent of delegates changing at each five-year term.

At the top, he says, "factional politics are strong." And the factions are becoming more important and more structured, as more positions slowly open up to contestability. Cheng Li, director of research at the John L. Thornton China Center at the Brookings Institution, has led the way in assiduously identifying members of two core factions: the "princelings" (*taizidang*), sons and daughters of party veterans, and supporters of the Youth League (the *tuanpai*), originally associated with Hu Yaobang and led until recently by Hu Jintao and Wen Jiabao.

Iseux also points to functional and geographic groupings. The former include the People's Liberation Army, the All China Women's Federation, and to a degree the party schools. Geographically, the most famous faction is the "Shanghai clique" led by former party chief Jiang Zemin. They became all-powerful following the suppression of the protests in 1989, in which Shanghai was deemed by Deng Xiaoping to have played a model role. Iseux says, "Shanghai people had never run China before" – although the Gang of Four was effectively headquartered there during the Cultural Revolution. Because so many other senior cadres had been discredited during the Tiananmen protests, Deng pushed the Shanghai leaders forward at the fifteenth National Party Congress in 1992.

Under Jiang Zemin and his Shanghai allies, some power was decentralised. Responsibility for taxes and financial services were handed to provincial governments and municipalities. Certain investment decisions could be approved at the regional level, without the involvement of the central government. But, says Iseux, Jiang Zemin "forgot that this could run the country into huge amounts of basic corruption." The next generation of leaders, Hu Jintao and Wen Jiabao, decided to clamp down on the Shanghai faction. The Shanghai party secretary, Chen Liangyu, was jailed in 2008 for eighteen years on charges of fraud, abuse of power and accepting bribery. Some decentralisation of economic decision-making has continued, but officials around the country are being more closely supervised, and party disciplinary structures have been given greater resources. Today, Iseux says, a "Shandong clique" from the country's ancient north-eastern province, the home of Confucius and a centre of military power, is also starting to acquire considerable strength, and is aligned with the Beijing-based cadres.

Holding a balance between the factions enables the administration to run comparatively smoothly, while the existence of local, semi-representative forums has helped to reinforce the party's legitimacy in recent years, Iseux believes. Nevertheless, no one is permitted to build such networks without the party's imprimatur. "Holding real power in China, its 3000-year political history shows, means having control of a network from top to bottom. That is the only thing that matters." So all networks, even those allowed some degree of independence, begin and end with the party.

When Iseux started working at People's University in 1999, he began asking his students annually if they wanted to join the party. Then, about thirty out of eighty said they did. Eight years later, it was 75 per cent. "That's not surprising," he said, "since important decision-making only happens within the party." The party's authority trumps that of the government administration, at both the national and local levels. Hu Jintao underlined this in June 2007, at a gathering of top cadres at the Central Party School in Beijing: "We have to insist on the party's leadership, the principle of people in charge and rule by law so as to push self-development and improvement of the socialist political system." The government implements policy, the legislature ratifies it – but the party determines what direction the country should take, and is not shy about reining in these other structures when it needs to.

The key decisions made at the party congresses are about who goes where and gets what. For decades, these reshuffles, promotions and demotions were informally agreed on by key factional powerbrokers during their annual trip to the seaside. They would stay at Beidaihe, a resort town three hours from Beijing by slow train whose prime feature is a fine beach that runs for ten kilometres from the Yinjiao Pavilion to the Daihe River. In 2004, Hu Jintao and Wen Jiabao decided that these decisions should be made in a more formal manner, in meeting rooms in Zhongnanhai, rather than in villas or seafood restaurants. But in 2012, on the eve of the National Party Congress that was to confirm China's leadership for the next decade, the mid-summer migration to Beidaihe seemed to be as popular as ever. They began to arrive, with their families, in late July. What happened there remained, and remains, off the record and essentially unknowable to outsiders. If many Chinese leaders continue to holiday in the comfortable government guest-houses at Beidaihe, and if they happen to chat with their comrades about current affairs, what's so odd about that?

These vast parallel bureaucracies – in the central ministries in Beijing and in the provincial departments, in the executive government structure and in the party structure – employ huge numbers of people and consume a large proportion of the national income. How is it all paid for? The answers, partial as they must remain – in a world in which all information is, at least in theory, owned by the state – come from an examination of how those with power tax those with less, at almost every turn.

Wu Si, the editor of the celebrated *Yanhuang Chunqiu* (*China Through the Ages*) history magazine and a party member himself, says that a large proportion of all taxes, charges, licences and other forms of government income goes into the party's own pocket. Typically, he says, out of the cost of a new real estate project, 20 per cent might be spent on real economic activity, 40 per cent will go to the developer himself, and the other 40 per cent is diverted to the approvals process, including to officials, to obtain access to land. "If you don't pay, they will delay a 'chop' [government stamp] for one or two years, or say the quality of your work is not good enough." "Just like robbers on the road," he says, "you must pay a fee for them to let you go, to refrain from hurting you." Sometimes literally: if, for instance, someone faces a jail term of five years, "the gift of a red bag [*hongbao*; a corrupt payment] could ensure it is just three."

In this environment, even getting a job costs cash. The uncle of a young woman who graduated with a top degree in economics from Nankai University in Tianjin told me of his immense frustration with her search for work. She was set on joining the state-owned Bank of China, perhaps the most modern of the country's four "pillar banks." But she was quietly instructed in the hard realities of life in modern China: although she was well qualified for the position, competition was tough; perhaps generosity to a certain executive might improve her chances. She was forced, embarrassingly, to ask her relatives – including her uncle – to stump up the 10,000 yuan required.

The party does not release, even to its own members, anything like a budget. It resents being asked about such matters – in part because of a presumption that such questions imply that the party and state could and possibly even should be separated. This was the core heresy for which the writer Liu Xiaobo, the 2011 Nobel Peace Prize winner, was jailed for eleven years. Imagine, then, the shock caused by a deceptively straightforward series of questions by a bold law professor at a 2007 conference organised by senior officials, in a venue in the Fragrant Hills on the western edge of Beijing. His questions would be seen as completely routine in most other countries, but in China they were considered unthinkably impertinent.

The professor asked, for instance, whether the party had registered itself as a social organisation – and if so, to which ministry was it accountable – perhaps Civil Affairs? All other organisations in China must be responsible to a particular government department or agency. Furthermore, he asked, how much was the party collecting in membership fees, and how was it spending its income? How did it fund its five-yearly national congresses? Did it hire the Great Hall of the People? And under what arrangement did the party leadership occupy its headquarters at Zhongnanhai? Did it pay rent to the government for this fabulously expensive piece of real estate, and for the immense opportunity cost of forgoing the construction of high-rise buildings in the centre of Beijing (no structure is permitted to overlook Zhongnanhai in any way)?

There was no answer, beyond the silent fury of the cadres.

Party expert Cheng Li says, "Such questions are legitimate and important. Prominent Chinese public intellectuals have asked about the party's funding. But in China, the party owns the state. All the state's assets are the party's in reality, if not in theory."

Since every branch of government bureaucracy contains a party committee, often comprising full-time paid staff, some of the party's income (as well as the wages of such staff) can be assumed to come from the government, as a form of payment for policy-making services. Other income derives from the party's notional "purchases" of land and property, and perhaps of state-owned company shares. For instance, I have learned about the sale of a prime piece of real estate in downtown Shanghai by the city government – which controls all the land in the city – to the municipality's party branch, for a nominal amount. The building on the land was old and run-down. The party called in a friendly developer and a soaring skyscraper now stands on the site. It is not clear whether the party sold the property for a massive profit or remains the landlord, collecting the handsome rents. Either way, the party is a big winner – perhaps the biggest winner – from the emergence of "capitalism with Chinese characteristics." Wu Si says, "The party's logic is this: we fought for power and won, we took control of China and so everything under the sky is the party's."

There is also revenue from income tax, although this is a work in progress: just 6 per cent of government revenues come from personal tax. Overall tax revenue has grown by 20 per cent a year in China in recent years, more than double the rate of the economy as a whole, but this is principally thanks to greater efficiency in collecting value-added and company taxes. China's tax office keeps launching drives to persuade the millions of people who are believed to avoid paying income tax to do so. One such push in 2007 only landed 3000 volunteers, almost half of them in Bejing. In some cities, not a single person has registered to pay. The pay-as-you-earn system, whereby tax is collected by employers before wages are paid, is only common in state-owned businesses.

The income threshold for paying personal tax rose in September 2011 to US$540 per month, leaving an estimated 24 million people eligible to pay it. The initial tax rate is 3 per cent. An estimated 500,000 Chinese now hold assets worth more than US$1 million, but few even of the wealthiest are prepared to pay income tax, with the top personal rate unusually high for Asia at 45 per cent. The government is now considering linking tax file information to identification cards and passport renewals, and to visas and work permits for expatriates, who are also being targeted.

Investors in China's rollercoaster of a share market do not have to pay tax on their earnings, although stamp duty on transactions is almost unavoidable. But they are now required to declare their annual income from share trading, which is arousing considerable anxiety about future tax imposts.

Some of those who decline to pay tax offer the "no taxation without representation" argument. A typical comment on the popular website sina.com said: "Housing, education, health costs, looking after aged parents, these are all becoming heavier and heavier mountains weighing down on our shoulders. Tax paying has become a treat for the few who can afford it."

Liu Xiaobo, shortly before his arrest, told me: "In the West, a member of parliament has the right to look into the financial record of the government, but an NPC delegate does not have that right." The finance minister presents a general annual report to the National People's Congress, but it lacks detail. Of course, like any administration, the Chinese government must maintain a detailed account of its expenditures, but this is not revealed to the public. As Liu put it, political activity "traditionally takes place inside a dark box in China."

What is clear is that the State Council (China's cabinet), the National People's Congress (parliament) and the Chinese People's Political Consultative Conference (an advisory body) are all governed by the Standing Committee of the Central Committee of the Communist Party. So are the legal services, including the prosecutors and the courts, via the party's "political and legal" committee. Ministers of national departments usually also act as party secretary of their ministries, and major departmental decisions are made by a party committee. If someone loses his position in the party, said Liu, "he won't keep the government job that goes with it. An important official must have positions inside both the government and the party."

At the party congress in 1987, Premier Zhao Ziyang proposed detaching the party committees from the ministries. The congress agreed and an experiment in the separation of powers began. Before too long, however, demonstrations escalated and the party committees were strengthened again. Zhao was placed under house arrest until his death sixteen years later.

Although the ministries are now as firmly controlled by the party committees as ever, it is not easy to keep the entire governance of such a vast country constrained. Gaps do appear between the interests of the central and local leaderships. For instance, Beijing wants smaller coal-mines to be closed, because of their widespread disregard for safety and for the environment. But in a poor province such as Shanxi, south-west of Beijing – a land of degraded and rocky soils and crevasses straddling the old Silk Road – this would mean reduced economic growth and higher unemployment. Officials in such places depend on bonuses for a considerable portion of their income, and these bonuses are tied to factors such as economic growth, employment levels and social order. Government officials at all levels in such places are deeply involved with the small mines, said Liu. "They have shares, or friends run them, or relatives work in them or, more directly, they get kick-backs from them."

Liu is hardly alone in saying so. But doing so from within China, where his words carry weight – he speaks in the measured tone of an upright gentleman scholar – caused the party considerable grief, as his arrest confirms.

CHAPTER 4: THE ENFORCERS

ONE SUNNY CHINESE DAY, DURING A VISIT TO THE OLD British enclave of the coastal city of Tianjin, a former treaty port, I was wandering with my family through a delightful park – full of the usual open-air Chinese pursuits: music making, table tennis, tai chi, chess, ballroom dancing – when a group of about 100 middle-aged and elderly people began to assemble on a street corner opposite.

They held up a banner and placards and began to chant in a subdued manner. Political activists? Unusually tentative Falun Gong practitioners? After all, this was the city where that group's encounters with the authorities had first alerted the party elite to what they perceived as a new threat.

Neither. They wore T-shirts printed with Chinese characters above English translations: "misery," "fear," "anxiety." Their cause was simple: their homes, just across the river, some of them historic, were being torn down to make way for a new development. All services had been removed and they were reduced to using polluted river water for washing and cooking. As I took a photo, a soldier guarding some nearby government offices came over to usher me away. Seeing us, one of the braver demonstrators shouted in English, "Post a photo! Let the world know what's happening here!"

These protesters simply had no other recourse. The courts, they well knew, were not on their side. They would have heard through the grapevine about a notorious case a few weeks earlier in the same city. Eleven residents had appeared in the Nankai district court house seeking to save their homes from similar destruction, even if only temporarily. Wang Ling, then aged twenty-six, a lawyer with the Beijing Cailiang law firm, was representing them; they had come to his firm's office only that morning, after receiving notice that their homes would be demolished the next day.

The notice, issued by the Tianjin Nankai Construction Committee, announced an extension of a demolition zone demarcated two years earlier and intended for subway construction, although the subway had already been completed. The judge ruled that the court could not accept a collective petition – "and even if they lay complaints one by one, I still won't accept them." The lawyer told his clients that he would appeal to a higher court on their behalf.

The judge became angry, rose up out of his seat and aimed a blow at the lawyer, although he later denied – "in the name of my twenty-eight years of Communist Party membership" – actually landing a punch. One of the residents took a photo. The judge ordered police to grab the camera. A melee followed. The judge approached the lawyer and warned him, "Be careful when you walk alone at night!" He then grabbed the lawyer by the neck and had to be pulled off him. A police officer said later, when asked about the assault, "We are several ranks lower than court officials. What can we do?" The judge's ultimate pronouncement as he left that day's non-hearing was, "I am the court, the court is me."

Despite such incidents, the legal system today exhibits more signs of fairness than it has during most of the country's history. It remains, however, ultimately subordinate to the party, which retains the right – and the power – to direct every institution as it feels necessary, from football clubs to the Catholic Church. An official tract published in 1958, *On the People's Democratic Dictatorship and the People's Democratic Legal System*, encapsulated what remains the prevailing ethos of China's justice system: "Party policy is the soul of the law." It is very difficult to imagine a judicial verdict that seriously embarrasses, let alone contradicts, the party. If somehow such a verdict were to emerge, a higher authority would repudiate or modify it. The party's single highest operational priority is to ensure that it controls China's law and order – through the courts, through the secretive disciplinary processes within the party itself, and ultimately through the disciplined security agencies, especially the People's Liberation Army.

Its success at keeping such control is a key difference between China and all the other major powers of the twenty-first century. It is also, however, the single subject that most alienates the Chinese people. There is little doubt that far more than democracy, far more than free speech, what those people who seek change most want is the opportunity to have their day in court. They look with admiration and envy at their neighbours – at the indictment, in Taiwan, of the wife of a ruling president, and the subsequent sentencing to life imprisonment of that former president himself, both for corruption; and at Hong Kong's Independent Commission Against Corruption. The adjective "independent" rules out the adoption of such an institution in China.

In 2010, Stern Hu, a cool, conservative Rio Tinto executive, responsible for selling billions of dollars of iron ore every year to feed China's voracious industrial machine, was arrested on corruption allegations. Hu is an Australian citizen, and concerns were raised by Australian politicians about the legal process to which he was subject. Liu Jieyi, a vice-minister in the party's international section, responded: "The Chinese government respects the independent judiciary of the Australian judicial system. I think we would expect the same from other countries."

However, no objective expert on China's judicial system believes it can be independent of the party apparatus. Jerome Cohen, author of *The Criminal Process in the People's Republic of China, 1949–1963*, has observed that in cases such as Hu's, the defence lawyer "is usually inhibited from investigating on his own and is precluded from seeing even skeletal relevant documents until the case reaches the procurator's [prosecutor's] office, and other documents until the case gets to court following indictment by the procuracy." Cohen notes that witnesses rarely appear at trials, with the outcome "normally pre-ordained after the accused has been formally arrested, indicted and brought to court."

The famous blind human-rights lawyer, Chen Guangcheng, who in 2012 escaped house arrest and managed to get to the United States via the American embassy in Beijing, has written that "cases of any significance are controlled at every level of the judicial system by a communist party political-legal committee, rather than by legal officials. From the Yinan County Basic Court to the Supreme People's Court in Beijing, it is this committee that directs the actions of the police, prosecutors and judges, transforming these ostensibly independent actors into a single, unchallengeable weapon." These committees, he said, have eroded "decades of progress in implementing the rule of law. This issue of lawlessness may be the greatest challenge facing the new leaders."

To make sense of the law in China today, let us first consider some history. Under the Tang code, the law of the dynasty widely viewed as a high point of Chinese civilisation (618–907), there were five possible penalties: beating with light or heavy sticks; penal servitude; exile for life; and death. Imprisonment was rarely used as a punishment. Most capital cases were reviewed by the central law agencies in Beijing, and all death sentences required approval by the emperor, who was obliged by his Confucian inheritance to emphasise *ren* – benevolence or humanity. There were public executions in late imperial China, but these, says Klaus Mühlhahn in *Criminal Justice in China: A History*, did not resemble the carnival-like public executions of eighteenth-century Europe.

Until surprisingly recently in Chinese history, torture was applied to secondary suspects or witnesses if necessary. In Imperial China, "pressing sticks" were frequently used by magistrates, causing fractures to fingers, ankles or shins. It was only in the early twentieth century, in the dying days of the Qing Empire, when modernisers introduced a new criminal code based on the German-inspired Japanese code, that torture, "slow slicing," the public exhibition of heads, the beheading of corpses, tattooing and other gruesome practices were abolished. Such cruelty – intended to underline the authority of the rulers – tended to be accompanied by what were, and still are, seen as humanising constraints, designed to show the caring side of the patriarchal state. In imperial times, for instance, limits were set on who was tortured and how. The elderly, the young, the disabled, the sick, and pregnant women were exempt.

Most crimes were dealt with by unofficial mediation within the family, guild or local community. Local jurisdiction was in the hands of a magistrate, who held open court on certain days of the month, when individuals could raise complaints or questions. The wonderful crime novels of the Dutch diplomat and sinologist Robert van Gulik (1910–67), featuring the seventh-century Judge Dee – a creation to rival Sherlock Holmes – accurately portray the investigative methods of imperial magistrates, not dissimilar to those of their counterparts in continental Europe today.

This core Chinese tradition, Mühlhahn writes, "was viewed not as a duel between opposing counsels but as a search for the objective truth, and not merely the legal truth." The adversarial structure of the British common law system is seen as especially exotic and foreign in China, whose rulers have always guarded their control of information, and their access to the truth, as key to their mandate from heaven. In this worldview, lawyers are seen as troublemakers. And indeed, a growing number of lawyers who choose to represent the wrong sort of clients – especially whistleblowers or critics of the party – find that their licences to operate are not renewed.

This was the legal tradition inherited by the People's Republic, and many aspects of this inheritance remain today. Under Mao, however, China experienced a formal legal vacuum, as these traditions were deliberately cast aside. The Chinese regime, like that of the Bolsheviks in Russia, became a theatrical state in which the boundary between internal and external threats was blurred. Vast numbers of people were declared "enemies" and incarcerated – or excised altogether. Social exclusion became the solution to many urgent problems as China set out on its convulsive, belated pilgrimage towards modernity. This began under the Kuomintang and intensified under the Communists with the *laogai* camps, which at their peak held 20 million people.

In the early days of the People's Republic, Mao introduced labour camps loosely modelled on the Soviet gulags, whose aim was *laogai* – reform through labour (short for *laodong gaizao*). Millions were consigned there, to work chiefly in factories whose output was sold – sometimes exported – by the state. The government also introduced *laojiao* – re-education through labour – centres across the country, with a similar ethos. Inmates of the latter did not need to have been charged with any criminal offence to be incarcerated. The government denies that *laogai* continue to exist, saying that they have outrun their purpose. But those who emerge from the prison system often attest that forms of *laogai* persist.

In the early 1950s, Mühlhahn estimates, about one in four people arrested – hundreds of thousands of people – was executed, usually in public. By the late 1950s, Mao decided that all laws had to be superseded as China entered a new stage of development. He wanted a more absolute power than even the emperors had been able to exercise. On Valentine's Day 1967, the party mouthpiece *People's Daily* carried an editorial under the headline "In Praise of Lawlessness." It said: "Party policy must take priority over law." A revolution was not a dinner party, Mao explained: "To right a wrong, it is necessary to exceed the proper limits." Counter-revolutionaries, he said, owed the masses heavy blood-debts. The rule of law was a tool, not an end in itself. One slogan screamed, "Kill, kill, kill until a bright, red world emerges." This process, writes Mühlhahn, drew everybody in; nobody was allowed to remain a mere bystander.

After Mao died in 1976, the National People's Congress began the painstaking task of rebuilding a legal structure, borrowing many elements from the past. Randall Peerenboom writes, in *China's Long March Toward Rule of Law*, "During the Mao period, China lacked even the most basic laws such as a comprehensive criminal code, civil law or contract law. The response has been a legislative onslaught, the pace and breadth of which has been nothing short of stunning." Between 1976 and 1998, the National People's Congress and its Standing Committee passed more than 337 laws. In contrast, only 134 laws were passed between 1949 and 1978, and only one during the Cultural Revolution (1965–1976). Moreover, of the 134 laws passed between 1949 and 1978, 111 were subsequently declared invalid and many others have been amended since 1978.

Post-Mao, Mühlhahn says, the party has ceded some authority to the courts and other institutions. The presumption of innocence, the right to defence lawyers and legal aid all featured in the *Amendments to the Law of Criminal Procedure* passed in 1996. Mediation is again being encouraged as a means of settling disputes, especially commercial issues, without needing to go to a full trial. The number of litigation cases registered in 2010 was more than 11 million, with civil cases comprising about half of them, up from 8 million in 2008. But, Mühlhahn concludes, "Good laws and well-designed regulatory systems do not mean much if Chinese citizens lack the means to protect their rights and interests through an independent judicial system that has the authority to enforce government and private compliance with the law." Today, the focus is not so much on the rule of law, as rule by law.

The precise number of people executed in China remains a strictly guarded state secret – so successfully guarded that even Amnesty International no longer gives an estimate, although it assumes executions exceed 1000 a year, more than in the rest of the world put together. Most of these executions are carried out by lethal injection using sodium pentobarbital. They mostly take place in execution vans – windowless,

24-seat buses that look like normal police vans on the outside and can be driven from prison to prison as required.

The authorities have reduced the number of capital offences and are taking other measures to limit the use of the death penalty. In 2011, the National People's Congress cut the number of capital crimes from sixty-eight to fifty-five – still a similar number as in Charles Dickens' London, and still including some property crimes. Later in 2011, the Supreme People's Court, the highest bench, ordered lower courts to suspend death sentences for two years and to "ensure that [the death penalty] only applies to a very small minority of criminals committing extremely serious crimes." For criminals, China's legal system is becoming fairer and not so relentlessly punitive. For dissidents, however, it is becoming harsher.

An important element of this system is voluntary confession: the accused must usually confess his or her guilt before a case can be closed. Such a confession can even lead to pardoning or release, if the offence did not cause irreparable harm. In confessing, the accused acknowledges the authority of the court and vindicates its decision to arraign him or her. The conviction rate in Chinese courts is among the highest in the world, with 98 per cent of defendants found guilty in 2005.

Prisons have come to be viewed as clinics. A person who commits a crime, especially against the state, is perceived to be in need of reorientation. This medical metaphor asserts the totalitarian capacity ascribed to state authorities. The reach of the state is pervasive and includes manipulation of the individual's inner world.

Both judges and lawyers are still expected to defer to the party's authority. In 2009 the president of the Supreme People's Procuratorate, Cao Jainming, declared that his department would "resolutely combat the influence of various misguided ideological trends" within the legal system. The justice minister, Wu Aiying, then one of the most senior women in the Chinese hierarchy, added that "the judicial system is determined by the political system … and the former also serves to confirm, safeguard and promote this political system." Willy Lam, a leading analyst of China based in Hong Kong, explains: "The top prosecutor was of course warning his colleagues against Western ideas such as the independence of the judiciary."

In 2010 Wu announced that of the 14,000 lawyers' offices in China, 2741 included no party members. Therefore, "guidance people … have been sent to all [these offices] in order to implement complete coverage by the party organisation and party work." In March 2012, the Justice Ministry ordered all Chinese lawyers to take an oath of loyalty to the party. In a statement, it explained that this was necessary "to firmly establish among the vast circle of lawyers, faith in socialism with Chinese characteristics … and effectively improve the quality of lawyers' political ideology." As a result, lawyers must swear: "I promise to faithfully fulfil the sacred mission of socialism with Chinese characteristics … to be loyal to the motherland and its people, and to uphold the leadership of the Communist Party of China."

What is it like to work within such a system?

Wang Ling was just twenty-nine when she became a judge in Nanchang, the capital of Jiangxi province in the south-east. Soon, she found herself condemning a rapist to death. In those days, the judge had to go in person to the killing field to give the order to the executioner. This time, the first gunman botched the job and a second shot was required. "The whole scene," Wang says, "felt like it happened in slow motion."

Wang is consumed by a rare passion inherited from her parents: a passion for truth, which led her into no end of trouble as a judge. When she was seven months old, her father, formerly a military judge and then a supervisor of a large number of factories, was sent to a remote rural region "to discipline himself through manual labour." His crime was to have defended a young man accused of criticising the party in a conversation with himself. The story was made up, said her father in vain. The young man was banished for thirty years, and Wang's father sent to a village in the mountains for four years. Her first memory of him, from a brief holiday he was permitted to spend at home, is of "his face nestled up against mine."

Wang won successive *san hao xuesheng* awards, for students who exemplified "the three goods": quality, study and health. This stopped with the Cultural Revolution, when formal classes were replaced by praise for Mao and the party through song and dance. One day her teacher pulled her to one side to say her dancing days were over. She had instead to attend classes for the *hei jiu lei zi nu*, the children of so-called "black" people: rich peasants, evil-doers, spies, traitors, intellectuals, et cetera. Wang's father had been branded anti-social not only for his own suspect behaviour, but also because his own father had been a fur dealer in the icy northern province of Liaoning. The teacher advised ten-year-old Wang, "You'd better make a clean break with him."

Later, Wang went to her father's workplace and saw him standing out front with a board around his neck. A banner was stretched across their house, declaring in big characters: "DOWN WITH THE POWER-HOLDERS! DOWN WITH LANDLORDS, EVIL-DOERS AND RIGHTISTS!" She tore it down. "I felt so proud afterwards. I suddenly understood how to distinguish good and bad, true and false, fair and unfair, love and hatred." The righteous judge was born.

The family was sent to another remote village, but Wang negotiated the obstacles and graduated from high school. She eventually made it to university at Hebei, reading English. One of the compulsory subjects was Communist Party history. "We got confused by its constantly changing," Wang says. One week a person was a "capitalist-roader," the next he was rehabilitated. "We couldn't keep up." Wang told her favourite teacher, Li, about her inner desire to be "an upright judge." Li responded, "Your ideal is beautiful, but it is unrealistic. How can you be a just judge in a society which has no proper legal system?"

Then and now, Wang was disturbed by Li's question. She became adept at regurgitating her lecturers' notes – "the way to get high marks" – and after graduating returned to her hometown, to work for the Nanchang Railway Transport Court. Working for a railway *danwei* or work unit was seen, like a job in a state bank, as a golden rice bowl. But this was not the prime attraction for Wang, who still burned to be a judge, "like a Western judge, lawyer and detective rolled into one." Soon after she started work, there was a *yanda*, a campaign against crime, in which 100,000 people were detained, most of them with prior convictions. Wang, now an assistant judge, went to the court, along with thousands of spectators, to hear sentence passed on forty such offenders. The prisoners were then taken out to the execution ground, ten kilometres from the city, where thousands more people were waiting to watch.

"Things happened quickly. In less than a minute, all the convicted were lined up on their knees. The first shooters lined up a metre behind them." Wang was a few metres away. The order was given, and the forty condemned fell down "at more or less the same time."

But "one old woman was found to be alive. She had fallen down before the bullet was fired. When the shooter turned her over, she sat up suddenly with terrified eyes, then knelt down again, begging to be spared. The shooter shot her at once, and as had happened with the others, her brains splattered out. I felt terribly sick and turned back to the van."

54

A year later, Wang was directing the execution of a rapist. After convicting the man, she had gone to his jail cell to take a final photo and verify his identity. "He took out his marriage certificate. 'Can you give this to my wife?' he asked. 'I wronged her, she is a good woman.'"

She recalls another case in which an eighteen-year-old was sentenced to death for robbery with violence; he stole a few yuan from a man he threatened with a knife. Crucially, Wang discovered, he had not used the knife. The trial judge was reluctant to talk about it: "I have handled so many cases, how can I remember such a small thing? I advise you not to spend too much time on it." "It's not a small thing, it concerns a person's life," Wang responded. The defendant eventually "escaped" with a twenty-year sentence, but only after a fellow judge warned Wang, "We may be called left deviationists if we punish criminals too heavily, but right deviationists if too lightly. The former is a mistake in working method, but the latter is a mistake in thought and attitude. It won't be a pity to kill one more from the dregs of society. And we don't want to upset the original judges."

Wang's next major case was quite different. The chief judge pointed to the defendant's name and warned her, "He is the nephew of a high-ranking cadre on the municipal party committee. You must take that into account." At the initial hearing, they did just that. For murdering his wife, the defendant was given just eighteen months, claiming she had attacked him first. Later, disobeying directions, Wang inspected the man's office. In a drawer, she found photos of a naked young woman and letters revealing an affair. Finally, in a dramatic courtroom moment, the man's calumny was revealed.

Wang's father remained a party member, despite all the ignominy the party had heaped on him. Wang herself has never been a member, although membership is generally regarded as essential for promotion. As a non-party judge she had to submit "thought reports" or self-criticisms, and perform "good deeds" in front of party members. She was eventually promoted and transferred to the commercial court.

One case involved US$180,000 in electronic equipment, supplied by an American company. The goods had been smashed during transportation by rail. Who should pay? Wang's superior had no doubts: "When one party is a foreigner and another is our state-owned enterprise, whose interests should we protect? ... We are the people's courts – shouldn't we protect our people's interests?" Wang managed to broker a compromise.

In time, after winning a scholarship to study overseas, she accepted the inevitable and abandoned her career in the law.

Cheng Xiaoxia, an associate professor at the China University of Political Science and Law, agrees with Wang that "to be a just judge in China is very difficult." The relationship between lower and higher courts is "like that between an embassy and its home government. You could strive to be a righteous judge, but your superior may tell you to rule a different way. You could be transferred or lose your job if you don't follow the required directives. You'd have to decide not to get promotion and to stay on the basic level through your career. Probably, if you had to support a family, you wouldn't have enough courage to go in the other direction."

Appeals are possible, but dates are not given for a decision. Cases just disappear over time. Says Cheng, "Some years ago, I went to file an appeal submission at an intermediate court. I had asked for an explanation for the original verdict, but none was given. They told me to go on a certain day to meet the president of the court.

"It was a very wintry, snowy day. Only a limited number of people could meet the president on that day, so I got there early to wait in line. I remember very vividly the person I met, who was the head of the [party's] disciplinary section of the court. I demanded a written statement so I could at least appeal against the decision. His response was, 'Yes, the law does say that we should do that, but we can't completely comply. That is just a goal we are working towards.' I said that constitutional rights had been infringed, but the official just replied, 'There's not much you can do.' There are not a lot of problems within the laws themselves. The system is pretty complete. All these laws seem to be empty, though. I was speechless after the disciplinary head talked to me."

The ties between judges and party officials are often close, notes Cheng. "It's very difficult for judges to be impartial. There is a different definition of corruption among them. If farmers go to court over inadequate compensation for officials taking over their land, judges would find many justifications for lower compensation. Some of the reasons would reach beyond the imagination. Why are the courts on the side of the developer? Almost invariably, the judges would have been bribed, usually with very large sums. Only a tiny number of such cases have been exposed."

"The greatest change China needs is for an independent legal system separated from the party," says Cheng. "Many judges today would be capable of making independent verdicts, given the freedom to do so. At the moment, only the court decision is made public, not the statements of the defence and prosecution. We should put these on the web. Then people can see whether the judge was impartial."

She says, "I was raised by the government and the party, and had a lot of respect for the national flag and emblems. After my first adverse encounter with the system, I recall facing the huge national emblem in Tiananmen Square, with tears streaming down my face. I couldn't control myself. I couldn't work out who to tell my story to, or how to get it straight."

A century ago, writes Mühlhahn, the country took steps towards meeting international legal standards, in order to help rid itself of foreign interference. In the many treaty ports, foreigners – and in practice many Chinese too – were exempt from Chinese justice, a privilege detested by China's rulers but literally a lifesaver for critics of the imperial system who found sanctuary there.

More recently China, while preserving its uniqueness, has not remained entirely aloof from international judicial practice. It has sent judges to observe foreign jurisdictions and invited overseas legal experts to visit China. China's accession to the World Trade Organization in December 2001 similarly led to a desire – still not effectively realised – for its courts to be perceived as offering fair redress for international commercial disputes. Hong Kong remains, however, the favoured jurisdiction for signing and registering deals between foreign and Chinese parties.

In 2011, Australia's then attorney-general, Robert McClelland, signed a memorandum of understanding on legal cooperation with the justice minister, Wu Aiying, updating a previous agreement signed in 1984. McClelland said, "The Australian legal and justice sector places a great degree of importance on its relationship with China," and closer cooperation would "help us better understand each other's legal systems." It would involve, he said, the exchange of legal materials, the development of education and training initiatives, and cooperation between members of the legal profession. Its most tangible expression would be a large number of exchanges "by ministers, officials, the judiciary, legal practitioners, legislative drafters, legal advisers, academics and law students."

Jerome Cohen commented: "Despite the huge dissimilarities between the Australian and Chinese legal systems, such exchanges are beneficial and should be encouraged, if only to bolster the morale of China's weakened law reformers and despondent criminal defence lawyers and judges. This is a difficult period for them." For such programs to be truly effective, however, they should not be restricted to judges and lawyers. He urged Australia "to include Chinese party and police officials in the exchanges, since they are the key players for many purposes." For the most part, however, the people involved in such exchanges are not those with the power to bring about real change, and the gulf between Chinese and international legal practice remains wide.

Insofar as the rulers of the new China feel the need to demonstrate accountability to anyone, it is to their own peers, via the party's disciplinary organs, usually in secret. Such parallel party institutions were first established by the Kuomintang under Chiang Kai-shek. But the failure to show loyalty to the emperor and thus the state, Mühlhahn points out, has long been a fundamental offence in China – in ancient days as now.

Let us take a rare visit to Scrutiny Central. The headquarters of the party's Central Commission for Discipline Inspection (CCDI) comprise two tower blocks – one brand new – within a large walled garden in Beijing's inner west. The forbidding wall is at least six metres high. China's top officials quake as they are driven through the gates for "discussions" about their financial dealings, their management practices or their private lives.

One of China's most feared and secretive organisations, the CCDI is responsible for investigating and punishing corrupt officials. Corruption has in recent years become a major cause of a sense of alienation among the Chinese *laobaixing*, just as it was in 1989. A National Corruption Prevention Bureau was established with some fanfare in 1997 to work alongside the commission, and the commission was made accountable to the top level of the party. But not much has been heard of the bureau since.

The Central Commission has a telephone hotline and a dedicated email address for people to report cases of corruption. Preliminary investigations may take place either at the national level or in one of the regional commissions spread around the country. The person under investigation is usually placed under *shuang gui* – "double demand" – which involves interrogation in a closeted venue over a set period of time. He or she is expected to confess within this period. In most cases, the commission aims to complete its task within six months, although it sometimes takes up to a year.

Liu Zhenbao, the deputy director-general responsible for reviewing cases, explains the commission's work. A poem by Mao Zedong, titled "Snow" (*Truly great men / look to this age alone*) adorns the wall, written in Mao's own calligraphy. Liu says that once the initial investigation is completed, his department examines the evidence and the commission's Standing Committee assesses the case. Then, if the green light is given, Liu's department determines the punishment. If a party member is found guilty of a serious offence, dismissal from the party is the key outcome. The accused is then handed over to the courts, which will impose a public penalty that can range from a fine to capital punishment (as happened to Zheng Xiaoyu, the head of China's State Food and Drug Administration, executed in July 2007 for corruption.).

In April 2011, the blogger Chu Zhaoxian described a visit to one of these interrogation centres. "A popular saying among Chinese government officials goes: 'Fear not the heavens or the earth, but fear the summons of the Central Commission for Discipline Inspection's Anti-Corruption Office,'" he wrote. "I had a rare opportunity to visit a *shuang gui* anti-corruption investigation facility. When the car reached the highway exit of another city, a police car appeared in front of us and led the way. We were driven through rugged and muddy mountain roads, until we were well within remote mountains. We entered an ordinary-looking courtyard and stopped before a small building, where People's Armed Police were standing guard." Then he passed through a security check and entered the building.

During my own tour of the commission, Xuan Hongyun, the deputy director-general responsible for "touring," explains that he heads a team of thirty-two staff, most of them aged under thirty. Only half of them are in the central office at any given time; the rest are in China's regions, leading teams investigating corruption claims in banks or other companies, or in provincial governments.

Records of the 60,000 cases handled by the commission since 1979 are kept under tight security in boxes fitted with electronic locks. Only staff with special clearance can examine these files. There are shredders on every floor, and the immaculate offices are virtually paperless. In the commission's garden stands a towering 350-year-old "locust tree," which in Chinese culture represents impartial justice. An official explains that "it is said to have a human spirit, so that cases heard under its branches will be decided justly."

★

Behind the legal structures in China, as in any other country, lie the enforcement agencies – the police, the army, and the many other branches of the security apparatus of such a vast party-state. Mao Zedong famously said that "All power comes from the barrel of a gun," and the army has always been crucial to the party's authority. Without the People's Liberation Army, the party could not have won power in 1949, and this has given the PLA a privileged position. One of China's problems, says the blogger Li Xinde, is that its government "doesn't have a foundation that comes from election, only from the gun." And the army has remained remarkably deferential to the party over the years. "The army must listen to the party, which also must approve the appointment of generals. No matter how high your rank, if you don't want to listen to the party, you'll be dismissed."

Li joined the party in 1978, as a soldier in the PLA, and remains a member. "I was really active. My unit built power plants and wharves for the navy. I had to work very hard to gain this party membership. Only 30 per cent of soldiers could be members. So besides the officers, who were mainly – maybe all – members, there wasn't room for many other soldiers to join. I placed high demands on myself as a member."

The army dictates how much of its soldiers' time should be spent on political education and how much on their normal work, Li says. Every military unit has a party committee. "I was on one that had five or six members, responsible for thirty soldiers. We had meetings once a week, usually on Saturdays. We listened to an official read documents sent through by our superiors. We discussed candidates for new party members and proposed those for higher level committees."

Wu Si, the editor of the party magazine *Yanhuang Chunqiu* (*History Review*), points out: "The party itself was a group that came to power through violence … The army was the very core resource in the control of the party. So the basic foundation of the party is to rely on the army … As long as the army is under the control of the party, its grip on power is solid. If the day dawned when that changed, it would become a symbol that China was becoming democratic and constitutional."

Calls to separate the party from the army have not been welcome. Liu Xiaobo's Charter 08 document called for China to "Bring the armed forces under state control. Military personnel should render

loyalty to the constitution and to the country. Political party organisations should withdraw from the armed forces … All public employees
including the police should maintain political neutrality." For his
efforts, Liu ended up in prison. In April 2012, the flagship military
paper *PLA Daily* published a commentary under the headline: "Ensur-
ing that the armed forces resolutely obey the party centre, the Central
Military Commission, and party secretary Hu Jintao." "The party controls the gun," it stressed.

The party is aware of the great debt it owes the PLA for saving it from
potential disaster during the waves of protests around the nation in
1989. It saved China from even worse anarchy during the Cultural Revolution, eventually being deployed by the party hierarchy to rein in
out-of-control Red Guards. But as a result of its bloody intervention in
1989 the army suffered a disconcerting collapse in its popular standing,
especially in Beijing.

Since then, the party has sought to repay its debt by improving the
armed forces. It has invested heavily in military modernisation. It has
reduced the number of soldiers from 4 million to 2.3 million, stepped up
entry requirements and curtailed the army's involvement in business,
which had come to subsidise its operations as well as enriching individual officers. For its eightieth anniversary in 2007, the PLA was given
newly designed uniforms costing US$1 billion, with a more modern,
Westernised look. The male soldiers' uniforms emphasise their shoulders (giving them a "T"-shaped silhouette), while female soldiers'
uniforms are a more figure-hugging "X" – designed, according to Xinhua, to make them look "sassier."

The party has also redoubled propaganda efforts to boost the PLA's
reputation. Media coverage of the 2008 Sichuan earthquake, for instance,
focused heavily on the army's role in rescue efforts. In a brilliant public
relations move, cameramen were deployed alongside almost every unit
working to free trapped victims. The opening ceremony of the Beijing
Games began with 2500 soldiers in ancient dress drumming up a storm
in the arena, beating in unison drums that lit up with each stroke. The
national flag was carried to the flagpole by a goose-stepping PLA squad.
The military also plays a key role in China's space program, which is
wildly popular; each new foray is greeted with the same frantic applause
as America once gave its astronauts. Meanwhile, the party has withdrawn the PLA from most domestic security functions. Instead, these

have been handed to the 1.5 million strong People's Armed Police, whose officers are especially well remunerated.

The PLA is the jewel in the crown of the party. In the absence of independent courts or parliament, it is the second most powerful institution in the country. As China gets richer, its funding keeps rising by double digits every year – and that is only the publicly acknowledged spending. Even after the global financial crisis struck, Beijing announced a downturn-defying 14.9 per cent increase in military spending in 2009, to US$109 billion, 6.3 per cent of the total government budget. In 2012, it rose by a further 11.2 per cent.

The PLA will be expected to play a prominent role in safeguarding the increasingly lengthy supply routes by which China obtains the resources it needs to fuel its economic growth. David Lai, a professor of Asian security studies at the US Army War College, wrote in *China Security* magazine that "the PLA's move to go global is a natural outgrowth of China's expanding power." He cited an editorial in the *PLA Daily* newspaper stressing that "China's national interests are spreading everywhere in the world, into the open seas, outer space, and even into cyberspace." Today, said Lai, "China not only has a territorial frontier, but also an 'interest frontier' that has no national boundaries."

Its focus has long been on building its capacity to invade – or to squeeze by blockading – Taiwan, against which it still targets 1500 missiles. The PLA's eightieth anniversary exhibition at Beijing's Military Museum featured a giant panorama portraying a seaborne invasion – an event that has not taken place since the PLA was founded. Since 1949 the PLA has fought the USA, Australia and other allied forces in Korea, as well as the Indians and Vietnamese, but always on land. The landscape in the panorama strikingly resembled a section of the Taiwan coast.

The secretary-general of the party leads the PLA by dint of chairing the Central Military Commission, which the constitution says "is responsible to the National People's Congress and its Standing Committee." The constitution does not state clearly how the chairman or the other members of this commission are to be appointed; in practice, throughout the history of the People's Republic, the party has always chosen the chairman and other members. The PLA is the ultimate political force, and it owes its loyalty not to the Chinese government or to the people, but to the party that appoints its commanders.

Together, the courts and the disciplined services form a mighty bulwark for the party-state. Both are adapting to the changing times and to China's new place in the world. But it remains inconceivable that they might not be responsive to the requirements of China's leaders, and therefore to the Communist Party.

CHAPTER 5:
THE MEDIA AND THE MESSAGE

IN 2008, CAI WU, THEN HEAD OF THE INFORMATION OFFICE of the State Council, China's cabinet, gave a televised press conference about the government's progress towards greater openness.

When questions were invited after the minister's presentation, the *Christian Science Monitor's* China correspondent, Englishman Peter Ford, stood up. He acknowledged that there were steps in the right direction: new directories of officials responsible for particular areas of information, complete with their phone numbers (there are no general telephone books in China, on or offline), and a loosening of restrictions on foreign journalists' movements. But, he said with characteristic firm politeness, the core problem remained: officials never tell journalists anything. They never provide answers to the most routine, anodyne enquiries, even if you can get hold of them. They still believe they own all information.

As soon as the press conference was over, Ford was surrounded by local Chinese journalists. Some were wagging their fingers at him.

"Don't get it wrong," they rushed to tell him. "It's not just you guys in the foreign media. We face exactly the same challenge. We don't get meaningful replies from the government either!"

In China, journalists are given some room to explore – especially when reporting on the environment and, to a degree, corruption. But many other rooms in the information palace remain firmly locked.

At the press conference, Cai also explained that the State Council was organising training courses for government spokespeople in Beijing and the provinces. He conceded that "people don't want more rhetoric and empty words; they want to be given facts." When it comes to implementing such policies, however, the Chinese government faces problems – even when good intentions are in place. Three examples demonstrate why.

First, the introduction, on 1 May 2008, of China's "national disclosure regulation," its version of freedom-of-information legislation. This did not mean that the government had conceded the citizen's right to know – rather, it had accepted that, in order to improve governance, its officials should be releasing more information. A pilot program was introduced in 2004 in Shanghai, Guangzhou and Wuhan, three of China's biggest cities. During the following four years, however, only one request was formally lodged by a journalist.

He was Ma Sheng, a writer on legal affairs for *Liberation Daily* in Shanghai, a newspaper owned by the city's Communist Party. He sought information – most importantly, a map – from a district-level planning bureau where, he believed, a corrupt deal had been made with a developer that involved the removal of many residents to clear the way for luxury apartments. His application was rejected, explains Cheng Jie, a professor of constitutional law at Qinghua University in Beijing, on the grounds that Ma was a legal and not an economic reporter, and so had overstepped the bounds of his field.

Ma responded that he had filed the request properly and still sought a reply. He was ignored. He then initiated a court action and wrote an open letter to the All China Journalists Association – the state-sanctioned, party-controlled national journalists' union – in defence of his bid. Published in the *China Youth Daily*, this letter attracted further publicity to the case, including from the Hong Kong media. The editors of *Liberation Daily* – Ma's employers – embarrassed by the suggestion of internal conflict, said that they had not authorised his request for information. Under severe pressure, he withdrew his bid for a legal hearing after a week. The final result was inevitable: Ma lost his job. The development went ahead.

The second example is the case of the Beijing photographer Wang Lili. He was sacked for creating a "political incident" by taking a photograph of his local mayor delivering a speech with his eyes apparently closed. Wang, aged fifty-two, formerly a "model worker," was assigned to cover Deng Naiping, the mayor of Tongzhou, presenting the annual "work report" of the local government. His photograph appeared on page two of the *Tong-zhou Newsletter*, a newspaper run by the district party committee.

As he was returning home from the hotel where the three-day meeting took place, Wang received a mobile phone call from his boss, who told him to write a deep self-criticism about the photo and to pay a 500 yuan (US$80) fine. Wang arrived home late morning, wrote the self-criticism over lunch and handed it in. According to *Southern Metropolis Weekly*, which provoked a storm of reaction by publishing Wang's story, his workmates presumed that was the end of the matter.

But at 4 p.m., an all-staff meeting was called and Wang was instructed to read out his self-criticism. Then his boss told him he was sacked. Colleagues gathered round to console him. One sobbed. Wang said he had received a note just before the meeting from his editor, explaining, "This affair has become a serious political incident. I cannot protect you. I too have been told by the mayor to write a self-criticism."

The formal notice of dismissal said: "Upon investigation, the news photo you took of Mayor Deng Naiping was misleading and had an extremely bad political influence. It is a grave dereliction of duty." A senior Tongzhou official told *Southern Metropolis Weekly*, "As a news photo, it was wrong in what it conveyed about the spirit of the meeting. It was not stimulating. Did the photo aim to tell the reader that work was done poorly in Tongzhou, that the mayor was bowing his head in acknowledgement of his guilt?"

An editor of the *Tongzhou Newsletter* was quoted as saying that Wang had been "insufficiently attentive," and so had failed to capture the instant when the mayor raised his head. He said that Wang had taken only six photos during the mayor's ninety-minute presentation. Wang said that he had been present through the speech and had taken eleven photos: "He basically read his text with his head bent. I couldn't ask him to look up so I could take a picture." The *Weekly* went on to report that Wang's colleague Deng Jie "lamented that everyone involved in Tongzhou propaganda knows that the mayor is not photogenic."

Wang, whose wife has retired, and who at first hid his dismissal from their student daughter, told the newspaper, "There's not much news to take in Tongzhou, it's all repetitive stuff. You have to wrack your brain to find some way to make the old stuff new again. For a news photo, you shoot what's there. I never thought that would lead to problems. If I had the chance to talk to the mayor, I'd say to him, 'If you had lifted your head just once, I guarantee I would have caught it.'"

A banner hanging in the *Tongzhou Newsletter* office at the time read: "Care for the people's lives, the people's feelings, and the people's will."

The third illustration is provided by a rare insight from a leading Chinese blogger, who explained why, in 2008, aged thirty-eight, he had quit a ten-year career at a prestigious national newspaper. He writes under the pen name Shiniankancai, although the authorities of course know his true identity. He wrote:

When I went to the Personnel Department to return my journalist pass, with its photo taken when I was twenty-eight, looking lean but spirited ... I reflected that I had given away nearly ten years of my life in this place, like throwing a stone into a bottomless well. I got weary of the job several years ago. Although I carried a journalist's pass around, I was hardly given a chance to fulfill that duty.

When I am unable to truthfully document what is happening, when I don't have freedom of expression, how is it possible for me to be a real journalist? I was doing the job just to make a living. It's time to say goodbye to such a "journalism" career.

He described his first reporting trip, covering a meeting at the headquarters of the People's Armed Police in the city of Xi'an. "There was hardly anything newsworthy to write about," he said. The same old statements were repeated again and again. He took notes carefully, since he was new to the business, but couldn't help wondering how he could write a story about this boring meeting.

Before the meeting was even finished, a propaganda officer of the People's Armed Police handed me a story, which he had written in advance of the meeting. I was told that I just need to make a few small changes to the article, put my byline on it, and send it to my editor for publishing.

So why did they invite me there? I figured it out later: my presence could help to add prestige to the meeting, since I was a reporter from a national newspaper.

After the meeting, the host showed him around the ancient city; they toured all the well-known scenic and historical places. But when they went to visit a memorial park dedicated to the Emperor Qinshi-huang, the gate was shut. A woman and two children in mourning clothes were kneeling in front of it. A group of angry people from the countryside stood behind them, shouting. Large characters were painted in lime on the wall of the park, reading: "He who murders must be prosecuted." Shiniankancai asked them what had happened and found out that the woman's husband, who was a farmer in a nearby village, had been beaten to death by police after he was arrested while trying to sell a few items in the park. His family members and relatives were trying to seek justice.

They all eagerly came to talk to me. But officials of the Armed Police accompanying me on the trip pulled my sleeve to move away. They said, "You are not here to mind their business." I had worked for the government as a civil servant so I knew some of its rules. I thought that I should show my respect to my host. And also, I didn't know what kind of trouble it could bring to me if I wrote a story without my editor's approval. So I sneaked away from the crowd.

Looking back on that first trip, he said, it set the tone for his journalism career.

It was not a reporting trip in the real sense. I didn't do much reporting. I was just playing a supporting role in a play directed by someone in the government. What I saw at the gate of the park has lingered in my mind like a shadow. Sometimes I try to console myself by thinking that I wouldn't have been able to get the story published even if I had stayed at the gate and written a story about the farmers. On the other hand, I think I should have tried to write it anyway.

Because his beat was government and politics, he often had to interview officials. Sometimes he had his picture taken with them. "Many reporters of state-owned papers love to do this," he said. "They seem to believe that appearing in a photo together with an official could give them some power."

Journalism as a career attracts many young Chinese, but it does not enjoy an especially high reputation among the professions. Journalists in the official media are viewed as reporters to the leaders, somewhat remote from ordinary people. Indeed, Xinhua employs many journalists whose only task is to provide discreet reports for the central government and party leadership, not for wider distribution. Corrupt opportunism thrives. Many journalists expect free meals and *hongbao* (red envelopes containing cash) in exchange for attending press conferences or launches. Some have been accused of blackmailing companies – they threaten that they will file a negative story unless the company, or individual, provides cash or buys advertising.

As Shiniankancai explained, officially sanctioned coverage of public events is generally restricted to good news. Most commonly, this means a leader opening a new building or conference or road, making – like Mayor Deng above – a speech while people applaud, smile and shake hands. Vast areas of life, such as politics and religion, are largely taboo for the mass media – although, it must be stressed, private conversations in China today range widely and can be extraordinarily frank. The old anxiety about speaking one's mind even to friends or relatives has pretty well evaporated. Public debate, however, remains scrupulously policed, to the extent that modern technology allows.

When any controversial issue emerges – and Chinese journalists know by second nature what this means – the usual response of an editor or TV producer is to leave it alone entirely, or else to use only the words or photos supplied by Xinhua or China Central TV. These are bound to be kosher. No commentary or analysis is attempted, at least not until the trend of the story has become apparent, or until a party-sanctioned academic or writer has shown the path ahead, leading the rest onto the dance floor. The media are expected to stay within the sanctioned bounds of a story. For instance, the Olympics were covered as a sporting event, and as an occasion of pride for the Chinese people. Forced relocations of residents in the lead-up to the Games were off-limits.

Cartoonists are still not permitted to draw party leaders. There can be nothing funny about being a leader of China, or of the party. Lower-level media are not licensed to report malpractices by higher-level bodies. A city newspaper cannot reveal corruption on the part of provincial officials, for instance. Almost all corruption stories are only reported after the party's own discipline department has released the news.

Foreign policy is a major area of state responsibility and as such is usually left well alone by media. Economic issues are more open for discussion – although again, within approved boundaries. Usually only party publications have the licence, and thus the confidence, to question government policies. But there are prominent exceptions in the economic media. Many of the most committed journalists work for business publications like *Caijing* magazine and the Caixin media group (run by China's most prominent female journalist, Hu Li), and these outlets break many important stories.

Ultimately, party propaganda departments administer all public media in China. The central propaganda department sends all editors of print, broadcast and internet media, often several times a week, lists of topics they are not permitted to cover. In April 2012, for instance, the United Nation released its *World Happiness Report*, which ranked mainland China as the 112th happiest country out of 156. Many websites posted the report, which was initially released by Xinhua. Swiftly, the State Council Information Office issued a general instruction: "Regarding 'UN Releasing World Happiness Report, China Ranked 112,' all websites are not to re-post the report. All existing posts are subject to removal."

In early 2010 the International Federation of Journalists published a report, *China Clings to Control: Press Freedom in 2009*, which listed sixty-two bans issued from January to November that year. At least seven orders were issued restricting coverage of the riots in the western region of Xinjiang in July 2009, in which almost 200 people died. Restrictions were also imposed on coverage of a corruption scandal involving the mayor of Shenzhen, on debate about political reform in Hong Kong, on the election of Macau's chief executive, and on the street protests following the election in Iran.

When Barack Obama visited China in November 2009, an order was issued that only official reports from Xinhua were to be used. Media were instructed to delete any reference to a forum in Shanghai at which President Obama answered questions. Other forbidden topics included: photos of the actress Zhang Ziyi topless on a Caribbean beach; the successful defamation case brought against a company by a journalist who had covered a miscarriage of justice case involving the firm; the sacking of a former Shenzhen party chief, Lin Jiaxing, for drunkenness and child molestation; the publication of the memoirs of Zhao Ziyang, the disgraced former premier; and issues related to the parents of children killed during the 2008 Sichuan earthquake. Entertainment programs on radio and TV were banned from discussing celebrity love affairs or "scandalous material." Meanwhile, an instruction was issued that "all media including internet must report positively on the book *Unhappy China*," which claimed that China was a victim of Western bullying and "should rise up and lead the world."

These were among hundreds of such edicts, the federation said. But despite the difficulties, "many journalists try to go out of their way to get the news. When pedicure worker Deng Yujiao was charged with murder in Yesnaguan, Hubei province, after she had refused 'special services' demanded by officials, some journalists went to the area to investigate, even though authorities had ordered them not to report it." The federation's general secretary, Aidan White, noted, "The IFJ list indicates that much as China's censors are maintaining a vigilant eye, they are also struggling to maintain a grip on information dissemination."

Sometimes, the federation found, stories were printed without restriction but were not allowed to be posted online – for instance, a report about land compensation in Suqian, Jiangsu province. Occasionally the reverse was true and authorities allowed coverage online but not in traditional media – for instance, a report by the Guangzhou-based Southern Media Group about a fight between Uighur and Han Chinese factory workers, in which two Uighurs were killed – an event that helped to spark the riots in Xinjiang.

Besides these specific instructions, self-censorship was also common, the federation said. "The main reason is lack of job security. The issuance of Administrative Press Cards to journalists by GAPP requires that they obey all regulations. If they do not conform, they risk losing their accreditation." In the cases of the twentieth anniversary of the massacre around Tiananmen Square and the fiftieth anniversary of the failed uprising in Tibet, "media did not need to be ordered how to report – they were very aware there was to be no independent reporting on these topics."

The federation's report also noted that the definition of a professional journalist was tightened during 2009, ensuing that "citizen journalists" would not be classified formally as journalists, making it all but impossible for them to have their work published in either traditional or online media. The explosion of the internet has, however, given many millions of Chinese people an appetite for direct access to the broadest possible range of information and opinions, with users of Weibo – China's equivalent of Twitter – doubling in 2011 to about 300 million.

In March 2012, the government imposed new requirements on Sina Corp, the company that runs Weibo. All users must now provide authentic identification when they register an account, including their real name and their government identification number, or their Internet Service Provider risks losing its licence. Every post by a user with more than 100,000 followers is now subject to examination by the net police. Any post deemed harmful or illegal is to be deleted within five minutes. The technical interface of the microblog would be made accessible to specialised search engines deployed by public security agencies and filters would be applied, removing keywords designated as harmful. Terms that have been banned include "leadership change," three variations of the word "dissident," "democracy," "one party rule" and "cultural revolution."

It's hard to keep up with the constant activism of the excitable authorities in this sector. Thanks to innovative and expensive surveillance technology – where China's research leads the world – the government can reach into almost every Chinese home by keeping tabs on the family's electronic devices. But China's netizens still contrive to stay one step ahead of them, usually through individual panache and ingenuity. It's harder for corporations or big organisations to succeed; they are usually not sufficiently swift of foot.

In 2010, China – at once the greatest beneficiary and leading driver of globalisation, and the chief champion of traditional nationalism – took on one of the great global corporations, Google, and won a points victory. During their six-month stand-off, Google engaged in a quixotic attempt to open up Beijing's internet boundaries – to demolish the Great Firewall.

David Drummond, Google's chief legal officer, stunned the world with an announcement that after a cyber attack on Google and twenty other large companies in the internet, finance, technology, media and chemical sectors, which Google attributed to Chinese agents, Google was "no longer willing to continue censoring our results on Google.cn." Its English site, Google.com, is also censored by Chinese "net police," but not with the company's active collaboration.

Drummond said, "Over the next few weeks we will be discussing with the Chinese government the basis on which we could operate an unfiltered search engine within the law, if at all. If it is impossible to operate an uncensored service within the law, we will close Google.cn.

We will obviously continue to offer Chinese-language search on our global search engine."

When Google entered the Chinese market in 2006, its co-founder Sergey Brin, whose family had fled Soviet communism, said that it accepted "a set of rules that we weren't comfortable with." Google had decided, Drummond said, that "the benefits of increased access to information for people in China and a more open internet outweighed our discomfort in agreeing to censor some results." By setting up in China through the official channels, Google provided a service for regular internet users. People who were especially eager to obtain uncensored information could do so by paying to route their searches through proxies. But only a tiny minority had the time, the know-how and the motivation to bother to do this. Most users were stuck behind the firewall. When a forbidden search hit the wall, the searcher would see a message advising that "Search results may not comply with the relevant laws, regulations and policy, and cannot be displayed."

By early 2010, however, the deal was becoming untenable for Google. There had been an increase in attacks on corporate sites launched from China. The credibility of Google's hugely successful Gmail platform was under threat, as was its unofficial motto, "Don't Be Evil."

Drummond stressed that the new policy "was driven by our executives in the US, without the knowledge or involvement of our employees in China." Some critics suggested that Google was just seeking to make the best of a bad job, finding an excuse for quitting China because it had only won 35.6 per cent of the search market there, while its dominant local competitor, Baidu, had 58.4 per cent. But that was still a huge number of followers, given the size of the market. And most of Google's Chinese revenue came not from advertising on its local site but from Chinese wishing to advertise globally.

Eventually, after six months' wrangling, Google repaired its bitter relations with the Chinese government by steering around censorship rules. The company won the renewal of its internet licence by acknowledging Beijing's insistence that it must not provide outlawed information. At first, Google said it would automatically redirect customers seeking banned information to an uncensored Hong Kong site. But later it agreed that it would instead simply alert these customers to the address of a Hong Kong site that might be able to help them. This rapprochement remains subject to annual renewal.

In 2010, Google expected to earn no more than US$500 million in China, out of its total revenue of about US$32 billion globally. But like other major companies, it knew that its shareholders would demand ongoing involvement in the world's fastest growing market, even if present profits were modest. Baidu's share price doubled when the row erupted; Google's departure would hand it virtually the whole search market in the world's biggest internet arena (at the time there were 400 million Chinese people online, and nearly double that number of mobile phone users). The renewal of Google's licence placed it firmly back in the game, albeit still as the underdog. The day after the announcement of the new deal with Beijing, Google's share price rose 2.4 per cent – trumping the free spirits in the online world who had applauded Google for at last living up to its ideals.

However, individual online mavericks continue to operate under the radar. Li Xinde, an almost obsessive investigator of perceived wrongs, has become one of the best known of this brave band. A stocky man in his fifties, he lives in a small flat up several flights of stairs in an outer Beijing apartment block. On his crowded desk is a black and white photo of himself as a soldier in the People's Liberation Army. He claims that his website – when he is able to post on it – is "the most well-known anti-corruption website in China." On it he posts detailed accounts of his investigations into local corruption.

He says, "I'm lucky, I haven't had any beatings so far. That's because I cover legal cases, rather than breaking news." He is still trying to obtain an official journalist's card. A card he was given by a newspaper in Anhui province was recalled after he used it to cover stories in other provinces. He had been investigating an explosion that killed more than thirty people at a site in Liaoning, where a coal business owned by Shanxi interests hid explosives.

Li says, "Some local officials were involved, so they complained to the central propaganda department and they ordered Anhui to take back my card. The newspaper announced it and faxed the announcement back to the department. I told the authorities I was going to print my own journalist's card. They said if I did, they would arrest me for fraud. I do have a card from an organisation registered in Hong Kong that has been issued by the China People's Publishing House, using their chop and the national crest. It cost me 2000 yuan. It's no more illegal than anyone else's. No one has a patent for theirs."

Li later exposed a case in Liaoning that led to the party secretary of the disciplinary commission of Fuxia being sentenced to eight years in jail. He was the protector of a mafia group there, Li says. The man launched a campaign to black out Li's website and ordered Liaoning police to arrest him. The legal authorities collected information on him but, finding that he was not an easy guy to catch, reported him to the Public Security Ministry in Beijing, hoping that its greater resources would lead to his arrest. But the ministry decided not to pursue Li. They said there was no political pressure to take action; Li was just a journalist writing articles. They told the provincial authorities they could take him to court locally if they wanted to. They didn't, and Li kept pursuing the story. A popular response grew to his online posts, and in the end the party secretary was charged by the local government.

He investigated another case where an official had acquired seven expensive cars and four villas, with no identifiable legitimate source. He recalls how the mayor of Jinnin in Shandong province kneeled down to apologise when his corrupt conduct was exposed. "The higher the rank of the corrupt official, the easier to pursue them, because they are more cowardly. It's taken them so many years to climb up. If they act against me publicly, I will respond secretly. Sometimes I take up cases to which I am referred by official media who have done preliminary investigations but can't go deeper because they were stopped. They pass material on to me."

He often locks his flat and heads off for weeks or months at a time, roaming China's corrupt badlands. "I travel a lot," he says. "I spent several months in Chenzhou city in Hunan with the victims of corruption there. In China people don't care much about what other people get up to or what happens to others, but if they are personally affected they will stand up. I work as the mouthpiece of those people and report, using evidence. I don't ask for comments from people who are not directly involved in a case."

He relies on individual supporters for his living. "I had some modest personal savings from a small business I ran in past years [selling Chinese medicines], but that can't support me now. So I get sponsorship, as well as some donations from home and abroad. And I charge a small amount for cases that people ask me to pursue." He claims that about 10 million people have looked at his website – which is still "closed down from time to time" – regularly since he began his work.

Of more than 100 cases he has recorded, seven or eight remain blocked, apparently permanently. "The Internet Service Provider just closes my sites down without giving a reason. Liaoning's public security office said that if I withdraw my article on the party disciplinary secretary, they would help ensure that one of my sites, run by an ISP based in nearby Shandong, would be able to stay open. I said I never retreat from my principles or from my websites. A friend wants me to transfer my blog to an Australian server, but I'm not keen to do that. Mao said you learn from the battlefield. That's how I'm still in business here. I still have another two blogs open somewhere."

Li, a stocky, tough figure, was born in Zhejiang province to a military officer's family and, growing up, lived on a naval base for ten years. "Many of my neighbours were heroes," he says. "Like Su Jichang, who shot down an American high altitude surveillance plane." He moved to Anhui when his father retired and worked behind the scenes in an opera house before joining the army. "I was only earning 6 kuai a week compared with 30 before, but I believed I was defending the country and all our families. I could be a hero. I left the military because there seemed to be no battles to fight." He has since found battles enough.

He joined the party in 1978 and remains a member. "Many older members like me are living kind of outside the system now. The members still attending party events and activities are mainly officers, or public servants and officials or staff of state-owned enterprises. I still see myself as working for the party – by fighting corruption, which is deplored by the Central Committee. We still uphold the revolution. Just like a Christian who even if he loses contact with his church still prays at home and has beliefs inside the heart.

"My personal belief is that I am true to my family background, even to my father's generation when they were all poor guys. He joined as a recruit for the Korean War. He borrowed a spare shirt from his older brother and they both went to war. Earlier generations were not only poor but also illiterate. The party came and changed that. I don't have a reason to oppose the party. Falun Gong organised a campaign for people to quit it, they came to me and I refused. China will not follow their request. I have told my children we should be proud of this great time. This is my true belief. The party gave my family education, something that my ancestors never had."

But there are problems, admits Li. "The party is deeply rooted in the land of China, in tradition and culture. If you move an orange tree from south of the river to the north, it will grow bitter fruit. Marxism spread to the USSR from the cities, but in China from the countryside. Our doctrine must be localised for local conditions. The collapse of the Soviet Union was a great shock to our party. Without economic reform the CCP will collapse in the same way. Hence Deng Xiaoping's opening up of the economy. But there are still a lot of problems because there's no political reform, which is needed as well – like having two horses driving a wagon."

Change is slow, Li says, because "many people within the party are afraid of losing their money if political reform is introduced. The *laobaixing*, the ordinary people, are not afraid. Barefoot people have no fear of losing shoes. It is people who have got hold of power who are afraid of political reform. And there is much explosive material on that in the internet. We need to talk about the distribution of wealth, and the centralisation of power. And rural corruption. The central party is working on such issues; they want to find a way out. But it doesn't have a good record for carrying out such reforms."

He says he doesn't know anything about politics, but he does know something about corruption, which "is happening because of the system. No doubt the party is sincere in fighting corruption. Like parents who give birth to a party official, who when he grows up is taken out and shot because of corruption. The party wants greater supervision. Some officials hate that and want to block it." So there remain constant tensions. Why not a multi-party system? "Because it is impossible. And a civil war is not something people would like to see."

But Li would like to see the NPC, China's parliament, become more than a rubber stamp, with more rights being returned to the people. "Chen Liangyu [the jailed party chief of Shanghai] was corrupt from the start, the higher he climbed, the more money he stole. Because there was no supervision. He had his favourite guys promoted by him and they naturally also wanted him as their supplier. There was no investigation of who promoted Chen or why. I have collected no evidence that any central leader is corrupt. But if somebody gave me the evidence I would investigate it.

"They want me to disappear but I will not. That's one of the benefits of the internet. I'm inconvenient."

The truth can be inconvenient in China – as it can be anywhere. Boundaries are being tested in the mass media, but this is a long, slow process. The party does not win every round in every place. But over time, it is finding ways to transform the new instruments of liberation, as they were originally conceived – the mobile phone and the internet – into instruments of control.

CHAPTER 6: ART AND CULTURE

MEET ARTIST YAO JUNZHONG, WHO DRIVES AN EXPENSIVE French car but lives in a very basic courtyard home in Songzhuang, an artists' village in the hinterland between city and country east of Beijing. His signature works for several years have been vast oil paintings, in startling colours, of his son Yaoyu, who was born in 1998. These portraits show the boy in settings or uniforms – often including People's Liberation Army olive green – that contrast with his good-humoured innocence. They sell for up to US$40,000 each overseas.

Pouring the first of dozens of tiny cups of tea during our meeting on a showery day, Yao says, "If you touch a political issue, your art will get sensitive, as the authorities say. But without any such touch, your art will be dull." Fewer than 1 per cent of his classmates from art college are still working as artists, he says. "Most are running their own businesses. A few are in the political circle."

It took Yao an exploratory decade doing "business paintings" – book illustrations, copies, adverts or commissioned works, working "from 8 a.m. to 1 a.m." – before he found his own way in 1996. Even then, the market wasn't ready for him until 2003, when overseas buyers began coming from Singapore, Hong Kong, Japan, Germany. He had just been banned from an exhibition of young painters in Shanghai. "They liked my painting of my son holding a gun, set in a renminbi coin. I named it *Qianjin*, which means advance, and also means money. I had to send three photos of it – to the organiser, the gallery owner and the cultural bureau in Shanghai. A cadre thought there must be a political element and told the owner it wasn't appropriate." Before exhibitions, he says, the bureau usually sends a list of taboos to the organisers and, through them, to the artists. "You will be told not to attack communism, not to attack the party. Sex is sensitive. So is violence. But not as much as politics."

Works featuring Mao are widespread in China. His image has become so iconic that the authorities see it as virtually beyond damage. But contemporary or even recently retired politicians are absolutely taboo. This is where the real boundaries of the Chinese avant-garde become clear, even in the celebrated Dashanzi 798 district in north-east Beijing – a great artists' precinct that has burgeoned on the site of a Bauhaus-style military factory (factory number 798), where the souvenir stores and coffee shops are now starting to outnumber the galleries. Any testing of boundaries there tends to attract foreign buyers; iconoclasm is a useful marketing tool. Although Yao has had several shows at Dashanzi, he worries that "too many of the artists there are specialists in the market – but they should look first inside themselves."

Yao now rarely sends paintings to Chinese galleries. "Accepting the taboos would mean just becoming a copyist. Working according to their rules means becoming propaganda tools. But I won't change my work; art is an expression of your own view. So almost all my paintings are abroad. It's a sad story, something I never intended and don't celebrate." In 2006, he says, the censors suddenly became concerned about an exhibition in Beijing and "several truck loads of paintings were taken away. But they were returned to the artists. They're not so inhumane as to destroy them."

As a result of this pressure, says Yao, painters tend to choose indirect themes, "leaving space for the officials to be not so oppositionist. Some people are trying to push the envelope, but not as strongly as earlier." And things are in some respects getting better: the government has set up an "arts promotion committee" to improve communication with artists, which Yao applauds. He moved to Songzhuang during a more difficult period, after police ejected the residents of his previous painters' village near the Summer Palace in west Beijing. Overseas collectors had begun beating a path there to buy paintings, and the resident artists were accused of "revealing state secrets to foreigners." "We didn't even know what state secrets were," Yao says.

Chinese people naturally pride themselves on their ancient culture – meaning, overwhelmingly, the Han culture. They honour artists, at least those who work within recognised traditions. They are avid consumers of mass media, reading more newspapers and magazines and watching more TV than any other people except perhaps Americans. Hundreds of millions are active daily on the net.

Just as big state-owned corporations are investing aggressively overseas, billions of dollars are being spent on a parallel program of global "soft power," promoting Chinese culture around the world. Hundreds of Confucius Institutes have been established to promote Chinese language and culture. (The phrase "soft power," borrowed from the American intellectual and ambassador Joseph Nye, is much used in modern China).

By co-opting and controlling cultural activities, however, the party diminishes some of their desired effects, just as forcing students to learn by rote undermines attempts to foster academic creativity. Thus Chinese painters, filmmakers and composers are winning awards and lots of money overseas, but seem to be losing their influence over hearts and minds at home. That suits the authorities. But it is a constant struggle to stay on top of a vibrant and often lateral-thinking creative world.

Few if any ground-breaking artists are in jail in China, although some – like the Nobel Prize-winning writer Gao Xingjian, author of *Soul Mountain* – have exiled themselves, in his case to France. The irrepressible artist/showman/cultural commentator Ai Weiwei was detained and subjected to – uncharacteristically for Ai – undisclosed treatment while under arrest, after he too-strenuously backed the cause of parents whose children were killed in collapsing school buildings in the Sichuan earthquake.

Many artists are still working hard in China and making a living, but some find the process of negotiating the space to express themselves exhausting. Their negotiating partner, the Chinese Communist Party, has had decades to fine-hone its skills of patronising, obstructing and marginalising its rivals in the struggle to shape the country's twenty-first century. Professor Miao Di of the Communication University of China in Beijing says that artists are better off now than ever, but "the general quality of output is declining."

China's artists also face big challenges beyond censorship. Some express concern that society's focus on materialism is producing an exile of the spirit. But this economic revolution is also delivering them new ways to reach wider markets, via new media, that sometimes leave the authorities gasping to catch up. In general, artistic creations that will be bought by foreigners, or command a largely overseas audience, are considered of little concern by the authorities. An exhibition of politically mischievous paintings in a Tokyo or London gallery will be met with a shrug; if the artist returns with a suitcase full of cash, so much the better. But work in Chinese, available to a wide audience in China, is a very different matter.

Overall, the party is determined to retain control over the world of ideas, which includes the mass media, art galleries, movies, books, history, music and even the internet. Surprisingly, it is still largely succeeding, even in the midst of China's present tumultuous economic and technological change. The process of control has become fluid. The rules keep changing. Artists who press against the barriers must second-guess what will be acceptable from one year to the next. Some apparently innocent works – like Zhang Bojun's book of profiles of Peking Opera stars – have been banned, while others that might seem more subversive are let through.

There is nothing new in the notion of state-control of the arts in China. In imperial days, although mavericks occasionally burst out, most artists were either independently wealthy aristocrats or artisans hired by the court. The highest praise was awarded for emulating styles of poetry, painting or calligraphy established by previous generations.

Suddenly, in the first half of the twentieth century, as the rest of China tore itself apart, the country's artists enjoyed an unprecedented period of openness. The greatest of Chinese writers, Lu Xun, produced his masterful short stories, while painters and other artists flourished.

Within a few years of coming to power, Mao called on intellectuals to "let a hundred flowers bloom, let a hundred schools of thought contend." It was a trap. Hundreds of thousands of artists and others, believing in Mao's sincerity, told him what they really thought about the party's casual cruelties – in the ancient Chinese spirit of believing that if only the emperor knew what his officials were really up to, he'd put a stop to it. Many were jailed, beaten or killed after speaking out.

Today's authorities have issued explicit instructions that Chinese media and writers must not refer in any way to this grim "anti-rightist" episode. In the decades since Mao, of course, China has changed massively, and the prospect of having a private intellectual life has opened up, at least for the hundreds of millions of people who have graduated from rural poverty. But every inch of public space remains closely defended by the powers that be.

The State Council has issued the following elastic list of forbidden activities: Opposing the principles in the constitution; endangering national sovereignty or unity; revealing state secrets or damaging the country's reputation; stirring up racial hatred; advocating cults or superstition; disturbing social order; advocating violence, gambling, pornography or crime; infringing others' interests or rights; damaging traditional culture; and encouraging any activities forbidden by law, regulation or the government in general.

The party's propaganda department operates a penalty system for arts and media outlets. Points are deducted for infringements of government rules; twelve points means closure. The Sanlian Publishing House lost a total of six points for an edition of its *Lifeweek* magazine that featured a photo of Mao's wife Jiang Qing standing trial, and for another that mentioned the 1976 Tangshan earthquake in which more than 250,000 people died. The party had banned references to either event.

The Ministry of Culture has also announced that it will introduce a certification system to cover thirty "industrial occupations" in the arts, ranging from film directors to singers. This system, reported Xinhua, "will become a basis for cultural work units to contract and hire talent as well as assess rewards and punishments."

The ministry also has its eye on popular culture. Wang Qing, party secretary of the ministry's artistic talent centre, warned that there were plans to "cool down all manner of talent events" – including *Super Girls*, the hugely popular Chinese equivalent of the *Idol* TV shows – "that are being conducted for commercial aims." On the whole, says Professor Miao Di, authorities are more relaxed about "the development of pulp culture, especially on TV, which is strongly controlled, while other arts are pushed to the edge." They do have some qualms, however. In 2007, the State Administration of Radio, Film and Television (SARFT) – queasy about the prospect of a *Super Boys* contest that promised to rival *Super Girls* for vulgarity – announced that only "healthy and ethically inspiring" songs should be performed on such programs in future. *Super Girls*, which attracted a peak of 400 million viewers, worried the authorities not only on taste grounds, but also because it invited the public to cast votes for the performers by email, phone or text message.

When *Super Boys* succeeded *Super Girls*, public participation was reduced and SARFT banned "scenes of screaming fans or losing contestants in tears," insisting instead that the show should "maintain a happy atmosphere." Contestants were to be aged at least eighteen, and "their hairstyles, clothes, fashion accessories, language and manners should be in line with mainstream values." Judges were prohibited from "mocking or humiliating contestants." The show attracted considerably fewer viewers than the *Super Girls* series.

Meanwhile a new TV talent program won plaudits from the powers that be: the *Red Song Contest*, which made its debut in the southern-central Jiangxi province, and in which the contestants performed Communist Party classics such as "Why Are the Flowers So Red," "The Red Star Sparkles as I Go to War" and "Liuyang River" (with lines such as *Mao is like the red sun in our hearts*). Some of the songs were from old films with patriotic or revolutionary themes; some were PLA marching songs. Jiangxi is a region with strong revolutionary connections. The People's Liberation Army's annual founding day honours an uprising in Nanchang, the provincial capital. And the communists established an early base in the Jingganshan Mountains here – an increasingly hot destination for "red tourism" to famous party sites.

The first contestants included an eighty-year-old man and a nine-year-old girl. Their performances were judged by a group of mature performers and composers famous for their own talents in this genre. Yan Su, a veteran army composer, told the official newspaper *China Daily*, "These songs, which were composed in the red revolutionary era, even make me, a 77-year-old man, feel excited."

Contemporary music, by contrast, is seen as something to be wary of – but also something to make money from. Diana Krall, the Canadian pianist and singer, one of the greatest jazz drawcards, was held up on her way into a Beijing theatre in 2008 by a scalper determined to sell her a ticket. He was so insistent, she told the audience later, that he wasn't deterred even when she told him it was her show. The sold-out concert was Krall's first in China. (She was outraged by the price he was demanding, but perhaps failed to realise she could have bargained him down.)

China is increasingly on the map for international artists, even though as a market it remains promising rather than lucrative. The party-state imposes a tax on every activity it knows about. In the case of cultural events, this greatly complicates budgets and imposes a hidden burden on genuine supporters of the arts. A substantial percentage of all tickets available at every venue usually has to be given by the promoter, free of charge, to the local party organisation, to the culture ministry or its regional offshoot (which must ultimately approve every performance), and to the state-owned enterprise or government agency that invariably owns the concert hall. The Poly Theatre in Beijing, for instance, was developed by the People's Liberation Army and retains close military connections via the Poly Group, which is a major corporation in China's defence industry.

This helps explain the ubiquitous *huangniu*, or scalpers. Tickets find their way into the hands of cadres who have no interest in the occasion. But they know someone who knows someone who may be able to get some money for the ticket. It also helps explain the sections of empty seats, usually the most expensive, near the front of the house, even at concerts where every ticket is ostensibly sold. The best seats have been "taxed" to officials, sometimes elderly, who may have little interest in attending themselves.

This was the reason for the extraordinary divide between sections of the audience at Krall's concert. The hollering and applauding fans were overwhelmingly in the cheaper seats. The behaviour of those in the US$240 seats was intriguingly different. Many were children, some of them clutching light-sticks that they did not switch on. It was clear that many had little notion of the music they had come to hear. Perhaps they had seen the promotional photos of Krall and imagined that a blonde Canadian of about forty must sing sentimental ballads in the vein of Celine Dion, the goddess of Chinese music fans, whose 1997 hit from *Titanic*, "My Heart Will Go On," has yet to hit an iceberg in the world's most populous country. Many of those in the expensive seats began to chat among themselves and even to walk out in the middle of songs.

The party hopes to boost the country's image by hosting international artists, but it insists on controlling the content of all performances. Even the Rolling Stones had to submit a playlist before their 2006 concert in Shanghai was approved. Classical music concert programs are scrupulously combed for works with any religious element, such as Mozart's *Requiem*. When Sonic Youth played in Shanghai, a little-known rule was invoked to halt a local rock band, Carsick Cars, from opening for them – a special permit was required, officials said, before Chinese and foreign musicians could appear on the same stage. Cross-pollination is viewed by the authorities as cross-pollution.

Nevertheless, large numbers of fans can be found for almost every type of music in China, and they are determined not to go without their musical pleasures, even if these find no place in the popular media. Chinese TV, despite its forty or so channels, plays mainly local adaptations of middle-of-the-road American pop, or else patriotic melodies. Thus when music enthusiasts get a rare opportunity to hear an exemplar of their favourite genre, they make sure the performer knows just how excited they are. The Romanian soprano Angela Gheorghiu, singing in the *Divas in Beijing* concert series during the Olympics, was called back for six encores. When the English soprano Emma Kirkby sang sixteenth- and seventeenth-century songs accompanied by a lute in the Forbidden City concert hall, a large group of Beijingers in their twenties hollered in delight. After the show, she came to the edge of the stage and engaged them in an intense discussion about early music.

Most older music lovers have survived terrible times, especially the Cultural Revolution, when their enjoyment of Western music could imperil them and their families. Their joy today at being free to listen largely to what they want to is moving – and stands in stark contrast to the cadres' families in the stalls.

In a society in which a single party has held power for more than sixty years, it is not surprising that many people would rather be inside the establishment than out, even – perhaps especially – if they have themselves spent decades struggling with the parameters set by that establishment. This appears to be the case with the filmmaker Zhang Yimou. Most Westerners have encountered Chinese film, if at all, in Zhang's intense, challenging stories set in the countryside, such as *Ju Dou*, *To Live*, and *Raise the Red Lantern*. It was he who introduced the luminous actress Gong Li to the wider world, through films that were international art-house hits despite receiving scant or no distribution at home.

But when the Taiwanese-American director Ang Lee, hugely admired in China, scored an international triumph with his martial arts epic

Crouching Tiger, Hidden Dragon, Zhang followed suit with a series of big-scale historical films celebrating national heroes. These films, starting with *Hero*, celebrate China's national unity and explain and excuse the brutality of its early leaders. His *Curse of the Golden Flower*, released in 2006, was at the time the most expensive, most parodied, most critically derided and most commercially successful film ever made in China. When Beijing won its bid to host the Olympics, Zhang was invited to produce the opening ceremony.

In an interview with the Guangzhou-based *Southern Weekend*, Zhang admitted, "Our program [for the opening ceremony] had the highest level of political review since the founding of the People's Republic of China." He said that reviews were conducted by the Central Committee of the party, which has 371 members, including the most powerful people in China. Zhang, who said he was not a party member, told the newspaper – "with my hand on my heart" – that even the highest leaders did not give orders. They only made suggestions, he said, telling him: "'Yimou, it is hard to please everyone. You directors need to take into account everyone's opinions, but you must do it in a way that works artistically. Which views to follow and which to leave aside, is up to you.'" Zhang said that this demonstrated how tolerant the leadership was, "how very understanding of the way art works." Nevertheless, he said, when a "very senior leader" gave his opinion after a rehearsal, "you do not have a chance to talk back. It is impossible to explain, nor can you say, 'Your opinion isn't up to much.' You have to analyse everything, then make the changes you feel necessary. But even if I thought sometimes that a modification wasn't necessary, I still had to do it."

The leaders, he said, made suggestions about everything, including the use of colour and the pace of the production. He said, "Often we had dozens of leaders come in at once. If an opinion was raised by more than three of them, I would definitely make the change they wanted. I realised that this was a test. The leaders knew this was a huge matter for the nation. They were all very clear-headed, all college graduates. We all think alike, we're about the same age, we had similar experiences, such as being sent to the countryside" during the Cultural Revolution. "The thing I said most often to my team was: leaders are human beings too. Let's not think of them just as leaders, but also as ordinary people, giving their opinion from the perspective of a member of the audience. Don't they also represent the views of many people in the audience?"

Zhang took notes whenever a senior leader suggested a change. "You can ask my team, when I returned to transmit their opinions, I always said the leaders were right." When he made changes in response to such suggestions, he would tell his team: "The audience throughout China, looking at the ceremony on TV, only cares about the result, not the process. No one will care why you made modifications, as long as it made the performance more lively and exciting."

Chen Qigang, the composer of the music for Zhang's opening ceremony, including "You and Me" (*You and me / from one world / we are family*), the sentimental theme song that was ubiquitous in China in 2008, has lived in France for twenty-four years. But while living in France, he said, "enabled me to find my true self ... we cannot forget our national character, and cannot forget the responsibility we should bear for the nation ... We made meticulous efforts to present a truly great China to the world."

Not all artists want to play the game. Jia Zhangke, winner of the 2006 Golden Lion, the top award at the Venice Film Festival, for his *Still Life*, is one. He is the doyen of the new generation of Chinese filmmakers and is openly scornful of Zhang Yimou's transformation into the most establishment of directors. Jia says, "We are bombarded by too many films in the name of gold. Films today are filled with people flying in the air, but my films are about people who walk on the ground."

Jia's films are gritty and grungy. They feature losers. They have a documentary feel. He doesn't use studios and works mostly with amateur actors in the streets and fields of poor provinces like his native Shanxi. He arrived at the Beijing Film Academy a couple of decades after Zhang, in 1993. "Four years after Tiananmen, no one really believed in communism," he recalls. "To be objective, that was the goal for understanding of the arts." He says: "Half my fellow students, while not lovers of the system, looked for work within it. I was on the other side. When I heard for the first time of independent filmmaking, I was excited. It means finding friends and partners to invest their own money."

In the nineties, the private economy was on the rise in China, so Jia dealt with "all sorts of businessmen" in his search for backers. His first feature film, *Xiao Wu*, made in his third year at the academy, was banned after he sent it directly to the Berlin Film Festival rather than submitting it through the official Chinese channels.

Jia says, "I wanted to find a way that Chinese people could see my movies," so he sent the screenplay for *Platform* to the State Administration for Radio Film and Television. "The reply was 'No, you can't make it.' I asked why not. They replied, 'Because you are too young to tell such a story, that talks of the decade 1979–89. Make it when you've grown older.' So I had to make the film on my own again – though it didn't prevent me from thinking that independent or not, movie people must have a kind of link with authority."

Public cinemas are controlled by the authorities, so Jia devised his own alternative distribution system, showing his films at universities and in bars and restaurants. "But we were acting like criminals, hiding ourselves." Then in 2003, SARFT sat down to talk with him. Why the change? "More independent filmmakers were emerging, new media were sprouting, my first three films were released in the US and Europe, so people pirated DVD copies and sold them everywhere, and others downloaded them. It all made them realise you can't any more ban a movie completely."

The authorities, he says, "wanted to build a culture industry. They had made some progress, but thought of movies as products." Seven or eight independent filmmakers met with the SARFT cadres and reached "a kind of compromise" whereby films already banned would remain so, but new films could be made openly. "But they are not stable in their minds. Sometimes they get extreme, sometimes they're surprisingly open to us. The forbidden areas are still unknown. But we just go ahead regardless … In receiving my award in Venice I said movies are always something we use to expand freedom."

When the director Lou Ye entered his film *Summer Palace* – which is partly set against the forbidden topic of the Tiananmen Square demonstrations – in the 2006 Cannes film festival without official approval, he was banned from making another movie in China for five years. Jia says, "If we don't touch the taboo areas we will have a lot of freedom. But then those areas will grow larger. The pity is, the economy is growing so rapidly, but breaking cultural taboos remains such a slow process. If your tactic is to guess what the censors are thinking, and try to avoid their concerns, you are ruined as an artist. Artists should have a spirit of rebellion. But we're living in a dangerous atmosphere, where many young people, captured by commercial culture, are quite resigned to being submissive. They are alienated from the rebellious culture of the 1990s."

Even Jia appears susceptible to the need for compromise, however. In 2009, he withdrew his short film, *Cry Me a River*, from the Melbourne International Film Festival. This followed the festival's decision to screen a biopic on the Uighur leader Rebiya Kadeer, who is viewed by the Chinese authorities as a dangerous "splittist" for leading – from Washington DC, where she has based herself in exile – the struggle for independence for her people in north-western China. The festival came under fierce attack from the Chinese authorities for showing the film, and for inviting Kadeer to speak at its launch.

Jia said at the time, "The political overtone of this year's Melbourne festival is getting more and more intense." Tensions between Uighurs and Han Chinese in China's Xinjiang region had recently exploded into violence. Jia insisted that he and another filmmaker (Emily Tsang, based in Hong Kong) had "decided to withdraw of our own wills. We received no instruction or even a hint from the government. When we read the festival program, we realised it has become a place not to talk purely about films, and this naturally diminished our enthusiasm to participate. We feel that appearing with Rebiya in a thoroughly politicised festival crosses the line of what our emotions and behaviour can accept. With the true nature of the tragedy in Xinjiang still unclear, we don't think it's appropriate to have Ms Kadeer speaking at such a festival. And to my knowledge, I have never heard of her being enthusiastic about film or [having] any movie achievements to her name." Their gesture did not, he insisted, amount to "meddling with the festival's freedom of artistic exchange. Withdrawing from Melbourne is, rather, a form of self-restraint."

Many of the films made in China – not just Jia's – are never seen in theatres, and there is an annual limit of twenty new foreign releases (plus, as of 2012, fourteen IMAX or 3D films). While China claims 36,000 movie screens in total, most of these are in workplaces, reflecting the old-school use of film to take political messages to the masses. In Mao's day, propaganda teams used to drive trucks around rural areas, tie up large sheets and present movies – the socialist equivalent of the drive-in, says Professor Michael Dutton, an expert in Chinese culture based at Griffith University. The number of commercial screens is rising rapidly, however, and by the end of 2012 had reached about 13,000.

Like so many areas of Chinese cultural life, film is in transition. But it lags behind many other fields, and SARFT is substantially responsible. SARFT, says Jeremy Goldkorn, the Beijing-based founder of Danwei, a pioneering marketing and media website, is one of the most conservative institutions in the country. In recent years it has shown some signs of accepting social change. For instance, the country's most financially successful film in 2008 was *If You Are the One*, a romantic comedy directed by Feng Xiaogang. A middle-aged bachelor, played by the veteran actor Ge You, advertises on Match.com and a string of hapless encounters follow. Unexpectedly, and not entirely credibly, he then strikes gold with the gorgeous Xiaoxiao, played by China's poster girl *du jour*, Shu Qi. Feng's similarly successful follow-up film, *Aftershock*, was set during the horrific Sichuan earthquake of 2008 and focused not on soldierly heroics (a theme always applauded by SARFT) but on a family fractured and then reunited.

In 2009, however, SARFT announced that it would strengthen its censorship criteria, in order to "purify screen entertainment." Out, according to Xinhua, were explicit sex, rape, prostitution "and the like," vulgar dialogue or music, sound effects with a sexual connotation, and content involving murder, violence, horror, evil spirits "and excessively terrifying scenes." Premarital cohabitation was out. So of course was frontal nudity, "abnormal sexual relations," the promotion of superstition, fortune telling, the worship of divine beings or incense burning, and anything endangering the integrity of the state,

Also out were films that "distort the civilisation and history of China or other nations, tarnish the image of revolutionary leaders, heroes, important characters, members of the armed forces, police and judicial bodies, reconstruct crimes or reveal police investigatory techniques, advocate nihilism, environmental damage, and the capture or killing of rare animals." (*Kungfu Panda* was thus an endangered species – but it managed to sneak onto the list of that year's twenty foreign releases, and proved immensely popular.) The final item on the list of banned topics was "other content forbidden by the state" – unspecified.

The Hong Kong director Er Dongsheng did not discover until he had finished shooting his film *Protégé* in China that love scenes must not last more than one minute. He was forced to cut large chunks of the film, but remained perplexed. "From which point is a love scene regarded as starting?" he asked. Bloggers wondered if this rule suggested that

Chinese lovemaking lasts only a minute. An earlier Er Dongsheng film, *One Night in Mongkok,* only passed censorship after a prostitute's line was changed from "I came from Hunan" – a Chinese province – to "I came from Southeast Asia."

Li Yu, one of China's most promising female directors, sobbed when her 2007 film *Pingguo* (released internationally as *Lost in Beijing*) was returned with dozens of excisions marked. Eventually, twenty minutes of the ninety-minute film were lost, including scenes of a child breast-feeding and the sale of a Cultural Revolution-era poster. Its producer, Fang Li, was banned from any involvement in the film industry for two years. Zhang Hongsen, deputy director of SARFT's film bureau, told a conference in Jiangsu that the film had been chasing international awards and in the process had insulted the Chinese people. "Our directors should consciously defend the honour of the motherland," he said.

Ang Lee's great masterpiece *Lust, Caution*, set during the Japanese invasion and the Chinese civil war, was a huge hit in China in 2007, although SARFT insisted that a seven-minute sex scene be removed. Thousands of mainland Chinese travelled to Hong Kong to watch the uncut version, helping to make it the most popular Chinese language film in Hong Kong that year.

During the annual meeting of the National People's Congress, however, a senior party cadre watched the film on DVD and was disgusted by what he saw as its "glorification of traitors and insult to patriots." He was enraged that the film's heroine, played by the brilliant 28-year-old star Tang Wei, warned her lover, a "traitor," of a plot by communist students.

As a result, several SARFT staff lost their jobs. Having been rapped over the knuckles, SARFT hastened to issue a statement "reasserting censorship guidelines," warning all film and broadcasting bodies that it was reviving its ban on films that "show promiscuous acts, rape, prostitution, sexual intercourse, sexual perversity, masturbation and male-female sexual organs and other private parts." SARFT also issued an internal instruction to China's TV stations and print media, ordering them to drop advertisements featuring Tang for Pond's skincare (a brand owned by the international giant Unilever), for which she was to have been paid about US$900,000. Tang emigrated to Hong Kong in order to continue working.

Zhao Guo-jun, the director of China Law Watch Centre, a legal NGO based in Beijing and with a prominent website, says that this case was typical. When the party decides to crack down, "There is no legal, public document, no formal procedure or hearing." There is no official film rating system in China. This unpredictable system "leaves the victim with no chance to make a formal complaint, or get legal help." The party's treatment of Tang was "obviously unfair, the more so because she has been punished after the film has been censored, and it has played widely in cinemas ... Of course, people in authority may exert their power. But they should do so in a public, transparent manner, inside a legal framework, and those being punished should have the right to legal assistance, and to challenge what is being done to them. Instead, the use of the ban today is random, it is unpredictable." As such, it encourages self-censorship. "No one knows what the standards or the limits are," says Zhao. "So the genuine artistic movie or TV products are very, very few." In the West, he says, if an artist is attacked by politicians or others in authority, he or she gains a higher profile. In China, it is the opposite. Like Tang, they disappear. Out of sight, out of mind. Nevertheless, Zhao holds out hope that the bounds of what is permissible might gradually expand.

Cui Wei-ping, a professor at China's premier film school, the Beijing Film Academy, says, "It's a question of the party still deciding the way history, the stories of the past, should be told. Generally, our students and film professionals simply hope they don't get caught up in such controversies." She describes a SARFT official who made a speech to students at the academy. He told them, "Whether you're an actor or a director, it's better that you don't touch a subject such as treachery." "It's a strange phenomenon" for an actor to be held accountable for the content of a film, Cui notes, but this is the reality for actors working in China today. "Academics like me sometimes sign letters about such issues," she says. "But actors, directors or photographers keep away. They don't dare, for fear their relations with SARFT will be strained."

In the West, our view of Chinese film does not always reflect what Chinese moviegoers are seeing. As Dutton says, "The least successful movies of the 1980s and 1990s within mainland China were usually the most successful ones outside China. Hence Western viewers have tended to be most familiar with the more art-house side of the Chinese industry." Within China, the theme of popular hits tends to be "saving the nation." Few independent, commercially sponsored films get made in China today. Most remain products of the state-run studio system. People at the top of the party hierarchy are particularly sensitive to criticism about economic or social policy, while cultural policy remains largely abandoned to the old conservatives. Complaints rarely get a hearing. And while movie stars are grade-A celebrities in China, as elsewhere, film-going is not the ubiquitous social activity that it is in many other parts of the world.

★

Ding Dong, a writer who left the Communist Party after 1989, makes a living from his writing on historical and contemporary affairs. Much is now published that would have been unthinkable in Mao's day, he says. But the development of democracy and, especially, the history of the party remain taboos. Sitting in the book-crammed bedroom-cum-study he and his wife share in a modest ground-floor flat in an ancient quarter of Beijing, he says, "However sound your research, if your viewpoint conflicts with that of the authorities, you still can't be published in this field. Ours seems a big room compared with Mao's day, but it isn't when measured against the UN constitution, or that of China itself."

In China today, all publishing houses are ultimately owned by the state. Private publications lack legal status, although a few may be distributed discreetly but not widely circulated. The authorities fix a total number of books to be licensed in any given year – usually about 200,000 – and then apportion these licenses to publishers. In giving out licenses, "those in charge will automatically filter viewpoints to align them with the party," Ding says. "They call it self-discipline."

But recently a new element has entered the equation: the market. Publishing houses "all need to finance themselves, they need to make a living. They are working between two pressures, that of the party and that to win a readership. So they have a certain impulse to speak the truth, which tends to appeal to readers more." This market pressure can also, however, make publishers more cautious. The government divides publishers into three categories, Ding says. Particularly trustworthy companies will be given more licences than the year before, while "the bad guys who publish books they don't like get a reduction," and the rest will get the same number as previously. There is thus a financial incentive to toe the party line. And the risks for crossing that line are real: publishing houses in Guangdong and Sichuan have been closed down, says Ding, simply for publishing one "bad book."

Before any book goes to press, publishers must send the title, author's name and a contents list to the local propaganda department. If the book is about historical, diplomatic, military or religious affairs, or mentions party leaders, the whole manuscript will require examination. The propaganda department will send it to a local "reading group" of retired cadres, all party members in their sixties or older, who will report back on anything they perceive as incorrect.

A new phenomenon in Chinese publishing is the on-sale of licences. The state-owned publishers increasingly function merely as rent-seekers, arranging the censorship approvals but then handing over the production, printing, distribution and marketing to private businesspeople. In Beijing, they can sell book licences for about US$5000 each – providing a further incentive for publishers to obtain as many as they can by pleasing the authorities.

The controls continue even when China's writers are sent overseas as part of the government's global "soft power" push. For instance, in 2011 ten writers visited Sydney and Melbourne via the Chinese Writers' Association, a government organisation funded by the culture ministry, for a four-day conference with some Australian counterparts. Formerly, Chinese writers travelled to writers' festivals as individuals, at the invitation of their overseas publishers. Now they are coming in teams. The writers – Mo Yan, Zhang Wei, Li Er, Zhaxi Dawa, Xu Xiaobin, Sheng Keyi, Zhao Mei, Hu Ping, Gao Hongbo and Shang Zhen – were accompanied by three officials, two from the ministry. The conference began quite formally and slowly but warmed up by the end, says Nicholas Jose, an author, a professor at the University of Western Sydney and a former "cultural counsellor" at the Australian embassy in Beijing. "It was an extremely interesting exercise – and also frustrating, because we came up against the limits to what real dialogue is possible."

Mo Yan, one of China's best known writers, opened the meeting by describing it as one between the panda and the kangaroo. He later expressed to Jose his intense curiosity about the latter – but Mo was unable to take time away from the group even to visit a zoo to see a kangaroo for himself. "It seemed poignant," says Jose. "When Australian writers have visited China, they have had very little contact with Chinese writers. People were very interested in what each was saying, but the gulf between the two literary communities became evident. Typically of this moment in China, the Chinese writers were primarily interested in themselves."

The Chinese writers were ferried everywhere by bus, stayed at a guest-house attached to the consulate in Sydney, and were not available for dinners or drinks with their Australian counterparts outside the formal sessions. Some of the writers then travelled to Melbourne for the Melbourne Writers' Festival. They left the country as soon as their official commitments were over.

Jane Weizhen Pan, a translator and interpreter, attended the Sydney conference. She and her collaborator, Martin Merz, had recently translated *The Magician of 1919* by one of the Chinese writers, Li Er. The Chinese visitors, she says, were "kept on a very short leash. They didn't get to see the real Australia. One of them told me that this was his first visit, but all he could recall was a conference room. It was such a pity, because they chose talented writers, but they might as well have done it by video conference."

Alexis Wright, an Indigenous author who won the Miles Franklin Award for her novel *Carpentaria* (which is now being translated into Chinese), had visited China two years before and "would have liked to talk with more Chinese writers then." She therefore seized the opportunity in Sydney, hoping to hear how Chinese authors coped with their restrictions. "I feel that Aboriginal writers in Australia are not easily heard either, and can be pushed out." Most of the Chinese writers, she says, spoke of their need to return to their traditions, which struck a chord with her, as did a paper on the sense of place. But, she says, "they stayed as a group, and I'm not sure what happened behind the scenes. I assumed that's the way they do things."

It is certainly how some artists must do things, at least some of the time. Typically, Chinese artists must migrate between worlds – between formal, organised encounters and the private world of the individual artist, who is sometimes self-consciously perched at the margins of her or his society. "The best works," Ding Dong tells me, "come out of artists who live in a small space, in the seams between the authorities and the commercial pressures."

CHAPTER 7:
CONTROLLING LEGENDS

IN A PARK AT THE CENTRE OF SHAOSHAN, IN HILLY, RURAL Hunan province in central China, "red pilgrims" gather to pay their respects to a ten-metre tall statue of the town's most famous son – the great communist leader and devout enemy of faith and piety, Mao Zedong. They move forward in step, one group after another. Some bow at the waist, some present wreaths, some place their palms together in a Buddhist *anjali* mark of respect. For some, it appears part of a jolly communal holiday; for others it is a tearful moment of contemplating the dreams, hopes and deep, deep emotional commitments they have made in past years, past lives.

This fits with the promotion of "red tourism" – as a tool to stimulate pride in the historic achievements of the party, as well as to boost incomes in the poor, remote regions where many of its founding legends took place, especially during the Long March of 1934–35 to escape annihilation at the hands of the Kuomintang. Red tourism began to be developed in 2005, and in 2010 thirteen cities agreed a "strategic cooperation declaration" to boost the phenomenon.

Keeping control of history is a core priority for the party. It views the Soviet party's loss of control of the memory of Stalin as a fatal step towards its loss of power. If it can own the past, the party believes, it can own the present and the future, both of which are shaped by how people understand their history.

Most red tourists come in groups, whose travel is often paid for by their employers – chiefly government agencies or state-owned enterprises –

or by their party branches. It is considered far easier for such organisations to gain budgetary approval for paid trips, especially in the face of rising concerns about corruption, when they can be viewed as "red" and therefore patriotic and educational. Xi Jinping, while visiting Jinggangshan in 2008, praised "the countless martyrs of the revolution who used their blood and lives to win over this country ... Under no circumstances can we forsake this tradition."

Some people dress in special garb to mark their devotion, in a manner that evokes religious pilgrimages. A group from Henan City wears the blue uniforms and caps of the early People's Liberation Army, as they travel by bus to view sacred Long March sites in a three-day "Spirit of Jinggangshan" (where the Long March started) study tour. Another group of state-owned enterprise executives, chiefly from Hunan's capital, Changsha, all wear bright red ties. Even Long March cuisine is available at hotels along the route. The three basic foods eaten by the red army were eggplant, red rice and pumpkin. Inevitably, the soldiers made up a marching song about them, which is now popular again among red tourists: *Chairman Mao stays with us every day, every day when we eat this food we think of Chairman Mao*, goes the chorus.

Shaoshan is the focal point of the pilgrimages, where in a lovely little valley nestles the apparent place of Mao's birth on 26 December in 1893. Modest investigation reveals that his birthplace, a substantial farmhouse complex, was mostly burned down in 1929 and has been rebuilt since. But Chinese attitudes to heritage sites differ from those in the West, and a building that seems to resemble the original will do perfectly well. An adjacent fish-farm lake is said to have been Mao's swimming pool; he is famously associated with swimming in the Yangtze River aged seventy-three. A voluminous pair of his alleged swimming togs takes pride of place in a Mao museum in another town on the red tourism trail, Zunyi.

The *feng shui* is perfect at the birthplace, on an elevated level with its back to a mountain and the lake in front – in contrast to the mess that has been made of the *feng shui* of Tiananmen Square by the construction in its centre of the great helmsman's mausoleum, where his embalmed remains are on display in a glass case.

At the birthplace, the queues of pilgrims are instructed to remain respectfully silent as they shuffle through. Signs warn that the cutting of words into the bamboo trees by the side of the house is strictly forbidden, as is cutting off the branches. Photography, smoking, "nibbling" and littering are also not allowed. Visitors are informed that Mao was a good son. He used to help his mother, Wen Qimei, with her household chores when he was a boy. And Mao Shun-sheng, his father, is described disarmingly in a sign in English as "hard working, thrifty, smart, and crackerjack man." A notice in the kitchen explains that "it was by the side of the kitchen fire that Mao had gathered the whole family together for meetings. He encouraged them to devote themselves to the cause of the liberty of the Chinese people."

The contrast, for Chinese people today as decades ago, remains stark: after a century of humiliation at the hands of foreigners, China "stood up" under Mao, and will not now take a backward step.

Another great shrine to that history – by turns glorious and gruesome, but always momentous – beckons red pilgrims in Shanghai. On 23 July 1921, thirteen young men entered a ground-floor room of 106 Rue Wantz (now 76 Xingye Road), in the bustling French concession in Shanghai, which was just beginning its brief effervescent heyday as a global centre of commerce, cultures and ideas. They weren't there to make money, like most people in Shanghai. They were there, inspired by recent events in Russia, to make revolution.

They formed the first National Congress of the Chinese Communist Party. The modest grey-brick house where they met was owned by one of the delegates, Li Hanjun, who had just finished building it the year before, in the then – and now – fashionable Shikumen style, a sort of Chinese-meets-European blend, with carved stone doorframes.

Today the house contains a waxworks representation of the thirteen founders; in an upper room, Mao stands in the centre addressing his twelve apparent disciples. But that inaugural congress actually chose, in absentia, Chen Duxiu as its first leader, making him the party's founding general secretary and then chairman. Chen, however, lost patience with Lenin and Stalin, becoming a supporter of Leon Trotsky and eventually losing the struggle for the leadership of the Chinese party.

The political rivalries of the 1920s were to determine the shape of the rest of the century for China. The Kuomintang dominated nationwide political life but failed to accommodate its own left wing, which would eventually shuffle into the CCP. While the Republic of China's forces dashed themselves against the Japanese invasion, the CCP was able to develop its own military force, which became the People's Liberation

Army. Whereas the Soviet communists' core strength lay in the urban, industrial proletariat, the CCP failed to develop as formidable a base as it hoped in China's cities, where industrialisation was less advanced than in Russia and where the Nationalists were already dominant. Instead, Mao, who replaced Chen as leader, developed the winning strategy of "surrounding the cities from the countryside."

Like the Russian monarchy, the Qing Dynasty in China, 250 years old, had been in the process of collapsing, like a car crash viewed in slow-motion, since the latter years of the nineteenth century. The last Qing emperor, the then five-year-old Puyi, finally fell half a dozen years before the last Tsar. But the dynasty – which comprised a foreign elite, the Manchus from the north-east – had never really recovered from the shock of being forced by the British to concede an "unequal treaty" following the Opium War of 1840, which awarded Hong Kong to Britain. It kept struggling to reject the foreign incursions that followed, but failed either to reimpose its rule convincingly or to learn from the foreigners whose rapid industrialisation had caught the empire unawares. In comparison, the ancient regime in Japan adapted to its own "shock of the new" with such eventual success that its people's average living standard remains more than twenty times higher than that of the Chinese. When an American naval commodore, Matthew Perry, sailed a small fleet into Edo (now Tokyo) Bay in July 1853, the response of the shogunate, then of the Emperor Meiji, was to seek to learn how the Western world had moved so far ahead, and to modernise.

During this era, educated young Chinese grew increasingly impatient with the imperial recalcitrance, and growing numbers went overseas to study – and to plot the regime's downfall. Most prominent among them was the charismatic medical doctor Sun Yat-sen (known in China as Zhong Shan), born in 1866, like many of that era's reformers in the southern province of Guangdong. He lived, studied and travelled in Japan, Hong Kong, Hawaii, Canada, Singapore and London, where in 1896 Qing agents succeeded in kidnapping him. The plot was foiled as they attempted to smuggle him from the legation back to China. He became in 1905 the head of the anti-Qing Revolutionary Alliance, which was especially strong among Chinese students in Japan.

The first Chinese version of Karl Marx's *Communist Manifesto* was published in 1906, the same year as a Japanese socialist party was also founded, heightening Chinese interest in this new thinking. The failed attempt at revolution in Russia in 1905 also helped. In that year, Sun travelled to Brussels, where he affiliated his new group with the socialist Second International.

The Qing regime finally imploded in 1911. A bomb exploded in Hankou, part of what is now the massive city of Wuhan, the capital of Hubei province in the heart of China, a centre of steel production on the Yangtze River. The bomb was being put together by a group of radical young people at their secret centre in the city's Russian concession. Those who were wounded were taken to hospital, but meanwhile Qing security forces arrived, killed the three comrades who had remained at the house, and discovered files listing many supporters. The historian Jonathan Spence explains what happened next: "The revolutionaries understood that unless they could launch an uprising rapidly, their organisation would be unravelled and many more members would lose their lives."

The radicals included soldiers in the New Army established a few years earlier by the Qing. Some mutinied and swiftly seized the city's ammunition depot on 10 October – the "double ten" day that remains the national day of the Republic of China, although it is celebrated only in Taiwan; the People's Republic adopted as its national day the anniversary of the party's 1949 seizure of power in Beijing, 1 October. Soon the mutiny spread to the adjacent Shaanxi and Hunan provinces, and the Qing court attempted to retreat to a form of constitutional monarchy. But Sun – who returned by boat from France, landing at Shanghai on Christmas Day 1911 – insisted on a republican structure, and was himself chosen as president by delegates from provincial assemblies meeting in Nanjing, where he assumed office in January 1912. On 12 February the child emperor Puyi abdicated, ending the authoritarianism – with a gloss of divinity – that had guided China for more than two millennia.

Sun stepped down the following day, acknowledging his military weakness in comparison with the forces loyal to Yuan Shikai, a modernising Qing general who then assumed the presidency and later attempted to have himself enthroned as emperor. In December 1912 China held its first election, for which Sun's party changed its name to the Kuomintang. Men over twenty-one who met certain property and educational qualifications were given the vote. About 40 million, a tenth of the total Chinese population, formed this electorate. The KMT dominated the results, winning 269 of the 596 House of Representatives seats and 123 of the 274 Senate seats. Song Jiaoren, aged thirty, who led the KMT campaign and was set to become the premier, was assassinated at a Shanghai railway station as he prepared to travel to Beijing for the first parliamentary sitting.

Yuan Shikai, widely blamed for the assassination, seized power and in late November Sun was again driven from China, travelling to Japan. But Yuan himself died soon after, in 1916, of illness. It was during the ensuing years of chaos and disappointment that Mao Zedong, born in 1893 in rural Hunan to a modestly well-to-do family, published his first essay, in the influential publication *New Youth*, in 1917 – intriguingly, it urged people to balance their mental efforts with physical education, which "not only harmonises the emotions, it also strengthens the will." The Bolshevik revolution that year reinforced the determination of young Chinese radicals like Mao to pursue more relentlessly the changes set tentatively in place by Sun, who remains universally viewed as the founder of modern China. Chen Duxiu, dean of Beijing University and editor of *New Youth*, ran an issue devoted to Marxism on 1 May 1919. Chen went on to become the Chinese Communist Party's first leader, appointed at that inaugural secret meeting in Shanghai.

Eventually, after they had fought the invading Japanese to a stand-still, the KMT was defeated militarily by the communists, who had assumed the Republican mantle first worn, along with his prototype of what Westerners now call the Mao suit, by Sun Yat-sen. The communists were to develop a narrative that made sense to the Chinese, especially to farmers, of their apparently purposeless suffering that for many began during the Taiping Rebellion (1850–64). That uprising, led by Hong Xiuquan, who claimed to be the younger brother of Jesus Christ, had claimed 20 million lives.

This narrative was one of dispossession by the landlord class, a category that had not previously been especially visible in China. But it enabled Mao, the emerging party leader, to blame village leaders – identifiable enemies, now branded "landlords" – for the woes of the rural population, and thus in effect to seize sovereignty in the countryside. At the local level, sovereignty was handed back to those with grievances, differentiated from the landlords with the label "peasants." Later, once the party was in control of China after 1949, they would take back that sovereignty and force those peasants into the great failed experiment of collective farms.

In the decades to 1937, when Japan invaded, about 10 per cent of China's gross domestic product was traded, accelerated by the vibrancy of the foreign-administered treaty ports. Technological transfers were boosted by the openness of Chinese society. Agricultural production grew twice as fast as the population in central and coastal China from 1890 to 1930. Chinese students outnumbered all other foreigners at US universities by 1930. Bilingual Chinese judges sat at the International Court of Justice in The Hague. In 1948, Chinese delegate Zhang Pengjun helped draft the Universal Declaration on Human Rights. Frank Dikötter, in *The Age of Openness: China Before Mao*, writes, "Religious expression was also allowed to thrive in a climate of relative tolerance, while culture bloomed in the absence of a monopoly on power and knowledge ... The era between empire and communism is routinely portrayed as a catastrophic interlude [but] the extent and depth of engagement with the rest of the world was such that we can see closure under Mao instead as the exception."

But what an exception. Mao's image still looms large. A gala celebrity concert was held in 2006 in the Great Hall of the People to mark the thirtieth anniversary of his death at age eighty-three. His face stared implacably at the concertgoers from his vast portrait on the Tiananmen Gate to their right, as they approached the stairs to the Great Hall, while to their left lay his mausoleum. The few guests without chauffeur-driven cars paid for their taxis with banknotes, each featuring a picture of Mao. The concert – some tickets to which cost more than US$200 – included 500 performers and began with a song that almost everyone in the audience joined to sing: *The sun is the reddest, Chairman Mao is the kindest.* Eleven poems by Mao were recited. The event closed with the song most associated with the Cultural Revolution, "The East Is Red," which includes the lines, *Chairman Mao loves the people, he is our guide* and *The Communist Party is like the sun, wherever it shines there is light, wherever there is a Communist Party, there the people are free!*

Although the party has since rejected Mao's disastrous economic strategy, its present leaders are convinced that his charisma remains a crucial source of the party's legitimacy. A leading party historian, Xia Chuntao, says, "In the early 1980s, the party issued an authoritative document that assessed Mao, with a very scientific definition of his achievements and his flaws. History since then has proven that this evaluation can stand by itself. No matter how many years pass, I don't think this will change." The party formally concluded that Mao was 70 per cent right and 30 per cent wrong.

What about Mao's role in society at large? For some, his image is now a familiar face, not even in its true sense an icon, although some taxi drivers keep a portrait on their dashboards for good luck, as some Catholics use medals of St Christopher. At Dashanzi, the trendy arts precinct in north-eastern Beijing, any number of contemporary artists make fun and money at Mao's expense, shoving flowers into his mouth, removing his head and creating statues of his full-to-bursting suit, feeding the market for Mao kitsch.

Most young Chinese know little and care less about what he thought or said. For the most part they shrug at – and shrug off – the past, which remains a dangerous place to visit. China's attitude to its history is perhaps complicated by the lack of tenses in its verbs. The present is the default mode.

Yet it's impossible to make sense of extraordinary, fast-changing China today without some appreciation of Mao. Sheila Melvin, a commentator on China's business climate – she spent seven years at the US China Business Council – has written *The Little Red Book of China Business*. She says, "Mao understood China and its people in a way that few others have. He was not an aberration of modern Chinese history, but a product of it."

Perhaps for this reason there is virtually no mention of the Cultural Revolution in China. The leaders maintain a strict silence on the topic, while tens of thousands of "net police" constantly patrol the web and block any mention of this ten-year black hole in China's economic, cultural and political life. Baidu, China's most popular search engine, warns those who seek Cultural Revolution sites: "Your search word could violate laws."

It is not surprising that the party should be so edgy about such a potentially painful discussion. President Hu Jintao, at a 2005 summit with Japan's then prime minister Junichiro Koizumi – who was strongly criticised for visiting the Yasukuni shrine, which honours war criminals among other war dead – urged Japan to "take history as a mirror and look to the future." But at home, says Professor Wang Dong-cheng of the China Youth University in Beijing, "The party is still trying to force people to forget about history. They are worried that any rethinking would amount to a denial of their legitimacy. The resulting task of Chinese intellectuals is a tough one. It is to refuse to forget. Or else we can't step towards democracy."

The party-state remains similarly anxious about the events of 1989, and allows no public reference to what happened. Xia Chuntao, who insists there is "only one correct and accurate interpretation" of historical events, says that the 1989 protesters were "anti-revolutionary rioters," and there the matter rests.

The anxiety also extends to more distant history. The party worries that allowing historians to publish new research or analysis of events – even long-ago events – about which the party has already pronounced a clear moral verdict might seem to place the party's legitimacy at risk. When China's chief censors gathered at the State Administration of Radio, Film and Television in 2007 to discuss the government's propaganda concerns, top of the agenda was getting history right. The censors were urged to "watch the erroneous trend of denying the historic achievements of the party and comrade Mao Zedong." It was crucial, according to a record of the conference proceedings released later, "to create the correct atmosphere for the 17th Communist Party congress [held in October 2007], to promote the main melody." Publishers were severely criticised for letting writers "run the red light" and for getting too close to taboo topics.

The most famous example in recent years was the sacking in 2006 of Li Datong, the editor of *Bing Dian* (*Freezing Point*), a leading intellectual journal, because it had published an article taking a new line on the Boxer Rebellion (1898–1900). This was a sign that the gloves had come off, that the party had decided that although it might have loosened some economic controls, it was going to tighten its grip on the country's cultural life, and especially on the telling of its history.

The article in question was written by Yuan Weishi, a courtly 75-year-old professor at Zhong Shan (Sun Yat-sen) University in Guangzhou and himself a party member. It was not about the events in Tiananmen Square in 1989, but about the more remote and bloody Boxer Rebellion. He says, "The Communist Party's propaganda department views the rebellion as a revolutionary action, but I think it was not. They think it was a contribution to social evolution; I think it was a crime. And the same goes for the Taiping Rebellion, too." Talking quietly in a trendy coffee shop next to the university campus in central Guangzhou, he turns off his tiny new mobile phone. There are "many trigger points that make the propaganda people upset," he says. "The official evaluation of Mao as 70 per cent right and 30 per cent wrong makes it very hard for historians" to rethink not only Mao himself, but also other emblematic figures and events in China's modern history. "This is too simplified a formula to describe any historical figure, especially one like him who played such a big role."

Today, he says, many people do support the party, "because of China's opening up and reform, and the improved life of the people. But people are unhappy with it at the same time, because of its monopoly of power, and the lack of freedom. The defenders think this continued monopoly rule is gloriously bestowed by history. They keep promoting their view that history has chosen the Communist Party. So they must maintain a tight grasp on the interpretation of history." Yuan has challenged his party critics to debate him publicly, on TV. But "the conservatives believe themselves too authoritative to discuss with others."

Lei Yi, a professor at the contemporary history research centre of the Chinese Academy of Social Sciences, says the party has always paid great attention to the ideology underlying its hold on power, as a crucial element of its legitimacy. The party's two lynchpins during the revolutionary period were that it was anti-feudalist and anti-imperialist.

Since Deng, he says, "Little by little, articles and discussions have extended freedom" to reconsider the past. "But this is restricted to academic study, not to popular publications or to the media. Even now, there remains a big gap" between the thinking and discussion tolerated on campuses, and in the wider Chinese society. He says that academics at universities sometimes shock students, who exclaim that "this is so different from what we were taught at middle school. That leads to two reactions – that the textbooks are wrong, or the university lecturers are wrong." History textbooks are still more tightly controlled than those of other subjects. "There has been big progress even there," says Lei, but certain topics remain off-limits. "We can openly discuss economic theory in public today, but not history."

The party historian Xia Chuntao says, "It's very natural for historians to have different views on events," and that Chinese historians have the freedom to express those views. "But there is only one correct and accurate interpretation, and only one explanation that is closest to the truth." Because Professor Yuan's critique of the Boxers only represents himself or a few people, "there's not much value to have a big debate." Xia says, "China is a very open society, academics can express their opinion through various channels. But a responsible academic should have a scientific and sincere opinion." Issues that are "quite clearly defined" are not in need of debate.

The government is taking "a very open attitude to academic disputes," Xia says. "But there's no country where academics can speak their minds without any limitations. They are citizens too, and must obey the law. And if they are a party member, they have to be restricted by party principles." Despite academic critiques such as Professor Yang's, "however much time passes, the party's general judgement" on such key events "won't change." This is especially the case with "contemporary history," the period since 1840. But that does not mean the party denies the "dark or weak points" in Chinese history. "We are talking here of a Marxist explanation of history. There have been a few academics who tried to interpret history from a very different perspective, but their conclusions are not convincing. We think history is our treasure, and history stresses the need for domestic stability. Because of our stability, this has become the golden era for China out of the last 150 years. Academics must have a strong sense of responsibility and of the need for such stability – and not provide absurd opinions that disturb people's minds."

Xia has been heavily involved in assessing TV costume dramas in China. Emperors can be divided into two clear categories, he says. Good emperors worked to unify China, and even if their reigns were bloody, they were justified. Bad emperors tolerated or failed to prevent division. This is why "the first emperor," Qin Shi Huangdi – credited with unifying warring kingdoms, starting to build the Great Wall, and imposing a single form of written Chinese – has become a hero in recent years. In previous eras he was for the most part vilified as a cruel tyrant, who for instance buried alive hundreds of Confucian scholars who had the impudence to disagree with him. His dynasty was swept away almost as soon as he was buried with his warriors, such was the antipathy he generated.

One of China's leading dissident intellectuals, Yu Jie, born in 1973, disagrees fundamentally with Xia about China's past and thus also its present. He has been a hugely popular author – his sixteen books each selling more than 100,000 and the first, *Fire and Ice*, almost 1 million – and has a master's degree in contemporary Chinese literary and philosophical history. But he became so outspoken, and won so much public attention, that he could not obtain a full-time job or publish his work within China. After increased harassment by the authorities, including house arrest and police interrogations, he finally left in 2012, moving to the USA.

Shortly before he left China, he met with me in a coffee shop near his flat in a new estate on the edge of Beijing. He told me that he was unequivocal about Mao, uninterested in whether he was 25 per cent or 35 per cent good or bad. "He was the worst tyrant in China's history. In world history, actually. Worse than Hitler or Stalin. Under his rule, millions of Chinese people died, far more than in the anti-Japanese war. The pity is, the interpretation of history is in the hands of the Communist Party, and ordinary people don't know about him."

Because "there is no real religion in China," he said, "one of the functions of history is to construct a religion, and official historians play the role of bishops in the West." Mao, he said, described the party's rule as based "on the gun and the pen – thus on force and a lie. And one of the important foundations of the empire of lies in China is the distortion of history, interpreted by Marxist thinking." The party was born from armed peasants. "So it needs to praise peasants' uprisings so it can dominate history. If the truth of historical events were revealed to the Chinese people, it might trigger a domino effect."

There was greater freedom in China in the 1920s, he said. "There was a lot of independent publishing, and private universities, and if people were censored they could escape to the treaty ports – which together with the missionaries, sped up the modernisation of China." Yu said an important turning point in the propaganda war came after 1989. "The focus shifted to patriotism. So if the truth of the war against Japan was revealed, this would undermine the party. There are also very few accounts of the extent of American aid to China during the war."

He continued, "As long as the Communist Party rules and its propaganda department retains its power, open debate will not be possible in China. It will only emerge if China comes into the democratic age and intellectuals get their independence." While he sees many academics being broken by the system, "they are not being sent to labour camps" any more. But this does not indicate a greater tolerance. "In recent years academic freedom has grown more restricted, and the situation has worsened. But people are not totally isolated, as long as their articles can be published in Hong Kong or Taiwan."

It took almost 100 years after Puyi was dethroned for China to regain a convincing sense of equilibrium as a nation, under a ruling party that is now relishing the country's newfound prosperity, and is demonstrating little interest in sharing power – including the power to write the country's history – for another century or more.

CHAPTER 8:
CONFUCIUS'S COMEBACK

N THE CENTRE OF THE TOWERING SOUTHERN WALL OF
Zhongnanhai, the large compound in the heart of Beijing which
doubles as the headquarters of the State Council and of the Chinese
Communist Party, stands the main gate, formerly called the Pre-
cious Moon Tower but now known more prosaically as Xinhuamen
– New China Gate. On one side is inscribed the slogan "Long live the
great Communist Party of China," on the other, "Long live invincible
Mao Zedong Thought."

Visitors enter, however, by a less dramatic gate to the north-west. Hopeful spectators seeking a glimpse of top leaders through the New China
Gate are doomed to disappointment, for their view of Zhongnanhai is
blocked by a traditional "spirit wall." On the wall, in massive characters in
the style of Mao's handwriting, is written, "Serve the People."

This simple and appealing slogan is found on entrances to party and
government buildings throughout the country. But its very location, on
a screen which prevents people from catching even a glimpse of the
secretive centre of power, hints at how problematic it is as a motto for the
party-state.

If not service – or not only service – what does the party believe in, in
the twenty-first century? And what do the people of China believe in?

Nearly all believe in their country's golden future. That is a positive
start. But they disagree to a surprising degree – given the close attention
paid by the party to fostering unity and obedience – about how to achieve
it. They believe in the family, in their teachers and professors, in owning

110

property, in Christianity, in Buddhism, in Confucius, in Mao, in good health, in good luck, in travel. And they can pursue all of these beliefs, in moderation – and as long as they do so along the signposted routes.

Traditional values and religious faiths were opposed during the Mao years as "counter-revolutionary." Confucius was vilified as the ideologue of imperial China. But the casual cruelties and destruction of the Mao years – the "Great Leap Forward" that killed 30 million people, about 5 per cent of the population, the repeated "anti-rightist" crusades, the Cultural Revolution – then drained most of the ideological commitment to communism that had previously motivated millions. What beliefs and values have taken their place?

In the twenty-first century, the party has embarked on a mission to rediscover meaning. But this journey has not yet taken it far. It has moved away from its roots, at least in terms of economic organisation, yet sometimes appears to regret doing so. In this chapter, we shall meet a number of Chinese people who are also engaged in this search for meaning. Some believe the party has the answers, while others think the party has failed to supply a credible, central narrative for China.

For most people in China, even for rank and file party members, politics is of scant interest, since for so long they have had little or no capacity to know what is really happening in the political realm, let alone to influence it. Since 1976, personal freedoms have steadily expanded and improved economic conditions have enabled people to exercise them. Materialism became for a time the new morality, the new source of inspiration. But after three tumultuous and largely successful decades, even that has begun to pall. For all their accumulation of material assets, many people – especially the younger generation – are increasingly expressing a sense of longing or insufficiency.

In 2007 Wang Wei, a marketing manager then aged twenty-seven, was among 8000 worshippers, most of them young people, attending packed masses at the Cathedral of the Immaculate Conception of the Blessed Virgin Mary in southern Beijing during Easter week. He was not a Christian, and his parents had no faith, but he explained that he was tired of the circular conversations of many of his friends: "Discussing the attractions of rival mobile phones, it just started to bore me." He had begun to believe that "there is a power above nature, but

I don't know exactly what it is. I started coming a year ago, because I'm interested in what happens here, in the music and the atmosphere and the sincerity."

Francis Xavier Zhang, the 38-year-old parish priest – he speaks fluent English and studied for four years in Europe – said that the church was thriving, with two thirds of the congregation under forty. "There's a vacuum in China today," he said. "It's too materialistic. Young people are saying there's no purpose in their lives, what they've bought has let them down. They are pursuing the real truth and seeking human values in the movies, in culture. They're reaching for real happiness."

As people are moving out of poverty and grasping for more in life than mere survival, religion has made a big comeback in China. There are five formally permitted religions: Buddhism, Taoism, Islam, Christianity and Catholicism. The latter two are peculiarly Chinese categories. "Christianity" means Protestantism, established as the "Three-Self Church," those three being: self-support, self-governance and self-propagation, principles first espoused by missionaries in the nineteenth century. The church's ethos is mainstream Protestant. The Chinese Catholic Church is not part of the Roman Catholic Church, but has increasingly close links with it; foreign Roman Catholic academics, including clergy, teach for instance at some of its seminaries.

In the nineteenth and early twentieth centuries, Christian missionaries helped to accelerate China's modernisation, including the education of girls, the introduction of science in schools and the foundation of hospitals with up-to-date equipment. There were criticisms; some churches were said to lure people to become followers in exchange for food – the so-called "rice Christians." But this all ceased with the creation of the People's Republic in 1949. The party was, and remains, devoutly atheist.

Now, however, it is tolerated; the party apparently feels that it is better to permit and control religious behaviour than to let it flourish dangerously underground. Bibles are readily available in Chinese. The Bible Society operates a massive printing press inside China, perfectly legally. But evangelism – by any religion, including Christianity – is frowned on, and most people in China grow up today without even the basic awareness of Buddhism or Taoism that remains commonplace in the Chinese diaspora, let alone any knowledge of Christianity. Christmas, however, has become popular, and canned carols can be heard in every shopping mall come December. Churches, most of them similar in size and set-up to old-fashioned Western cinemas, are often full, usually hosting several services each Sunday. The government effectively pays the wages of the clergy in these churches and contributes substantially to their training. This does not mean that those clergy lack sincerity, but they cannot criticise – or appear to criticise – the party-state consistently or forcefully. There are also "house churches," which have no formal connections with the established churches and are technically illegal but tolerated in some provinces.

The religious situation varies massively around the country. Some local officials are relaxed and may even be surreptitious believers. Others are hardline opponents. Yet more are simply pragmatists. A local party chief in Shaanxi province, disturbed by an increase in gambling, called in the town's Three-Self and Catholic clergy and asked them to help in return for a little more leeway from local officialdom for Christianity. They preached fiery sermons – also, inevitably, long ones, considered "good value" in China – and the gambling tide turned.

But some officials remain fierce in their secularism. In 2007, a ban was announced on the public performance of religious music. Handel's *Messiah*, which had for several years been performed at Christmas in Beijing, was cancelled. A prominent Italian orchestra, visiting China, was told there was nothing wrong with Bach's *St Matthew Passion*; the music was fine – they just needed to change the words to excise references to Jesus and God, and it would receive the censor's tick. In general the party retains a suspicion of religion, for religious faith raises questions about where the adherent's loyalties truly lie.

Confucianism, the prototypically Chinese philosophy, is safer; it fits more comfortably with Beijing's 21st-century focus on quality of life, on balanced development and social cohesion. In early 2011 there was much excitement about the sudden appearance of a 9.5-metre high statue of Confucius, clasping his hands together in front of him and wearing traditional robes, outside the newly rebuilt National History Museum. The museum stands at the north-east corner of Tiananmen Square, so that Confucius's bronze face stared almost directly at the vast portrait of Mao on the gate of the Forbidden City. The sculptor, Wu Weishan, who has made more than 200 statues of the philosopher, told the AP news agency that "the rise of a big country requires a cultural foundation, and Chinese culture upholds the spirit of harmony" – handily echoing the catchword of the Hu Jintao era. Wu said, "The essential thoughts of Confucius are love, kindness, wisdom and generosity. And peace and prosperity are what the people are striving for."

As Wu was completing his statue, the state was financing a biopic simply titled *Confucius*, starring the ebullient Hong Kong actor Chow Yun-fat. Globally, China's "soft power" thrust is helped along by hundreds of Beijing-funded Confucius Institutes. Confucius's sayings are now providing the philosophical platform for the confident nation to project its influence throughout the world.

Four months after it was placed on its plinth on the northern side of the museum, however, as Beijing entered spring, the statue disappeared as suddenly as it had appeared, like snow that melts overnight. It had been moved to a courtyard inside, where it is not visible to passers-by. It was widely speculated that the intense debate set off by its arrival had been a step too far for many in the old guard. Confucius might be back, but he was still on probation.

His return wasn't welcomed in all quarters, and not only among the residual Maoists. The restoration of Confucius reinforces to the nation's minority ethnic groups, especially the Uighurs, Tibetans and Mongolians, their distance from the Han Chinese mainstream; it reminds them that the new nationalism is essentially a Han nationalism. His return played out better in the rest of East Asia, in Japan, Korea and Singapore, for instance, where Confucian culture has never been banished as it was from Mao's China.

In Qufu, however, which is proudly Han – all the more so for being on the frontier – there are no signs of such querulousness. There, Confucius is the conquering hero. China Central TV now regularly broadcasts live from Qufu to the whole country the colourful ritual – invented in the twenty-first century – to celebrate his birthday, which is also handily used to celebrate the whole of Shandong province and its economic boom. About 1500 students in orange uniform flank a procession of leading officials from the national, provincial and city governments, and large numbers of residents dress as they might have 2500 years ago, with horse-drawn carts, ancient musical instruments and silk banners. The culmination is the burning of armfuls of incense at an altar in front of a vast statue of the philosopher in the final hall of the Confucius Temple.

This great show of national respect is no mere stunt. The fourth generation of communist leaders, under President Hu, who grew up in a Confucian household, made the Confucian concept of harmony its touchstone. This marked a major contrast with the class warfare launched by Mao. The fifth generation, led by Xi Jinping, is following Hu's path. And the readiness of the *laobaixing*, the ordinary Chinese, to embrace at least a pop version of Confucianism was revealed by the extraordinary response to a series of televised lectures, starting in 2006, by Professor Yu Dan of Beijing Normal University. Talking directly to camera, she re-presented Confucius for modern China and built a national audience of scores of millions, to whom she has already sold 4 million books, becoming en route a celebrity throughout the Chinese-speaking world.

Professor Kang Xiaogang of People's University, one of the leading proponents of the new Confucianism, says a new survey in nine cities shows that Confucius has more impact on people's minds than Marxism, liberalism or Taoism, China's traditional religion. He says, "In the past, China belonged to one [imperial] family. Today it belongs to one party. But it also needs an ideology. Leninism provided such a system in the past. Now is the hour for Confucianism, which should be adopted not only as a theory but as a national religion," with its temples of learning becoming community centres. (Although some "new Confucianists" might see their cause as akin to a religion, the evidence shows that Confucius himself was not a believer, although he valued religion's structures and rituals.)

Since the days of Deng, says Kang, "the Communist Party has been replacing public with private ownership, and the planned economy with the free market. When a party's conduct and theory are at odds in such a way, it shows the theory no longer works. Confucianism is not contrary to this free-market economy which China needs, nor to a peaceful world. It is flourishing again after thousands of years. It has more vigor than Marxism and Leninism. We're not advocating a return to ancient times, but pursuing the Confucius spirit and principles for modern society." He says that today's leaders have grown up in a very different era from Mao's, one in which "Chinese people are more confident in their own culture and tradition. Since the economy is going well, people think, the political system can't be bad either."

Kang believes that the official embrace of Confucianism will be gradual, because the party's legitimacy remains to a degree tied up with its own (secularist) history as well as on today's economic success. "The party is doing something about it, but not talking about it. They are pushing the renaissance of Confucianism quietly," still testing the public response.

Kong Xianglin, a 75th-generation descendant of Confucius, is another quiet promoter of Confucianism. He is vice president of the magnificent Confucius Research Institute in Qufu. The unique continuity of China's ancient culture can be attributed substantially to Confucius's influence, Kong says – and Confucianism is more relevant today than ever. China may have bounced back economically, but "getting rich is not an adequate goal in itself. We also need courtesy, knowledge and culture. And Confucius believed a country should be governed with kindness – with low taxes, high education, and less punishment." If Confucius were alive today, he believes, he would focus on morality, "because its level has lowered in China in recent years." When pressed by a female Chinese journalist about the common perception that his ancestor promoted patriarchy, Kong responds, "I think Confucius would support the equality of women." The patriarchal interpretation relied on a single saying whose context has been lost, he says, and the great Kong family tree, which shows 4 million descendants, is now being redrawn to include women. It was only 900 years after Confucius, in the first Song Dynasty, that male domination became entrenched in China, he claims.

Confucius was a scholar named Kong, whose disciples called him *Fuzi*, or master. Hence *Kong Fuzi*: Confucius. His "analects" were recorded and collected, in a modest 12,000 characters, by his disciples and their disciples about seventy-five years after his death. He was born in 551 BC and died in 479, a period during which China comprised many countries with a largely common culture, much like modern Europe. He was born to a semi-aristocratic family that had fallen on hard times, and his father died when he was three. He travelled widely, attempting to find a local ruler who would allow him and his followers to govern a region according to his precepts. He believed that when others saw his successful model, his ideas would be widely adopted. But it was not to be. He never gained the official roles he sought. No one knows precisely where Confucius is buried, although a tomb was built in his name in Kong Lin cemetery, a 200-hectare wooded area just beyond the walls of Qufu. Members of the Kong family have been buried there since their famous ancestor died, eighty-three generations ago.

As China fell apart at the start of the twentieth century, many progressive Chinese thinkers turned their backs on Confucius, blaming his "feudal" thought in part for their nation's ignominy. But Confucian scholars today insist that this was a misreading of the ancient philosopher. In his introduction to *The Analects of Confucius*, Pierre Ryckmans, Australia's leading Sinologist, writing as Simon Leys, refers scathingly to Singapore's founding father Lee Kuan Yew's efforts to propagate "the magic recipe [supposedly found in Confucius] for marrying authoritarian politics with capitalist prosperity." But Ryckmans writes that "imperial Confucianism only extolled those statements from the master that prescribed submission to the established authorities, whereas more essential notions were conveniently ignored – such as the precepts of social justice, political dissent, and the moral duty of citizens to criticise the ruler (even at the risk of their lives) when he was abusing his power, or when he oppressed the people."

This broader understanding of the philosopher's legacy has wide appeal in China, far beyond the elite. Duan Yanping, a 39-year-old electrical engineer from Qufu, has founded a non-government organisation to promote Confucianism. When he was growing up, "Confucius was still taboo and despised. But I was enthralled by the stories my parents and neighbours told me about his life." His group now has several hundred members. They wear Confucius badges and meet twice a year for weekend conferences, at which they plan ways to promote Confucianism and conduct a ritual of their own invention in the sage's honour: they don ancient dress, burn incense and kowtow ten times. Duan concedes that some of his colleagues are puzzled by his enthusiasm, but he points out to them that Confucius advocated innovation and did not criticise businesspeople *per se* – only those who "used tricks and deceptions."

It had long seemed that Confucius was irredeemable. He was especially reviled by Mao, who sought a clean slate for his own communist dynasty and admired the totalitarianism of Confucius's ancient nemesis, Shi Huangdi, the "first emperor" whose grave near Xi'an was defended by the terracotta warriors. Mao boasted, "Shi Huangdi buried 460 scholars alive; we have buried 46,000 scholars alive. You [intellectuals] revile us for being Shi Huangdis. You are wrong. We have surpassed him a hundredfold." Calling for the "smashing of the four olds" – Old Customs, Old Culture, Old Habits and Old Ideas – Mao initiated an anti-Confucian blitzkrieg. A detachment of Red Guards from Beijing's Normal University, led by the fiery Tan Houlan, was deployed to smash Kong Lin in 1966. Tan supervised an assault on the Confucius Temple – the second largest historical building complex in China, after the Forbidden City – and the destruction and desecration of tombs with a manic zeal that still causes a shudder when described by people who live in Qufu. The Red Guards hauled out the body of the most senior of the seventy-sixth generation of Kongs, hanged it, hacked it and burned it. His son, Kong Decheng, became the most venerable Confucian of the early twenty-first century; until his death in 2008, he refused countless appeals from Chinese leaders to return from Taiwan to participate in the rehabilitation and glorification of his ancestor.

Even after the destruction of the Kong family's cemetery, however, an uneasy sense lurked at the back of revolutionary minds that the great man was not out for the count. An official broadcast from Beijing in 1974, towards the end of the Cultural Revolution, said, "Although Confucius is dead, his corpse continues to emit its stench even today. Its poison is deep and its influence extensive." Prophetic words. For Confucius is now back, big time. At the opening of the Beijing Olympics, People's Liberation Army soldiers dressed as ancient warriors chanted one famous Confucian saying after another. Others were flashed onto vast, high-tech discs mounted high around the Bird's Nest Stadium.

Despite his resurrection, it is doubtful whether the philosopher would have enjoyed the tenor of the Games. He wrote, "A gentleman avoids competition. Still, if he must compete, let it be at archery. There, as he bows and exchanges civilities both before the contest and over drinks afterwards, he remains a gentleman." China's Olympic shooting team had as its motto, by contrast, "Die in the fight for gold. There's no point in merely participating." Shooter Zhu Qinan wept at the podium when he was being awarded a silver medal, knowing that he would be judged a loser by his teammates and his nation, who were hungry only for absolute success. Nevertheless, the Games marked the first official statement by the country's top leaders that, after a century in the communist wilderness, China's greatest philosopher was to be restored to the nation's heart. They needed him.

There is a Chinese saying – not one of Confucius's – that "culture provides a platform for business." This is an idea that the town of Qufu itself, with its old walled city and its famous ancient citizen, is certainly embracing. Five million tourists visit Qufu every year. Confucius trinkets are on sale everywhere. Above the tollbooths of the six-lane highway leading into the city, a huge banner welcomes visitors to "The holy cultural city." Popular among parents of young children are imitation jade tokens with the child's birth sign on one side and a blessing from Confucius on the other. Some tourists complain that the souvenir portraits of the sage do not make him handsome enough.

Yue Shihe, a 41-year-old taxi driver from Xinyang in Henan province, was among the tourists at the Confucius Temple during birthday celebrations for the philosopher in 2007. His family originally came from Qufu and returned for a reunion specially timed to coincide with the event. He was keen for his ten-year-old son to learn about Confucius, "because he's the number one master of education in China." Meanwhile Liu Fang, nineteen, studying English at Qufu Number 1 University, didn't learn much about the sage at school but said she was catching up quickly; she would be singing Confucian sayings along with hundreds of fellow students during the celebration.

Hou Duan Min, the vice mayor of Jining City, which encompasses Qufu, says, "We know China is a communist country, but all our beliefs are also based on China's traditional culture ... We are now rethinking our lives, and our role in the world. We can't be a world power through our economy alone. We have to be culturally strong too." This argument makes sense. For as China's economic, military and diplomatic power grows, it is starting to attract the sort of vilification the USA has experienced for being so strong. Meanwhile at home, where the party-state claims credit for everything that succeeds, it also cops the blame for anything that goes awry. Since Deng, rapid modernisation has become a crucial source of the party's legitimacy. But what if China's magnificent new economic machine winds down? And what to do about the growing gap between rich and poor, now more severe than in the USA? A sullen, if now no longer starving, underclass of hundreds of millions represents a real threat. Then there are the other challenges that come with economic success, including terrible pollution and the epidemics of affluence, such as heart disease and various cancers.

These are tests that would challenge any ruler. The party is well aware that overseeing a spurt in national development is no guarantee of permanent popularity. Suharto in Indonesia, the military presidents of South Korea and the Kuomintang in Taiwan all demonstrate this. A Confucian touch might soften the party's image and deepen its appeal. Hence the move to broaden the ruling ethos from Deng's "to get rich is glorious" to Hu's "harmonious society," which echoes Confucian humanism and which urges the elite to accept a sense of *noblesse oblige*. "Authority without generosity I cannot bear to contemplate," said Confucius – and "When you have faults, do not fear to abandon them."

A search for moral meaning, of course, need not always entail a return to religion. It was widely assumed internationally, especially in the lead-up to the Beijing Olympics, that China was starting to embrace what are widely viewed, especially in Western countries, as "universal values," including a growing list of human rights. But this has been explicitly challenged by public intellectuals in China, who have portrayed "universal values" as a Trojan Horse for Western control, as pernicious as the opium that was pressed on China by Britain and other countries in the nineteenth century.

In the opening chapter of this book we met Wang Xiaodong, the charismatic commentator based at the China Youth and Juvenile Research Centre and a champion of China's new nationalism. Wang believes above all in China. His China is not everyone's, but it has become a popular brand. He says that after the Great Leap Forward and the Cultural Revolution, "the Chinese, especially the intellectuals, lost their belief in their own country and culture, and developed a kind of reverse racism" against their own heritage. "Westerners were angels, we were demons."

The younger generation is different, he says. "They are seeing China's economic development, the increase in living standards. They have more contact with the West; they understand it better. They know Westerners are not really angels, they realise that they are different from us not only in ideology but in national interests." They are told by the West that media should be objective – but then discover that Western media are biased against China, "so they get angry; they're not happy. We can't bear the prejudice and hatred from the West."

Wang believes this resurgent Chinese nationalism will have "a pro-found and long-lasting significance, like the May 4 movement in 1919," when students gathered at Beijing University to draft a manifesto against foreign incursions. He says, "Some Westerners are saying that Chinese must make an effort to make themselves accepted by the West. That is an outdated opinion. The West must learn how to make itself accepted by the Chinese." The new generation, he says, rejects Mao's socialism but embraces his nationalism, while also tentatively re-adopting some traditional Chinese values.

In 2010 Wan Songsheng, a researcher in the Cultural Research Institute of the China Art Academy, caused a convulsive shock in intellectual circles with his book *China Stands Up*, written under the pen name Moluo. This book marked a turning point for the "new left" in China, an amorphous movement that sought a better deal for those left behind by the country's economic growth spurt. They had at first identified themselves with the great writer Lu Xun (1881–1936) and other members of the "New Culture Movement" of a century earlier and had spoken up for dissident writers such as Yu Jie, who was eventually exiled in 2011.

Moluo had been an exponent of these seemingly liberal politics. But in *China Stands Up* he focused on the "excoriation of the New Culture and May Fourth movements," rejecting "Lu Xun's forensic examinations of Chinese national character," writes David Kelly, a visiting professor at Beijing University. In doing so, Muluo revealed the extent to which many Chinese intellectuals are now "sailing with the nationalist tide."

Belief in universal values has faded, the historian Xu Jilin says. In its place has emerged a new nationalism, celebrating "'Chinese values,' the 'China model,' 'Chinese subjectivity' and other narratives of nationalist authenticity … The artillery fire of their critique of the West is aimed, not at the Machiavellianism of becoming rich and powerful – which they in fact regard with awe – but at the Enlightenment values of freedom and democracy."

Of course, says Kelly, "contemporary China has already become a hybrid of foreign and local cultures. In order to obtain a national community free of Western pollution, some extreme nationalists deliberately enlarge the binary opposition between China and the West, seeking to … extract a pure, clear China." Thus after *China Is Unhappy* became a best-seller, a series of popular books emerged, one after another, "forming a spectacular 'China chorus'": *China Has No Role Models, What Is China to*

Do, China Stands Up. These authors often argue that the state is central, and that the core objective of modernity is to enhance its prosperity and capacity. As representative of the people's interests, the state has the highest sovereignty: supreme, indivisible and non-transferable. This ideology may revisit, Kelly warned, "the disastrous tracks of twentieth-century German and Japanese statism – otherwise known as fascism." Other statist thinkers draw on Confucianism. Whichever form it takes, statism essentially reduces democracy to providing "responsible authoritarianism" with legitimacy.

Beyond nationalism and statism lies celestialism, a belief that the divine favours certain dynasties. A much-studied figure on Chinese university campuses today is Carl Schmitt, Adolf Hitler's "crown jurist," a famous critic of liberalism, parliamentary democracy and liberal cosmopolitanism. Richard Komaiko, writing in the *Asia Times*, says, "According to several Beijing college students, the word 'Hitler' does not evoke images of anti-Semitism or genocide, but rather, strong leadership and nationalism. They say that they admire Hitler for his ability to unify his country and restore it to a position of respect in the international arena." In 2008 Song Hongbing's book *The Currency War*, which relayed conspiracies about how the Jews were manipulating world events, became a bestseller after the global financial crisis set in. And in 2001 a bizarre rumour spread around China that Hitler was raised by a family of Chinese expatriates living in Vienna, the Zhangs. In one survey conducted on Kaixin (the Chinese equivalent of Facebook), this was believed by 38.8 per cent of respondents.

Mark Lilla, a professor of the humanities at Columbia University, wrote in *New Republic* magazine in December 2010, after a lengthy visit to China, "Leo Strauss [a political philosopher who questioned whether freedom and excellence can co-exist] and Schmitt are at the centre of intellectual debate, they are being read by everyone, whatever their partisan leanings; as a liberal journalist in Shanghai told me as we took a stroll one day, 'no one will take you seriously if you have nothing to say about these two men and their ideas' ... Everyone I spoke with, across the political spectrum, agrees that China needs a stronger state, not a weaker one – a state that follows the rule of law, is less capricious, can control local corruption, and can perform and carry out long-term planning. When my turn to talk about American politics came, and I tried to explain the Tea Party movement's goal of 'getting government off our backs,' I was met with blank stares and ironic smiles."

The pragmatic, mostly non-ideological party leadership is unlikely to embrace the more fervent of the nationalist ideas swirling around Chinese campuses and online. Nevertheless, it may seek to harness aspects of the new nationalism. Xu Youyou, a researcher with the Chinese Academy of Social Science, says that the government "realises the problem of a lack of values in China," so is strengthening "selective aspects of traditional culture – but also, in doing so, over-emphasising the particularity of China." In 2009, three years before he became party leader, Xi Jinping impressed the new nationalists when he responded testily to international criticism of China: "There are a few foreigners, with full bellies, who have nothing better to do than try to point fingers at our county. China does not export revolution, hunger, poverty, nor does China cause you any headaches. Just what else do you want?"

On the other hand, in April 2012 a popular nationalist website, Utopia, was officially closed for a month. The following notice was posted on the site: "This morning, the Ninth Bureau of the State Council Information Office, the Beijing Municipal Network Management Office, and the Beijing Municipal PSB Network Security Corps told our website maintainers that the Utopia website had published articles that violated the constitution, maliciously attacked state leaders, and speculated wildly about the 18th Party Congress. Acting jointly, the three agencies requested that the website shut down for a self-inspection beginning from noon on 6 April 2012, to be brought back online after an examination was passed. Our maintainers asked for a list of articles that went against the constitution and said we would cooperate to deal with them. They did not have any specific articles or evidence. In the end, the conversation terminated."

The problem for the party in embracing any set of values, except for such vague notions as "harmony," is that this might identify it with a finite cause or program, and so imply limits to its authority. The party, although it in some respects has clearly defined aims, also in some ways resembles a semi-mystical body, taking decisions on people's behalf much like the mediaeval Catholic Church did, with no obligation to spell out its guiding philosophy or justify its priorities. But there has been no ideological equivalent of the Protestant Reformation in China. There is a secular equivalent of a "God-shaped blank" at the heart of China's political realm – which in indifferent or self-centred hands might manifest itself more as a heart of darkness, as it did during some of the Mao years.

"Communism is not love," insisted Mao. "Communism is a hammer which we use to crush the enemy."

Most people in China continue to enjoy better material lives, as they have since the 1980s. The party sees itself, in this sense, as still answering Mao's injunction to "serve the people." But the people's needs are evolving. After obtaining their first car, many are seeking something more beyond a second. The world of ideas is opening up, in part through access to the democratic universe of the internet. The party, while still cleverly adaptive in terms of day-to-day policy, seems frozen in terms of these big-picture driving forces, caught between nationalism and Confucianism and statism and celestialism and the rest – anxious lest it chooses too narrow a path, down which it will struggle to persuade the rest of China to follow. Or worse, that people will start marching off in different directions.

All power appears still to reside in Zhongnanhai. The party continues to control the world's largest nation – partly through wielding those hammers beloved of Mao, although usually more subtly, and partly by seeking to maintain its grip on the world of ideas. But this is becoming more difficult as the party itself appears, to many people, to have lost its own way in that world.

CHAPTER 9: DOING BUSINESS

EVERY CHILD'S DREAM AS SHE OR HE COUNTS DOWN THE sleeps to Christmas is to find the place where toys come from. It's easy enough to do.

First, fly to China's great southern centre of Guangzhou (formerly Canton), then take a brief commuter flight east. You arrive at a small airport, then drive through a landscape pleasantly warm but so polluted that sunlight rarely seems to penetrate. You pass ten-storey buildings, at the base of which are convenience stores, beauty parlours, mechanics' workshops. A massive poster urges people to *Learn English the Easy Way*. Another strongly suggests a diversion to Budweiser Amusement City. And another, proudly protectionist, shouts: *Source from China!*

You drive past a large training centre run by the cosmetics firm Amway. In the middle distance are hills pockmarked with quarries. Banana plantations tended by people in conical hats are bisected by a golf driving range.

This is Shantou, a pulsating manufacturing centre of 4 million people about 300 kilometres east of Hong Kong, on the coast in Guangdong province. It has been home to busy merchants for far longer than Hong Kong. The East India Company had a trading post on an island in the harbour 250 years ago. In 1860 it became a treaty port known as Swatow.

Today, it is well known for two reasons: as the birthplace of the wealthiest man in Asia, Li Ka-shing (known as "Superman" in Hong Kong, where he has lived since arriving there as a penniless thirteen-year-old in 1941), and as Toytown. Like the rest of China, Guangdong is of course changing quickly, and the provincial government is intent on guiding the province upmarket, towards a high-tech, service-based future, while factories shift inland to chase cheap labour.

In this chapter we shall look at what China has become best known for – its role as the world's factory, as the engine room of global economic growth – at the people who have made this happen, and at their plans to build a new economy based on domestic consumption rather than exports. We shall meet some of those who have been left behind. And we shall see how the party is enlisting the country's new entrepreneurs through the vast state-owned corporations that still dominate most strategic sectors of the economy. China's economic world is brimful of such apparent contradictions.

Yasheng Huang, professor of political economy and international management at Sloan School of Management, Massachusetts Institute of Technology, explains in his book *Capitalism with Chinese Characteristics* how the reforms of the 1980s advanced the private sector, especially in rural China. And how since then, economic changes have advanced the state sector in the cities. The wealth of Shanghai, Professor Huang points out, which so impresses visitors with its apparent dynamism and openness, comes chiefly from state-owned enterprises, foreign corporations and resources sourced from other parts of China.

China supplies about 70 per cent of the world's toys. Guangdong's toy exports account for about 75 per cent of all such exports and earn the province US$15 billion every year. Almost half of these toys are produced in Chenghai, a scruffy town of 700,000 permanent residents, plus many migrant workers, in the Shantou district. In other words, one toy in every four in the world is made here. But a dusty roadside billboard depicting Santa carrying a sack is the only clue a casual visitor gets.

On a Saturday afternoon, scores of young workers ride their small motorbikes past the cheap restaurants and mobile phone shops that line the road outside, and turn in to one of Toytown's biggest factories. None wears a helmet. They rush past the Buddhist shrine by the gate to clock in before 2 p.m. These are the clerks and middle managers, nearly all from local families. The factory workers, 80 per cent of whom are migrant workers, live in dormitories onsite, in a high-walled cluster of white buildings five storeys high. They have come to Chenghai from far-off provinces, seeking to make their fortunes – or simply to help their farming families survive.

Guangdong Xinning Technology Toy Factory employs up to 500 people, peaking in mid-year when, with the weather at its hottest and stickiest, the big Western markets require Christmas stocks to start flowing. The factory exports about 2000 containers a year. It is clean, well lit and well ventilated. Large signs admonish: *No smoking, no spitting, no food or drink.*

Santa is on everyone's minds here. They are stitching up Christmas stockings, decorating snowmen, assembling singing Father Christmases in rocking chairs. The workers, mostly young women, are focused on the job at hand but are able to have a laugh, too. Most sit in groups, working by hand. Some are operating machines. Chinese Canto-pop music, not "Winter Wonderland," is playing in the background. This is not an oppressive workplace. Workers are paid by the hour, not by the piece. The workers on the lowest rate take home almost double the legal minimum wage.

The factory director, Lin Jing-ru, says that although the cost of wages and of materials is rising by double digits annually, it is hard to raise prices to match: "the market is so competitive, and our clients wouldn't accept it." Ninety per cent of the factory's products – 6 or 7 million toys each year – go to the USA.

Guangdong Xinning has been in business since 1982. During its first decade it produced souvenirs for the domestic tourist market; only since 1991 has it been making toys for export. The firm was the first in the city to gain an export licence, in 1999. Before then, it had to sell through state-owned agents. Lin says the company welcomes inspections by its clients. Because the factory mainly makes soft toys without a high-tech content, "it's a mature market, and everyone knows the profit margins – which are not merely low, they're micro" – so there is "not much room for bargaining" on price. He believes that competition is so fierce, the number of factories in Toytown is likely to drop. "Most of them are smaller. They're really family workshops."

The showroom is a vast Aladdin's cave. There are toys and novelties and decorations ready for Easter, for Thanksgiving, for Valentine's Day, for China's National Day of 1 October, for the Spring Festival and Chinese New Year, but most of all, of course, for Christmas. The factory employs a design team to dream up new ideas and respond to customer suggestions. The designers visit trade shows and toy stores and look at websites to get a feel for what colours and shapes are attracting the market each season.

On the ground floor, workers are loading cardboard boxes onto a pallet. Addressed to Nantucket, USA, the boxes are pre-printed "Walmart: Trick or treat kids. Made in China."

Walmart, the world's biggest retailer, is the factory's biggest customer, although all business is done through a Hong Kong or American agent. On a typical US$2 sale, the factory makes about ten US cents' profit. Overall, Lin says, "the US market is shrinking rapidly, with orders down 20 to 30 per cent from their peak. European prices are better, but their orders are very small."

Meandering through Chenghai is a creek that has become an open drain, clogged with garish industrial waste, blues and yellows and reds. Children play on the banks while their mothers sit sewing and hungry dogs scavenge. People burn incense at a green-roofed temple, while in a nearby workshop mechanics fix scooters, watched over by a portrait of a godlike Mao. A little further on, young men play pool under a tarpaulin that covers a bar of sorts.

Chenghai is eager, increasingly desperate, for more workers. Banners announce that one factory needs female staff, while people on the pavement distribute recruitment flyers for the Electronic Toy Company: "No experience needed, but must be keen to learn, salary more than US$200 a month, paid on time on the tenth of each month, free accommodation and meals." Off a side-alley, in a gloomy workshop with an oil-stained cement floor, a couple of women are pressing out plastic toy cars, while a man with a cigarette dangling from the corner of his mouth fits them with rubber tyres. This is the assembly line of a family-based business.

Nearby, up a few flights of decrepit stairs – the lift is broken – in a building less smart than the average car park, is the Le Yuan factory, which employs about fifty workers. Shirts have been hung up to dry in the entryway. The supervisor, Chen – he doesn't want to share his given name – enters the small office and sits down next to a slab of beer and a slab of cola. A closed-circuit TV shows him the stairway, so he can keep an eye on any goods being carried out.

He says, stubbing out a cigarette in an overflowing ashtray, that he has more people around the city doing out-work for him, assembling electronic cars and games. Most of the toys are designed by the owner and his family, sometimes inspired by products made by others. Ceiling fans flicker and pop music plays as the men and women assemble the toys adroitly with electric screwdrivers. Some are pasting in circuit boards with bowls of glue and paintbrushes.

At the end of the line, a worker tests remote-controlled toys, sending helicopters flying up and down. The price of these electronic toys at the factory door ranges from US$1.50 to 5. The employees here are paid per piece and earn around US$200 per month, says Chen, "if they are experienced." Most of them have come to Chenghai from inland farming provinces.

Chen Guangfeng, aged thirty-four, owns the Fengze Toy Shop in the busiest street in town. Changhai is crammed with similar stores, which are essentially wholesale display rooms. Buyers come to these outlets, negotiate a price, and then leave it to Chen to obtain the products at the agreed price from the "several thousand" toy factories in the district. Chen owns his own factory, too. He says, "This is my village. My parents were farmers here, growing rice and vegetables. Then in the 1970s one or two Hong Kong factories shifted here, using their own generators because there was no electricity." He is concerned about the environment in which his son and daughter are growing up; he worries about the pollution, and the crime rate. "How can I say if the change has been good or bad?" he says. "We're richer, but when we had no money at least we had clean air. Wealth is not evenly distributed here. There are extremes. In some factories, the boss is a worker too, but in others he lives some way away, perhaps in the big city of Dongguan. I prefer the life of my childhood, riding my bicycle round the fields."

Liu Cheng-rong, aged twenty, and Li Jun-wun, eighteen, are both from Hubei province in central China but met in Chenghai. They are squatting by the roadside near a fast-food stall on the edge of town. They have quit their jobs "because the factory was not too good." They both came to Changhai almost four years ago, because "there are no jobs at home." Since then, they have occasionally made US$200 in a month, but usually less. Liu has not been home since arriving in Changhai. He says, "I have to write to my family that everything is fine. I haven't managed to build up savings, but I can't return without taking the family some money." The bottom line for Liu? "I feel sorry I came." There are no elves in the real Toytown, and there is more elbow grease than magic.

Shantou will not remain Toytown forever. Change is coming via more capital-intensive industries. The shape of this Chinese future can be seen at a vast industrial estate south-east of Beijing, where Richard Chang, an American who grew up in Taiwan, has built a US$1.5 billion microchip-making factory. His 2000 staff work in "clean rooms" constantly tested for dust and humidity. The machines, made in the USA,

Japan, Germany or Holland, cost up to US$37 million each. All staff must be able to read the instructions, which are invariably in English.

About 55 per cent of the staff have degrees, and 10 per cent are hired from overseas. All have three months in-house training before they begin work. Semiconductor Manufacturing International Corporation (SMIC), which Chang founded in 2000 after working for twenty years with Texas Instruments, will provide an interesting test of China's ability to move into more sophisticated manufacturing. Typically, the state threw a heap of incentives Chang's way to ensure he got up and running – free land, syndicated loans, research and development incentives, zero tax. Between 2004 and 2010, the plant's capacity doubled.

In striking contrast to the noisy toy-works, this factory is as silent as a library. The "clean rooms" can be viewed from glass corridors that circumnavigate the building. The staff wear head-to-toe sterilised white uniforms, as if in a radioactive environment. They work twelve-hour shifts, two days on and two days off; the plant operates around the clock. Construction took two years, a long time in China, where whole cities are made over in that time. But the precision machinery needs an especially stable foundation. Microchips, the building blocks of the electronic and information industries, are constructed out of minuscule strands, some the diameter of one thousandth of a human hair, that are built layer by layer into wafers. They are transported by overhead rail from one stage of the manufacturing process to the next. Human contact is reduced to a minimum. The specifications for each item of equipment are planned by a central computer, which is linked to every step of the production process by a local area network.

Today in China, most state-owned enterprises have abandoned their old cradle-to-grave provision of services for employees, from housing to kindergartens and schools to clinics and pensions. But the big new private-sector firms, including SMIC, have tended to take over such services, as a way of retaining well-trained staff. Most of SMIC's Beijing employees are housed in a staff compound, where the company provides a gym, a beauty salon, a basketball court and tennis courts, as well as schools. In Shanghai, SMIC provides 6000 apartments for its employees.

While Mao Zedong still looms over the centre of Beijing, where SMIC's factory is humming so quietly, at the other end of the country, Shenzhen,

China's great new southern city, is dominated by a different figure: the diminutive Deng Xiaoping, forever striding forward in a massive bronze statue on the top of Lotus Hill Park.

Overall, there's no contest. This is palpably Deng's day, not Mao's. China began to modernise during the Republican era following the overthrow – or the disintegration – of the Qing Dynasty. Then Mao drove the country down a cul de sac of collectivisation. With Mao gone to meet Marx, Deng launched a reformist period that brought rapid growth and new jobs, via labour-intensive export industries, to compensate for the closure of old-style, state-run heavy industry.

Now the fourth wave is getting under way. The best place to view it is from alongside Deng's statue. For Shenzhen, which was a mere fishing village when Mao died in 1976, is today a city of 11 million with the highest average annual income in China – more than US$10,000. Once dismissed with a shudder by neighbouring Hong Kongers as a polluted, shanty-crammed haunt of corrupt officials, concubines and cheap knock-off goods, its administrative centre is now a green zone of boulevards and exciting new buildings by the world's most expensive architects. And it is attracting growing numbers of middle-class migrants from Hong Kong.

It – and the Pearl River delta of which it is a part – is driving China's transformation from the world's factory into a high-tech, services-based economy. One of the reasons why this megacity, which stretches out along the Pearl River from Guangzhou down to Hong Kong, is developing so quickly, is that it is so far from communist party HQ. The old saying went, "The mountains are very high and the emperor is far away." If experiments go awry in Guangdong province, the rest of the nation will not be convulsed. The party can afford to loosen the reins here. Shenzhen was chosen to be the first "special economic zone" as China threw off, under Deng, its Maoist economic shackles. When the reformist Wang Yang became Guangdong's provincial party secretary, he echoed Deng by urging officials to "further emancipate their minds." It was no coincidence that Walmart chose Shenzhen as its base from which to place its orders, establishing the characteristically low-key Walmart Global Procurement Centre. This is can-do country, and it's a landscape that Americans recognise.

Small manufacturers are being replaced by large global firms. For instance, while European and American car makers established factories in China earlier and built their plants further north – often losing large amounts of money – the world's leading car makers, the Japanese, have focused their efforts in Guangdong, with Toyota, Honda and Nissan all building new factories here. High-tech companies in Guangdong pay only 15 per cent tax, compared with the general rate of 25 per cent. Newly established ventures receive three years' tax holiday, then pay only 7.5 per cent for the next three years.

The flagship is Huawei, based in Shenzhen, which has rapidly become, alongside Siemens, Nokia, Cisco and Ericsson, one of the world's leading suppliers of telecommunications and internet equipment. The standard entry requirement for a job with Huawei, at its pristine, park-like "campus," is a bachelor's degree; new graduates are paid US$20,000 a year, and many live in the company's housing estate, in hotel-style rooms of thirty square metres each, with access to a gym, tennis courts and a swimming pool.

The rewards for workers are considerable – but so are the expectations. The founder and CEO of Huawei, Ren Zhengfei, urges his staff to embrace an aggressive, deal-winning "wolf spirit." Each employee is given a copy of Jiang Rong's best-selling novel *Wolf Totem,* set on the steppes of Inner Mongolia. The firm uses an individualised, incentive-based pay structure – a very different model from the group-based template that drove Japan's industrial growth. Huawei – its name means "Say yes to China" – inhabits elegant, modernist buildings set in a vast, impeccably manicured park. They have tall ceilings and marble-lined foyers. It is quiet, temple-like. There are few people about, and those who are speak in polite, low tones. The firm is increasingly outsourcing its own manufacturing and reducing its production capacity.

My guide, Amy Shi from corporate affairs, has bought a home in downtown Shenzhen. Shenzhen is an ideal base, she tells me, so conveniently close to Hong Kong. A shuttle bus takes staff from the Shenzhen campus to that more famous city. Stock in the corporation is mostly owned by the staff, who are entitled to buy shares after a few years' employment. The board mostly comprises the founders – Ren and his original partners, some of whom now run the firm's larger operations in 100 other countries. Crucially, buried inside the somewhat opaque company structure is a Communist Party committee which, while not steering day-to-day business, has a veto power over strategic decisions.

China is also home to the world's second largest white-goods manufacturer, Haier. Its Asia-Pacific president, Philip Carmichael, addressed the Hong Kong Foreign Correspondents' Club in Hong Kong in 2011, insisting that "while there are party members who work with me and for me, it doesn't have any impact on our business." The chief executive of Haier, which is based in the former German treaty port of Qingdao, happens to be a senior party member, Carmichael said, and party membership in the company has been rising. And yes, he said, there is a party committee within the company, and its office is right around the hall from his. But it does not direct quality control or other managerial matters.

What about the workers? If there is a party office inside a company, is this a guarantee the workers will be well treated? Until recently, wages and welfare spending were restrained while the earnings of state-owned enterprises boomed, with little going back to the government as tax or dividends. That is changing, as firms are having to compete harder for labour. China has a workforce of about 813 million people, about 200 million of whom are migrant workers. The Australian economist Ross Garnaut says that China is approaching the "turning point in economic development," at which there is no longer abundant surplus labour in the countryside, as happened decades ago in Japan, Korea and Taiwan. When this happens, employers must pay much more to attract staff. But China is not quite there yet.

Anecdotal evidence suggests that there has been an increase in unrest involving workers. Hu Xingdou, an economics professor at Beijing Institute of Technology, says, "The local government has become the frontline of conflict. But there is no channel to allow people to express their will. They lack the right to speak, the right to organise and unionise to represent their interests, therefore they can only use an irrational way by demonstrating or rioting to solve problems."

Liaowang, a magazine published by Xinhua, reported at the start of 2011 that, partly because of rising living costs and inadequate pay rises at a time when profitability had soared, "mass incidents stemming from labour disputes have dramatically increased, and taken a more violent form." Wages have fallen as a share of China's gross domestic product, from about 17 per cent in the late 1970s to about 11 per cent thirty years later. Thus, says blogger Liang Jing, "the greatest beneficiary of China's sweated slave-labour system is not international capital and foreign consumers, but the government." Huang Yiping, a professor of economics at Beijing University, says that "households' share of the economy has slumped from 52 per cent to 40 per cent or less in the first decade of the twenty-first century, with the corporate sector, led by state-owned companies, and the government increasing their share."

There is a trade union movement in China – monopolised, of course, by the party. The All-China Federation of Trade Unions, which is an arm of the CCP, has been given a boost by recent restlessness among workers and by a tough new labour law that, from 2008, forced foreign firms like Walmart to allow chapters of the union onsite. Foxconn, the giant Taiwan-owned corporation that makes most of Apple's products, had to increase wages by between 16 and 25 per cent in 2012 alone. William Hurst, assistant professor of government at the University of Texas, who has published a book on Chinese workers' politics, says, "The state and party have looked to reinvigorate unions as a way to both increase control over workers and insert their apparatus more deeply into the operations of foreign and private firms."

Appearing to take on foreign firms on behalf of Chinese workers has obvious political benefits for the party. Such disputes give the leaders a chance to "burnish their nationalist and populist credentials, gain leverage and deeper control over otherwise unwieldy companies, and generally establish themselves as vital players in any arrangement leading to labour peace." When it comes to locally owned private companies, however, things are more complicated. Such firms "often have strong ties to local officials or agencies." And "they are so numerous and widespread that encouraging worker activism" risks sparking a much broader movement for workers' rights. Few Chinese workers are thinking, yet, in terms of independent unions or of greater militancy.

Torrents of edicts have been issued from Beijing to local governments all over the nation: maintain rapid growth, attract new industry, boost the service sector, cut pollution and energy use, close old state-owned loss-making factories, reduce unrest by laid-off workers and by farmers who have lost land to industry. In short, somehow create a Confucian "harmonious society" from a host of apparently contradictory priorities. And fund it all yourselves. No wonder local officials are blamed by many of the disgruntled poor. They are being asked to create mini welfare states overnight, with scant taxing powers.

Such rapid change has inevitably produced casualties, people left floundering between the old socialist and the new modern worlds. Many of them are people doubly damned. They lost their education to Mao Zedong's Cultural Revolution; then at the turn of the millennium they lost their "jobs for life," their "iron rice bowls," to the economic revolution triggered by Deng Xiaoping.

Yan Qinghai is one of them. He and his friends live in dingy, corroded flats behind Red Flag Street. They are focused on surviving each day, placing one foot before the other, while the approaching months or years are clouded by questions about their income, and about how they will afford treatment if they or a family member falls sick.

A nearby river that was once the most prominent feature of the neighbourhood, along which lovers strolled and children played, has run dry, its water "stolen," says a resident, by a power plant and a brewery. The brightly lit modern stores on Red Flag Street itself are mostly empty, but shoppers are crowding after work into a street market to buy food to cook for dinner – kebabs, plucked ducks, a hundred varieties of mushrooms, seeds and spices, fish gasping to breathe in a couple of inches of cloudy water.

Inside a tiny lean-to store nearby, a handful of laid-off workers are sitting on upturned crates. Yan, aged fifty-nine, worked in a large state-owned machinery company, making pumps for bellows, until he was laid off in 1996 when the factory was corporatised; before that, he says, it only survived thanks to government subsidies. He hasn't managed to get a job since.

"If you hear high officials talk, everything's great," he says. "It's not. Society is so unbalanced. People don't feel it's fair. How can we even pay for medical insurance or for pensions – where can we find the money?" He says he has heard that cadres are paid as much as US$1500 a month. "But we have to have *guanxi* [connections] to get a job." His 28-year-old son is a graduate, but remains unemployed and still scans the newspapers every day looking for work.

Yan likes the idea of setting up a business, something people out of work are encouraged to do. "But we don't have the funds for that. We have thought of migrating elsewhere in the country, but we're already getting on, and we don't know where the job opportunities are." And most of the people running the nearby market stalls have moved to Dalian from elsewhere, "so we can't imagine other places have more opportunities."

Pan Hong, sixty-two, who worked in a factory for twenty-three years until it was merged and then made bankrupt, says he has had several jobs since then, but none has lasted long. He earns US$58 a month now. He hasn't been able to pay the annual heating fee for two years, and says the lowest contribution rate for health and retirement cover is almost US$50 a month.

His flat is miserable. The bed in which he and his wife Dong Yan sleep is against one wall, that of their 25-year-old son against another. His wife has a US$100-a-month pension after losing her thumb in a work accident, and their son is jobless. His mother, aged eighty, with Alzheimer's, lives with them. They have no TV, no hot water, no electrical appliances.

Li Kai-jiang, fifty-two, is the best-off member of the group – his wife is in work and his parents have a US$150 monthly pension, considered handsome in China's struggletowns. He is drinking a warmish bottle of the local beer, for which he has just paid about 20 US cents. His cheeks are hollow and he coughs uncontrollably. He worked for a shoe factory for twenty years, until it was closed down in 1999. "Usually companies just look for people aged eighteen to thirty-five," he says. "After that, the only work you can get is as a house cleaner. Even then, you have to have good connections." He says, "I switch off my TV when I see those cadres talking with their loud voices. We're not opposed to the Communist Party. It's a good party. But its policies are not worked out well at the grassroots level."

Sun Xiuqin, the woman who runs the store, says, "There is a retraining project. But it's just a show. And you have to pay. After that, anywhere you go they will turn you down anyway." She says that in this neighbourhood, most people used to work in government factories but are now laid off. "If people get sick, they just buy drugs. They can't afford to see a doctor or go to hospital. We're all neighbours and friends, we help each other out."

Yan, Pan, Li, Sun and their friends, struggling to survive the present, have essentially given up on the future. But downtown, on Gorky Road, 8000 people a day, their faces optimistic, visit a thriving, high-tech job centre. It is named after Qi Xiuyu, a charismatic "model worker" who was working in a far more modest job centre here in the late 1990s when Mayor Bo Xilai chose her to help turn it into the city's prime centre for placing laid-off workers into fresh careers.

Today, the initial rush of workers from the closed-down factories has subsided. The centre is now also taking on migrants, who pour from the surrounding countryside into Dalian seeking a new start, as well as young people, including many graduates, and a growing number of workers with sufficient experience and education to keep hopping jobs in search of more money and responsibility.

Newcomers to the centre – which occupies two floors, and is accessed directly from the street – fill out a form and provide a photo, which is scanned into the database. The 280,000 people currently on file are informed about relevant jobs through three channels: the centre calls them, the potential employer calls, or they can drop by the centre itself.

Downstairs is a row of forty touch-screen terminals where jobs can be searched by sector or qualifications needed or locality or wage. Some housing compounds around the city host similar terminals. Upstairs, there are old-fashioned noticeboards, electronic panels displaying scrolling lists of jobs on offer, and a large screen in front of rows of plastic chairs. The same jobs are advertised through all these different channels. The software was developed by a local company at the direction of the centre, which has since on-sold it to similar institutions around China.

A large screen displays the number of people currently looking for jobs – 593 – and the number of vacancies – 7797. At the peak, says Qi, 18,000 vacancies are advertised in a day. The centre is even starting to place people overseas; recently, it found forty cooks for a restaurant chain in Britain. Small loans, up to about AU$15,000, are available through the centre for people wanting to start their own businesses. Just under AU$10 million has already been lent out, including to a category the banks tend to shun – groups of laid-off workers who wish to set up a venture together, who are eligible for a maximum AU$75,000.

The casualties, says Qi, have come not only from state firms that have gone broke, but from businesses that can no longer meet increasingly tough environmental criteria, and those that have automated, sometimes cutting their workforce from 500 to as few as fifty. The government, she says, provides jobs for some of those who appear incapable of retraining – as cleaners or gardeners, or community security guards, or traffic facilitators. And it subsidises some jobs for older people, paying employers directly. She says that the government pays 92 per cent of the pensions of women over forty and men over fifty, as long as workers contribute the other 8 per cent – a sum that remains an obstacle, however, for many.

Domestic help is one of the fastest growing categories of new work, Qi says. Much of China's middle class employs live-in maids. One terminal at the centre advertises jobs as cleaners, tutors and baby-sitters for about US$77 a month. (The highest paid job available, as a senior engineer, pays US$3000 a month.)

Qi herself, fifty-two, used to work in the human resources section of a shoe factory, until it was closed down. She has seven brothers and sisters, several of whom have lost their jobs. This helps her empathise with the plight of the laid-off, she says. There is an inevitable gap between the expectations of both sides, with workers seeking jobs close to home, with fewer hours and more pay, while employers are looking for people who have all-round skills, high qualifications and immense capacity for work – and who are young. On the whole, the balance has shifted over the last ten years, she says, and workers have more choice today.

Dalian's mayor, a fifty-year-old former finance professor, Xia Deren, smiles when he hears about my visit to Qi, whom he knows well, and takes in his stride my description of the woes of Yan and Co. He is a busy man, running a region of 6 million, including 2.5 million in the city proper. This evening he will host two banquets, the first for American diplomats, followed immediately by a meal with businesspeople. His survival strategy: he eats only from every second dish.

Dalian's economic transformation involves upgrading rather than merely demolishing its old established industries, he says. Under the new government drive for "scientific development," "we are supposed to get rid of businesses that harm the ecosystem as soon as possible, and to upgrade the technology of the rest so that they become competitive." At the same time, Dalian – like other cities – is expected to welcome new higher tech and service industries. It is attracting research and development centres, including for integrated circuits, new materials, energy saving and electronics. As a port, it is also naturally focusing on logistics and international shipping. New industries, Xia says, are supposed to consume less energy and resources. And the bottom line is that "we would like to pay more attention to the real needs of citizens, so they can benefit from economic development. We want to provide better social welfare and resolve urgent needs, including medical care and education costs."

The key solution is jobs, he says. Just 2.5 per cent of working-age people are registered as unemployed, although he is aware that the true total is many more. "Up to a dozen years ago, most people in Dalian were working in traditional industries such as chemicals and shipbuilding. At that time, the workers had hoped their employer would take care of them for life."

That burden has now shifted to the city government, as it has throughout China. Local officials have had to find ways to provide the medical, educational, housing, pension and other needs formerly met by the state firms, whose workers lived on site. The central government did little to help. No wonder that fees, commissions and other charges proliferated among local officials, further alienating many of their own residents. In Dalian, the government had to introduce special budgets to deal with spiralling welfare, health and educational costs – but today, mayor Xia believes, the provision for these things is "quite adequate." Ultimately, it is only "through healthy economic development that the government can meet people's expectations."

Xia presents me with a copy of *The World Is Flat*, a bestseller by the American author Thomas Friedman, a prolific champion of globalisation. City mayors all around China, but especially on the coast, are grasping eagerly at globalisation as their best chance to transform their cities from rustbelts into boomtowns. There is a bookmark on a page where Friedman writes, "Dalian has become for Japan what Bangalore has become for America and other English-speaking countries: outsourcing central. With its wide boulevards, beautiful green spaces and nexus of universities, technical colleges, and massive software park, Dalian – with more than 200,000 students – would stand out in Silicon Valley." Xia himself has a cameo in Friedman's book, where he is described as "dynamic ... with a charmingly direct way of describing the world. 'The rule of the market economy,' this communist official explained to me, 'is that if somewhere has the richest human resources and the cheapest labour, of course the enterprises and the businesses will naturally go there.'" Friedman describes a ten-course dinner he enjoyed with the mayor, but does not seem to meet a single Yan.

The mayor himself knows better. He understands that while China may be outrunning the many perils that could pull it back, the race against poverty and destabilising resentment remains a marathon. He is well aware that "outsourcing central" can only be a way station, not an ultimate goal.

So long as the economy is still moving, however, and despite the glum prognosis for Yan and his down-and-out friends, much of China is focused on ways to get ahead. Take Xu Leiguang. Grasping a Honghe (Red River) cigarette, he stabs his fingers at the graph on his computer monitor. It shows how he once lost US$12,000 on a Black Tuesday in China's casino-like share market. Now aged fifty-two, he was an engineer in a coalmine until he narrowly escaped death in a crippling blast. He has since spent almost every day in one of the hundreds of trading rooms that have sprouted all over China since stock exchanges were reopened in 1990. Xu receives a disability pension of about US$165 per month, and in nine years' share punting has turned this into a US$65,520.54 trading account – a substantial fortune in China.

Xu and two friends together own US$165,000 in China Satellite. This communications firm is their great hope, although Xu laughs at the very idea of being allowed to attend a shareholders meeting ("We're too small to be allowed in.") The three men sit at a row of screens in the "middle-level investors" section of the China Securities Company's vast trading room, beneath a hotel in Beijing's Dongzhimen district. They operate in an area screened off from the dimly lit zone for general punters, where about 500 people are milling around or sitting in rows of plastic chairs. On a vast wall of large screens, red, green and amber lights trace the fortunes of China's 1400 stocks, as well as the situation on the Shanghai and Shenzhen exchanges. When they are ready to trade, punters rush to one of the scores of booths that line the walls and key in their passwords before buying or selling. The booths are linked to the mainframe computer of China Securities, which is one of the country's top three stockbroking firms, and is owned in turn by the government-owned conglomerate CITIC.

It is a chilly winter's day outside, but the trading room is well heated. Some of the punters sit in groups, cradling their flasks of tea. Middle-aged and elderly women knit as they watch the stocks flick from red (a loss) to amber (no change) to green (a gain). Half-a-dozen male investors are having a smoke outside – only middle-level investors and above are allowed to light up inside.

For forty-year-old Ding Zhelu, a part-time electrical mechanic, this is like a club. He meets his regular acquaintances here almost daily and swaps notes. He owns two stocks in shopping malls, one in a nickel mine. They all slumped on Black Tuesday, although the mine has since recovered its lost ground. "But this is not a stable income. I wouldn't make a living out of it," he says. He tends to keep his stock for several months, but a friend "starts to worry if he hangs on to a share more than one day."

Wu Fengli, aged fifty-five, has been a regular punter since retiring from her job in a factory personnel department. She believes that the fortunes of the Chinese market are tied to the global economy, and so keeps a close eye on the USA's Nasdaq exchange as well. She spends a lot of time reading market commentary in the newspapers, and has attended some weekend classes run by China Securities. She sees herself as an investor who looks to the long term, hanging on to her stocks for an average three months.

Behind the general trading floor, past the section reserved for middle-sized investors, are stairs leading to the high rollers' rooms. Since it is the Chinese New Year period, a massive red and gold *fu* character – for good luck and/or wealth – is hung on the landing, upside down because the character for "upside down" sounds the same as that for "come." Thus good luck's arrival is greeted. Up the stairs, a quiet room with screened-off individual desks houses punters with at least 1 million yuan (US$165,000) in their trading accounts. And beyond, opening onto a maze of corridors, is a score of private rooms with opaque glass walls, hat stands, fridges and sofas, for those trading more than 5 million yuan.

Everyone, in the modern People's Republic as in ancient China, knows his or her place, although they covet dearly the opportunity to move up a rung or three. China's registered retail stock investors hold about three quarters of the entire market. There are now about the same number of share traders – about 80 million – as there are members of the Communist Party, and the two groups overlap substantially.

Yin Guohong, who holds a PhD from the prestigious Chinese Academy of Social Sciences, is assistant manager at China Securities' HQ in Beijing – a building whose entrance is flanked by two massive *chi-lins*, a mythical, conglomerate Chinese animal said to enhance *feng shui* and thus wealth. He says his firm has 1.7 million clients around China, including the hundreds in the trading room at Dong-zhimen. The latest trend is towards trading by mobile phone or online, where the fees are lower. The trading halls have lost much of their buzz since 2008, when China's share markets took a severe hit.

All investors have to go through brokers. Shares are sold in lots of 100. On average, a stock is traded every six months, says Yin; many are sold more often. He says that institutional shareholders assess companies' performance, while retail investors mostly watch out for new government policies or regulations that will impact on the market. The fall on Black Tuesday was the result of rumours about the latter, he says, especially about a capital gains tax being introduced – a policy the government has since denied.

Yin says that at least half of his firm's clients now have their own accountants or financial planners. They are eager to shift their savings from the state-owned banks, which offer interest of only 2.5 per cent or so. The largest three groups of punters, he says, are office workers (especially from firms within the finance industry itself), retirees and students. At first, says Yin, when investors were new to the market, they would come into his firm's offices and confront the staff to complain if a stock fell. But now they tend to be better informed, "and the Chinese market is operating increasingly like those of the rest of the world." But he accepts that speculation will continue to drive the market for some time, during which "it won't really reflect the economy."

An obviously over-simplified but amusing formula, offered by students at Beijing University, sums up China's relationship with the market:

In 1949, only socialism could save China.

In 1979 (after the Cultural Revolution), only capitalism could save China.

In 1989 (after the demise of the USSR), only China could save socialism.

In 2009 (after the global financial crisis), only China could save capitalism.

But China's is a very particular form of capitalism. While the market has been growing, so has the size and influence of the Communist Party. Sheila Melvin, the author of *The Little Red Book on China Business*, says of this apparent contradiction, "The Communist Party is China's most important business organization; it has ultimate approval over every investment, and branches in all state-owned enterprises and 85 per cent of private enterprises. Party members are present at the negotiation stage of any major deal ... If you want to succeed in China, you must understand how the Communist Party works, what it wants, and what it can do for you." Mao said, "Our basic concern is with internal problems." Melvin writes that today, domestic issues continue to dominate, including in the commercial sphere. She warns foreigners, "Neither your business nor your nation is as important to China as you may think it is."

Carl Walter and Fraser Howie, American bankers who have spent decades working and living in China, including together leading China's first joint-venture investment bank, agree. They point out in their seminal book *Red Capitalism* that "party leaders believe they are better positioned than any market to value and price risk." China's financial system remains Soviet inspired, they say, "an empire set apart from the world." They argue that there is little or no evidence that the Chinese financial structure will be opened up, as Chinese manufacturing was so successfully in the 1980s.

There was a watershed, these authors argue, in 2001, during the premiership of Zhu Rongji. Zhu oversaw China's accession to the World Trade Organization in December 2001, pushed extraordinarily rapid modernisation of state-owned industrial corporations, and appeared poised to facilitate the steady opening-up of the financial sector. The main chance for change was lost, however, as towards the end of Zhu's premiership the political factions lined up on the conservative side against him, so that in the financial sector today, "no one is able to take a position opposite to that of the government."

Those who opposed the further opening up of the financial structure felt vindicated by the global financial crisis. But Walter and Howie write, "We do not believe in the recent triumphalism of China's bankers and many of its leaders; this is only a diplomatic ploy. China's banks survived the GFC, as one senior banker has publicly stated, simply because the financial system is closed off from the world. With a non-convertible currency, minimal foreign participation and few overseas assets beyond US Treasuries and commodity investments that will neither be marked-to-market nor sold, why shouldn't the system survive a major international crisis better than open economies?"

They point out that China's banks are not exposed to private-sector ups and downs, because the country's stock, bond and loan markets "cater only to the state sector, of which the 'National Champions' represent the reddest of the Red." Growth still depends heavily on debt-financed capital investment. Reforms that had edged forward for a decade were kyboshed by the frantic "policy loans," a tsunami of debt that comprised China's chief response to the global financial crisis. This has ensured that interest rates, exchange rates and foreign participation will remain severely restricted and subject to state direction for years to come.

An example is the spending on high-speed trains, whose take-up rate by passengers has so far been disappointing because of high ticket prices. Research published by the leading Chinese business media group Caixin says that the resulting outstanding debt hit US$248 billion in 2011. It asks the underlying question, "Will newly built high-speed trains generate the additional cash needed to service the debt? Maybe not. But banks may not mind, since railway construction is a national policy issue for the government, and the Ministry of Railways is a good customer." Even if it can't repay its debts.

It is the party that effectively allocates such debt, Walter and Howie point out, and "one cannot simply assume that words such as 'stocks' or 'bonds' or 'capital' or 'yield curves' or 'markets' have the same meaning in China's economic and political context." They describe the process of shifting debt around in China as a "precarious shell game."

When in 2009 a state-owned giant, Chinalco, wanted to pump US$29.6 billion into the global mining corporation Rio Tinto to become the company's dominant shareholder, the vice president of Chinalco, Lu Youqing, said that he did not yet know in detail how the deal was to be funded – even though it would have been by far China's biggest ever foreign investment anywhere in the world. He said that some Chinese financial institutions had been contacted, and they had expressed an interest in participating in what *China Securities Journal* described as "Chinalco's luxurious bet." Lu's lack of concern about the details underlined forcefully how such deals work. The vehicle used by Chinalco to buy its original holding in Rio Tinto a year earlier was appropriately called Shining Prospect. The leading Chinese business magazine *Caijing* said that such deals, which "related to the nation's energy strategy and foreign relations, are directly decided by the State Council, China's Cabinet, without following corporate governance principles." It quoted a bank staff member as saying, "From the perspective of national strategy," they have to be funded "whether profitable or not."

China's extraordinary growth has been largely investment-driven, funded from both within and without the country. China insisted from the start of its opening-up that foreign capital come in the form of direct investment. Foreigners had to build factories or hotels in areas preferred by the party. These large and lumpy assets could not be withdrawn in a crisis. If foreign investments were not in the party's nominated development zones, they had to be in joint ventures with Chinese companies. Many inefficient and sickly Chinese state companies were thereby married to foreign firms.

In the 1990s, China began grooming selected state-owned enterprises to compete with overseas multinationals. Some 120 large enterprises were chosen by the State Council. These new national champions were characterised by their dominant role in strategic sectors such as telecommunications, energy, transport, mining, iron and steel, aerospace and aviation, chemicals and shipbuilding. They were given tariff protection and favourable financial treatment. Western investment banks such as Morgan Stanley and Goldman Sachs were brought in to repackage these companies in line with international legal, accounting and financial requirements. They then listed on international stock markets.

China's state-owned enterprises look, at home, like a new wave of business success, 21st-century style. Sometimes, however, they have struggled overseas as they follow the government's direction to go out and conquer the global corporate world. Michael Komesaroff, an Australian who has worked in Asia's minerals industry for more than thirty years, mostly as a Rio Tinto executive but also with a Chinese state-owned giant, explains that China has not been able to replicate internationally the model that has succeeded at home. The difficulties stem, he says, from a common perception that they can solve any challenges by deploying their existing in-house skills. Yet the approval process for investing offshore is often dysfunctional, as it frequently "mixes commercial with political imperatives."

Within China, he says, many success stories are the result of simple, well-understood processes, combined with weak regulatory institutions (such as environmental regulators), an abundant and compliant workforce, and multiple networks of known and experienced suppliers. Overseas, however, China's state-owned enterprises tend to come up against complex, unfamiliar processes in states with strong institutions, less docile workforces, and unfamiliar or undeveloped supplier networks. At home, many problems can be solved by throwing more people at them. There is also an expectation that the government can broker relations with landowners and unions and other social groups. The same conditions don't usually exist overseas. There have been clear overseas successes, such as at the Channar iron-ore joint venture or the Portland aluminium smelter, both in Australia, but other state-owned enterprises have not been as quick as they might to learn from these.

Early in the "open-door" era in China, Komesaroff says, decisions about investing were made at the top levels, and on a somewhat subjective basis. Then, as restrictions were relaxed and decision-making was devolved during the 1990s, local governments plunged into "a rash of investment," some leading to notorious over-capitalisation. A centrally imposed approval and monitoring process was introduced as a result, to staunch losses.

Komesaroff, who is a regular contributor to the prestigious *China Economic Quarterly,* says that the balance of risks and rewards became asymmetrical, with "punishment for failure outstripping reward for success." Indecision and procrastination were often the result. A more formal procedure was introduced in 2012; mineral projects of more than US$300 million and non-mineral projects of more than US$100 million are now required to undergo a four-step approval process: registration with the State-owned Assets Supervision and Administration Commission (SASAC) and the National Development and Reform Commission (NDRC) and then, if they give the green light, a feasibility study, formal approval, and regular progress reports. This process now applies to the 121 state-owned enterprises that report to SASAC and comprise more than 80 per cent of China's entire foreign investment. The feasibility stage involves all parties likely to finance the project, or needed to provide approvals, and takes place within a punishing schedule – approval must be granted or refused within twenty working days.

When companies seek approval to go offshore with particular projects, the NDRC will consider whether they are the most appropriate firm to represent China. Sometimes the NDRC will force a marriage between two competitors for the same or similar projects. Sometimes they will seek to create "national champions." These national-level enterprises are ranked from A to E on the basis of performance and promise. Those few that are relegated to the D or E levels are the least likely to be given approval to go offshore. The Ministry of Foreign Affairs is also brought in to the discussion, evaluating the value to China of the country being targeted for investment. "If it's in a war zone or has been the target of international sanctions, it will receive much greater scrutiny," says Komesaroff, who describes China as "a Leninist state where the party shadows the government at every turn." One of the challenges for SASAC, he says, is that it is regularly outranked by the companies that it is required to manage, because many of them form the commercial arms of ministries.

Komesaroff says that the top two or three employees of the SASAC-guided enterprises are monitored carefully by the party's Organisation Department, and that every year between forty and fifty of them shift into senior positions in the government or party, or back again. The party constantly, he says, rotates talent between industry and government, a process that takes in ministerial and vice-ministerial positions, provincial governors, party secretaries, top business executives, university chancellors, heads of academies and others. He says that managers of the top state-owned enterprises receive a base salary that is typically just a third of their total package, with bonuses comprising the other two thirds. About 60 per cent of the bonus is usually paid immediately, the other 40 per cent on retirement from that role. He concedes that while state-owned enterprises have become more market-focused, "their political heritage is undeniable."

The party was challenged to change these structures in a report produced jointly in 2012 by the World Bank and the Development Research Centre of China's state council. This outlined what came to be seen as the core challenges for the new leadership under Xi Jinping. The report, very widely circulated within China, said that after more than thirty years of rapid growth, "China has reached another turning point in its development path when a second, no less fundamental, strategic shift is called for." It went on to identify six key challenges: to strengthen the foundations for a market-based economy by redefining the role of government; encouraging innovation; going green; extending social security; strengthening the fiscal system, especially at the local-government level; and becoming a "pro-active stakeholder in the global economy."

Hu Shuli, the founder of Caixin Media and China's leading business journalist, was among those who backed this program. In 2012 he wrote that China's economy had hit the limits of its outdated model of development, which was driven by investment and by cheap labour producing goods for export. She said, "Whether China can now re-engineer a new path of growth and avoid the middle-income trap [a stage of development at which many emerging countries find themselves stuck, unable to move up a level to become South Koreas or Singapores] will depend on its determination to transform itself."

Zhang Zuhua, who worked alongside former leader Hu Jintao but later left the party, believes that such a transformation will occur. Although the party may seek to absorb businesspeople, in time these entrepreneurs will start to erode long-cemented party ways. "Mutual penetration of party and business in the medium term gives the party tighter control," he says. "In communist terms, this will enlarge its social base. But in the longer term, it will change the structure of the party," allowing China's economic transformation to get back on track.

In opening itself up to the business world, the party may be getting more than it bargained for.

CHAPTER 10: MEET THE LEADERS

THE LEADERS OF THE MOST POWERFUL ORGANISATION IN the world today, the Chinese Communist Party, are almost as mysterious to most of their 1.3 billion fellow citizens as the emperors of old.

When the party unveiled China's new leadership team at the National Congress in 2007, there was a genuine air of excitement as the nine members of the new Standing Committee, in dark blue suits with white shirts and red ties, filed into the Great Hall of the People. This was like a very formal version of *Chinese Idol*. The previous party leaders had all been anointed by either Mao Zedong or Deng Xiaoping, who together dominated communist China for almost fifty years. But Xi Jinping and Li Keqiang, the new leaders, emerged from a process of consultation with a wide range of influential party figures, although the then general secretary, Hu Jintao, retained ultimate veto power.

The official communique from the 2007 congress described the leadership structure as "a system with division of responsibilities among individual leaders in an effort to prevent arbitrary decision-making by a single top leader." Jing Ulrich, the chairman of China equities with J.P. Morgan Securities, explains, "Despite one-party rule, a number of checks and balances exist in China's political system … Factional politics is less a zero-sum game in which the winner takes all, and more a process of deal-making and power-sharing."

During a tour of Japan in 2008, Hu Jintao visited a school and was asked by eight-year-old Songtan Haoji, "Grandpa Hu, why do you want to be president?" After the laughter subsided, Hu replied, "I want to tell you, I myself did not want to be the president. It was the people in the whole country who voted me in and wanted me to be the president. I should not let the people throughout the whole country down."

His answer was of course misleading. China is not a totalitarian dictatorship, but nor is it a democracy. The party system has been portrayed as a meritocracy, and those who have met today's leaders confirm their intelligence, but both the criteria for promotion and the method of selection remain unknown beyond a small circle. The public remains on the outside, looking in through frosted glass.

At a press conference during the 2007 party congress – held at the "media centre" set up for the occasion, ten kilometres from where the congress itself met – a journalist asked how many positions were open for the party's Central Committee, when and how the voting would take place, and how the new Politburo and Standing Committee would be elected. Ouyang Song, the deputy head of the party's Organisation Department, smiled tightly and answered, "A string of interesting questions, about which I'm sure all the people in the hall take enormous interest. But maybe my answer will be disappointing to you. The central bodies of the party are elected according to the party constitution and relevant rules, so changes in leadership can only be known following the elections.

"But I can tell you, the members and alternates of the Central Committee will be elected by the delegates and specially invited delegates through a secret ballot on the basis of the election method adopted by the party. Both the elections are based on competitive elections. But how large the size of the competition will be determined by the election method which is just being drawn up, so I am not in a position to tell you that.

"As for the Politburo, they will be elected by secret ballot by the first plenary session of the [new] Central Committee. Intra-party democracy is the lifeline of the party, but unity and solidarity within the party is also its lifeline." He concluded by adding, almost mischievously, "Thank you very much for your interest in the central leading bodies of the Communist Party of China." (The electoral procedure was in fact formally decided by a "presidium" of 237 people – an ad hoc group of party movers and shakers led by general secretary Hu, whose own choices were guided by a much smaller presidium Standing Committee, consisting of the party's inner circle.)

The 2012 party congress saw the peak ruling body, the Politburo Standing Committee, reduced from nine members to seven. Although the process excited greater international interest than ever, with considerable speculation about the "new leadership team," in fact the seven had all served on the Politburo for the previous five years, and the top leaders, Xi Jinping and Li Keqiang, had also been on the Standing Committee.

The other five were Zhang Gaoli, aged sixty-five, party secretary of the port city of Tianjin; Liu Yunshan, sixty-five, head of party propaganda and previously a Xinhua journalist in Inner Mongolia; Zhang Dejiang, sixty-five, an economist who trained in North Korea, and who replaced Bo Xilai as party secretary of Chongqing; Wang Qishan, sixty-four, formerly chief of the economy and now in charge of the disciplinary commission against corruption; and Yu Zhengsheng, sixty-seven, Shanghai party chief. Just two of them appear to be members of Hu Jintao's *tuanpai* faction; the rest are protégés of Jiang Zemin. Three are princelings and one is a princeling by marriage. The next party congress in 2017, however, when most of this Standing Committee must retire, may see Hu's followers take up more of the top jobs.

The average age of Central Committee members is fifty-six. Of the 205 full members, only 5 per cent are women. The Politburo now includes two women, but the Standing Committee has none. There are no members of "minorities" on the Politburo; all are Han Chinese. Geremie Barmé from the Australian National University has argued that despite its 83 million members, the party is effectively controlled by 200 to 300 influential families. These families hold powerful positions in the corporate world, in the upper ranks of the People's Liberation Army and in all levels of government.

The party congress of 2012, however, did mark a watershed in one important way. For decades, the leadership group had deferred to a gerontocracy of Long March veterans and other legendary party figures. These veterans have now nearly all "gone to Mao," and Xi Jinping has a clear path to promote his own program, essentially free of speculation about "the power behind the throne." Xi himself is on the throne, and there is no one lurking behind it.

He still remains a remote figure for most people, however. Zhai Hongwei, aged thirty-five, a textile salesman from Harbin, was touring Beijing by bicycle on the day Xi was promoted to the Standing Committee. He told me, "I'm not very concerned about the faces in the committee. We just hope they can benefit the *laobaixing* – doing something practical for us." Li Xiaohong, a 45-year-old laid-off worker, was acting as a volunteer to organise passengers into queues at bus stops. She said, "We hope the new leaders can do something about unemployment. People like us, older than forty, can hardly find any work, and prices are rising sharply."

Neither Zhai nor Li, nor other passers-by in west Beijing, some of whom had stopped to take their lunch breaks near China Central TV, the heart of the country's news media, knew anything about the newly named "fifth generation" leaders. They had never heard of them. But they had heard of Xi's wife, Peng Liyuan, China's most famous first lady since the notorious Jiang Qing, Mao's fourth wife and one of the Gang of Four, who committed suicide in her jail cell after the gang fell from grace.

Hu Jintao, Xi's predecessor, remained, throughout his years at the top, perhaps the least known Chinese leader since the Qing Dynasty. This is a tribute both to the party's successful culture of secrecy and to the innate caution and self-deprecation of Hu himself, who spent his whole working life in party roles, except for a few early years as a water engineer. Journalists, domestic and foreign, unearthed remarkably little about him or his family, considering he ran the world's most populous country for ten years. There is virtually no single proven anecdote about his life. His only recorded joke came when he was visiting the USA shortly before he became general secretary. When the then governor of New Jersey, James McGreevey, told Hu – whose hair is jet black – that he did not look his fifty-nine years, Hu replied, "China would be happy to share its technology in this area."

He did also once playfully remark, when interviewed by a group of foreign journalists, including myself, on the eve of the Beijing Olympics, that if he were to play in the Games, it would be at table tennis. "But since the Chinese table tennis team is already finalised and made public, it seems my wish will not be granted." In the event they managed well enough without him, winning all four gold medals and the men's and women's silver and bronze as well.

In the lead-up to his becoming party chief, the journalist Ma Ling was assigned by her then newspaper to write a profile of Hu. She was completing the piece after extensive research when she was suddenly told that instructions had come from on high that such a personal story was unwelcome. Ma had become so intrigued and impressed by Hu, however, that she quit her job and began to research him for a bigger project – a book, which eventually had to be published in Hong Kong because it was "unauthorised." It remains the only dedicated biography of Hu. Ma travelled to all the places Hu had lived for any reasonable period and talked to people who knew him. Even then, his personality remained elusive to Ma, although she became an admirer of his dedication and focus.

One thing about Hu became clear very soon after he took power: despite rumours before his promotion that he was a closet radical reformer, he was not a Mikhail Gorbachev, ready to usher in changes that would weaken the party's monopoly on power, or even to test its popularity through elections. Zhang Zuhua, a former colleague of Hu's, says, "His personality is highly circumspect. He will not take risks. He is good at listening, at summarising a meeting, and picking up the focus of a group." This low-key style helped Hu to survive politically for so long.

Like Hu, Xi has been labelled a reformer with a streak of decency. Hu presided over continued rapid economic growth – the core of the contract between party and people, which survived even the global financial crisis – but also over the maintenance of stern party controls of many areas of life in China. Most at the top of the party expect no less from Xi in return for his elevation. There is great risk and scant gain, in contemporary Chinese politics, from introducing reforms unless they are deemed essential for the system's very survival.

Xi is the third successive leader of China to emerge from the most peaceful transition process in the nation's millennia of history. He is the son of the late Xi Zhongxun, who was a Long March general, a vice premier and a staunch supporter of Deng Xiaoping. Xi is therefore naturally associated with the informal *taizidang* or princeling faction within the party, consisting of the children of communist veterans. But he has also demonstrated consensus-building skills, and these enabled him to clamber to the top of the tree.

He is a burly, open-faced figure, aged fifty-nine when he became general secretary in late 2012. He had previously been in charge of some high-profile assignments, especially sorting out the mess left after top-level corruption was exposed in Fujian and Shanghai. China's leaders rise to the top through such provincial roles, much as US presidents are often former governors. He speaks some English, and as party chief in booming Zhejiang, south of Shanghai, he became friendly with a number of international business leaders including former US Treasury Secretary Henry Paulson, who described him as "the kind of guy who knows how to get things over the goal line." He only just scraped over the line in his first really important election, when he became an alternate member of the Central Committee of the party in 1997: he was elected with the lowest number of votes of all of the 151 successful candidates, according to Cheng Li, a political scientist at the Brookings Institution. Since then, Xi has worked assiduously to build trust within the broad party base. At Chinese New Year in 2010, for instance, he sent a "personal" text message to about 1 million officials around China.

During the Cultural Revolution, Xi and his siblings were sent to the hardscrabble Shaanxi countryside, home of the terracotta warriors, where he lived for seven tough years. Xi eventually graduated from Qinghua in Beijing, one of China's top five universities, in chemical engineering. He later became a doctor of law from the same institution, specialising in Marxist theory and ideological education.

He worked in Hebei province near Beijing and then in coastal Fujian, and in 1999 was appointed acting governor of Fujian in the wake of a massive corruption scandal. In 2002 he became party chief – the top job, senior to the governor – in booming Zhejiang, just south of Shanghai. He was then shifted temporarily to Shanghai as party secretary. In 2007 he was brought to the centre of power, joining the Politburo Standing Committee as the heir-in-waiting with the strong support of his fellow princelings as well as of the "Shanghai faction," led by the former president and general secretary Jiang Zemin.

Kerry Brown, executive director of the University of Sydney's China Studies Centre, has written in *Foreign Policy* magazine, "The Chinese system is not set up for someone with big, bold ideas, but for the ultimate insider, the person with the best networks and the biggest vested interest in making the system work. And that person is Xi." Hu Jintao was the ultimate committee-man, expert in building consensus through long party meetings, and his successor has similar skills. The party today covets continuity and detests surprises, and Xi is expected to maintain the gradual shift in focus, begun under Hu, from physical infrastructure (the country's "hardware") to the human side (the "software").

Xi's first marriage, to the daughter of a former ambassador to Britain, ended in divorce in the 1980s, and she now lives in Hong Kong. He and his second wife, Peng, have a daughter, Mingze, who enrolled at Harvard University in 2010. Peng joined the People's Liberation Army Song and Dance Ensemble when she was eighteen and has risen to the rank of major-general. The core of her repertoire as a soprano is patriotic songs in praise of the motherland and the army, such as "I Belong to China," "My Soldier Brothers," "Daughter of the Party" and "We Are the People of the Yellow River and the Mountains." She has also sung Western operatic works and has performed often overseas, including in the USA and Canada. She has recorded many albums and until recently performed almost daily.

A long interview with Peng in a small city newspaper, *Zhanjiang Wanbao* in Guangdong province, provided a rare insight into China's first family in 2007. The article was republished on China Central TV's website, giving it the official seal of approval.

Peng said that her glamorous stage presence "has a lot to do with my family. If I didn't have a happy marriage, which would potentially wreak havoc on my heart, I would not have been able to maintain such a shiny public image ... Career and family are both important for a woman. My family is just like everyone's family. It is an ordinary family, a happy family."

A friend introduced her to Xi in late 1986, when he was working in Xiamen, a thriving coastal city in Fujian. Aged twenty-four, she was already famous and was based in Beijing. She said she had deliberately worn a pair of unglamorous army pants "to test whether he cared only about appearances." She did not fall for him at first sight. Not only did he look like a farmer, she said, "he also looked a bit old."

But he asked intelligent questions about her music. They chatted for a long time and arranged a second date. She recalled, "I was touched. 'Is he the one I want in my heart?' I asked myself. He had a simple heart, and he appeared thoughtful. He later told me that in that forty minutes' chat, he already recognised me as his future wife."

He told her at their second meeting of his ambition, of the long hours he was likely to spend at work. Peng said, "If career is taken care of, family will be taken care of too. They are complementary." Her parents were anxious about the prospect of being caught up with such a high-ranking family, but Xi persuaded her that this was no barrier: "My father is a peasant's son ..."

They married on 1 September 1987, in Xiamen. At the wedding banquet, the local party chief recognised the famous singer and asked Xi why she was there. "Because she is my wife," he replied. She said that their work had caused them to be separated for long periods, but that their relationship had strengthened in the process. "Perhaps because of the [nine-year] difference in our ages, he treats me like a little sister," she said.

At home, they are not political leader and singing star, only husband and wife, she said. He had never asked her to stay at home. "'As long as she's fine,' he says, 'I'm happy whether she does the housework or not.'" He hasn't tended to take her with him to occasions where spouses are invited, because she is so well known. Trading on her fame would be frowned upon in straight-laced party circles.

She said he was too busy "on the frontline, battling against floods" to be with her when she gave birth to their daughter. She had wanted a boy, Xi a girl. "But looking at how happy they are together, how can't I be filled with joy? Our daughter is a lot like him. When she was younger and I looked after her, she always acted up. But when she was with her dad, she behaved like an obedient kitten."

Before Xi's promotion to the top job, Peng often sang on national television on the eve of Chinese New Year, a timeslot that commands the highest TV audience in the world. Websites have featured many calls for her to do so again, with some viewers saying they will switch off if she doesn't perform. But it is unlikely to happen. As her husband is now in the spotlight, she is expected to step back. The covers are being drawn across the cage of this celebrated songbird.

China's new number-two leader, Premier Li Keqiang, was groomed by Hu for a couple of decades; they first worked together in the party's Youth League. Like Hu, Li comes from the inland province of Anhui, where his father was a rural official. Labelled an "intellectual youth," he spent two years in a rural commune at the end of the Cultural Revolution. He graduated in economics from Beijing University and later earned a doctorate, also in economics. There, he joined a free-thinking group of intellectuals, studied the law, and helped translate *The Due Process of Law* by British jurist Lord Denning. He was not involved in the Tiananmen Square demonstrations of 1989, although friends from student days took part.

After graduation he worked in rural Henan province, during the period when many thousands of peasants contracted AIDS through a blood-donor program, a scandal that was at first concealed. In 2004 he became party chief of Liaoning, a rustbelt province in the north-east. He accelerated Liaoning's economic make-over, attracting Intel and BMW to set up large plants there, and hosted World Economic Forum conferences in the prosperous city of Dalian. He facilitated massive central-government spending on infrastructure and set Liaoning up as the key province for pilots of new pension and welfare schemes. In 2012 he told the Boao Forum, an annual conference held on Hainan Island involving political and business leaders from across Asia, that "China's reform has entered a critical juncture."

Under the previous leadership group, high hopes were pinned on Premier Wen Jiabao as the humanising, egalitarian and incorruptible element of the team. In his straightforward political career, the single event that stands out is his televised visit, on 19 May 1989, to Tiananmen Square, just sixteen days before the troops cleared it with tanks and bullets. As a leading adviser, he was accompanying the then general secretary, Zhao Ziyang, who boldly, belatedly and vainly attempted a compromise deal with the student leaders of the protest movement – tragically, just as other leading party figures, marshalled by Deng, were already opting to use the iron fist.

That Wen's subsequent career scarcely skipped a beat testifies to his considerable political skills. He found fresh patrons and refocused his efforts on economic reforms. Until the Bo Xilai scandal in the dying days of the Hu—Wen administration, he exemplified the modern party's distaste for extended internal bloodletting of the kind that disfigured the Mao decades.

When I interviewed him inside the government HQ, Zhongnanhai, Wen exuded quiet charm and intelligence. He was palpably bright and across his briefs, answering my questions for a full hour without consulting his notes or the advisers who sat opposite. He then showed me around the Purple Light Pavilion where we had conducted the interview, on the north-west shore of the "Central Sea," one of the three Zhongnanhai lakes. Originally built during the Ming Dynasty, it was rebuilt in the eighteenth century by the great Qing emperor Qianlong. In February 1921, Mao held his historic meeting with Richard Nixon there.

The comparison most commonly drawn to describe Wen is with Mao's long serving – and long suffering – Premier Zhou Enlai, who attended the same high school as Wen in Tianjin. Zhou somehow survived those years of purges and tyrannical turbulence with his reputation intact as a modest, honest representative of the ordinary people, a sort of Chinese Jimmy Stewart or Tom Hanks. Wen inherited some of Zhou's populist mantle, which also recalls centuries of imperial tradition, when peasants in remote villages would pay letter writers to tell the emperor how much they respected his fatherly concern and how shocked he would be by the corruption of local officials.

During an annual session of China's parliament, Wen described an unannounced visit he had made to the Jiangsu countryside. He candidly admitted being surprised when the villagers failed to recognise him. They did not lay on a special welcome for the visiting cadres, he continued – in fact, "those villagers were apparently not happy." A local woman told reporters accompanying the official party that the cadres "could not solve the people's problems." Now, Wen told the parliamentary delegates, his voice choking with emotion, every time he visited Jiangsu he wondered, "Are those peasants happy now?" This, he said, had become "an obsession in my mind."

These rural peasants are the people who spawned Mao's party – not the urban workers who drove the Soviet revolution. Wen was well aware that if they continued to be locked out of China's rapid wealth creation, their noses pressed enviously against the glass, the risk of a second rural revolt – this time against the party – was real. Hence his scrapping of centuries-old rural taxes and his attempt to redirect resources from the comparatively wealthy coast to the country's heartland, its 600 million farmers. His New Deal-style rhetoric – building a harmonious society, focusing on the quality rather than the pace of growth – was sound, and his good intentions plain. But when Wen smiles – which, as "the nation's grandpa," he does a lot – his eyes remain watchful. He more than anyone is acutely aware that the challenges he identified have not yet been resolved.

The extent of these challenges acts as a lid on the party's factional rivalries; everyone is aware that division would threaten the whole project. China's leaders know just how dangerous a time this is for them. Nevertheless, factions remain.

Cheng Li, the most thorough chronicler of these divisions, identifies two core factions, which he prefers to call "coalitions" because they are loose-knit groupings rather than formal alliances. There are the *taizidang* or princelings, in the blue corner, and the *tuanpai*, or Youth League followers, in the red corner.

There are some ideological or policy elements to this divide – for instance, the princelings are more market-disposed and more inclined to look to the economy for legitimacy, while the Youth League faction is more state-focused and more inclined to use nationalism to stir up support. In general, the *taizidang* tend to live in the richer coastal provinces, while many *tuanpai* have worked in less developed areas inland. But these are not battle lines. When it comes to the crunch, they will pull together and put the party first. Although power sharing is always difficult in practice, they need each other and they know it.

Cheng Li writes in *Asia Policy* that "the two coalitions may take turns in the 'driver's seat' of Chinese politics. Occasionally one camp may inflict 'casualties' on the other by firing one or two political rivals on charges of corruption or incompetence. Each side, however, will need to make these political moves through compromise, negotiations and deal-cutting, to avoid causing a systemic crisis."

They are also aware of the dangers of negative public perceptions. The princelings, for instance, risk being criticised for unearned promotions or appointments, especially of family members educated overseas, often at US Ivy League universities. The children of the top leaders accumulate dynastic stakes in strategic industries. Jiang Zemin's son has focused on telecommunications; Li Peng's family, power; Zhu Rongji's son, banking; and Hu Jintao's son sold the Beijing city government the new automated subway ticket machines it introduced shortly before the Olympics. The website of the news agency Bloomberg was blocked in China for a considerable period in 2012 after it detailed wealth amassed by the extended family of Xi Jinping, including investments worth US$376 million – though not, Bloomberg stressed, by Xi himself. In the *New York Times*, David Barboza similarly detailed the wealth accumulated by Wen Jiabao's family – and provoked a similarly outraged response from the establishment.

The emergence of this hereditary ruling caste bothers many of China's independent commentators such as Zhang Yaojie, who teaches at China Arts Academy, and whose writings – although confined to academic publications – have a strong following. "Even in the countryside the party secretary of the village has to pay the party secretary of the county to get his position," he says. "Often you don't give money directly, but to a project or to supporters, relatives or contacts. And many family members of important leaders are in charge of big projects. If you go to provinces and municipalities, you can see that the officials in charge of telcos and electricity and other big state companies are often relatives or contacts of state-level leaders. Anyway, they have *guanxi* [networks].

They do have a competitive system to select leaders," but the competition is often among those relatives and contacts.

Zhang says, "I don't think there is any document saying how to select party leaders or senior cadres. But there are unwritten standards. They have a hidden rule for selection. The rules within the party are mysterious and terrifying. No one gave them the right to say they can represent us." He is confident that democracy will be realised in the future, but in ten, twenty or thirty years. "China introduced a democratic system after the Qing Empire was overthrown in 1911. But then the leader of the Kuomintang, Sun Yat-sen, overthrew the democratic system. Then the Communist Party overthrew the KMT. For now, the Chinese people are not strong enough to claim the country back."

He frets that "the good part of Chinese tradition and history is got rid of, and the bad part is continuing. Everybody wants to be emperor. No one wants to be responsible." He believes that the CCP would win an election because it has no rival – but "party members are not confident enough to allow elections. They are interest-driven." However, a small group "standing and shouting slogans for a political campaign" won't benefit the country. "I will support the Communist Party if it opens itself to elections. Because so-called dissidents who want to organise other parties might not be any better." China does not need another Mao, he says, but a Gandhi, a Martin Luther King jr, a Gorbachev or a Chiang Jing-guo (the son of Chiang Kai-shek, who conceded democracy in Taiwan).

The official selection criteria for leadership might not be publicly known, but Xi Jinping has stressed four crucial qualifications for leading cadres: "Political beliefs and resoluteness; principled political viewpoints; sensitivity in political discrimination; and reliability in the area of political loyalty." No Gorbachevs need apply; they will be rooted out.

Another criterion that has emerged in recent years is an informal age limit of sixty-five for provincial chiefs and seventy for the very top jobs. Those who are at or near this age when they are promoted to the Central Committee or the Politburo can expect to be replaced after only a single five-year term. This ensures a turnover and the emergence of new talent, although senior figures can remain influential into their late eighties.

There are various ways into a party career. Princelings have often begun by working as personal secretaries (*mishu*) to top leaders who were comrades of their fathers. Xi Jinping, for instance, worked as *mishu* for Geng Biao when he was defence minister. Willy Lam, a leading expert on the party based in Hong Kong, has published a report on the sixth-generation cadres – those who will come to the fore after Xi and Li, running China from 2020 through to 2030 and beyond. He points out that a record number of senior party posts are now held by senior managers of state-owned enterprises, especially from the petroleum and automotive sectors. Others are filled by the 300,000 Chinese expatriates who have returned since the mid 1990s with degrees from American, European, Japanese or Australian universities. But, says Lam, these graduates still "face a class ceiling as far as promotion to top-level posts" such as the Politburo. Party apparatchiks, rather than technocrats or professional administrators, still dominate the top ranks. Nevertheless, a degree remains useful. In 2009, says Lam, the party recruited 130,000 graduates. A spell in the People's Liberation Army also helps, and the princelings in particular have found success within the ranks of the PLA, where favouritism and family connections come in for less public scrutiny. And while Hu Jintao is not generally seen as a strongman, "he has been successful in methodically filling plum central and regional level posts with his protégés from the Youth League," says Lam. Top leaders thus play a major role not only in picking their own successors, but also sometimes the successors of their successors.

Cheng Li has written in *Asia Policy* that for most of the history of the PRC, the ruling elite was largely homogeneous in terms of social and professional backgrounds. "Communist revolutionary veterans with backgrounds as peasants and soldiers comprised the first and second generations, while engineers turned technocrats made up the third and fourth generations. The emerging fifth generation [led by Xi and Li] is arguably the most diverse elite generation in the PRC's history in terms of class background, political association, educational credentials, and career paths" – potentially making it more difficult to maintain that strongly desired consensus. Most of this cohort belongs to the "lost generation" whose education was interrupted or undermined by the Cultural Revolution, leading them to value endurance, adaptability and humility. Their political socialisation was rigorous; no one from a "bad background" was considered for party membership when they were starting out. Cheng Li points out that people from China's eastern provinces – especially from Shangdong and Jiangsu – have always been over-represented in the leadership, and this remains true today: 40 per cent of the Central Committee members in 2012 came from these two provinces.

On major issues, all significant factions are consulted until a consensus emerges. If someone with an especially firm conservative position reaches a top position, however, they can veto or delay reform for years. Cadres with strident personalities (*gexing ganbu*) are viewed with caution. This was demonstrated dramatically in 2012 by the ousting of Bo Xilai, then aged sixty-two, from Chongqing, the vast metropolis (population 29 million) in south-western China. Bo was the son of Communist Party royalty: his illustrious father, Bo Yibo, was one of the party's "eight immortals," a guerrilla hero from its founding era and a vice premier after Mao's demise. But Bo Xilai failed in his bid to be elevated to the vice premiership after a term as commerce minister, and was instead dispatched back to the provinces in 2007. As a former Red Guard, he took heart from his hero Mao Zedong, who in 1919, in the wake of the Russian Revolution, wrote, "The world is ours, the nation is ours, society is ours." "The world is ours" became Bo's mantra. He believed that, like Mao, he could build support in regional China and return in triumph to the capital.

He pursued this strategy in a surprisingly literal – and initially successful – manner, using revolutionary songs and the paraphernalia of the era most associated with Mao. Stages were set up at schools and workplaces, decorated with the national flag, and local cadres and party members were encouraged to lead the singing of "red songs" including "Road to Revitalisation" and "Good Men Should Become Soldiers." Karaoke bars specialising in these songs were set up , and local TV and radio stations were asked to introduce "red singing" into their schedules. New statues of Mao were erected. Officials were encouraged to wear Mao-era uniforms. Bo texted "red messages" to Chongqing's 13 million mobile phone users, often comprising quotes from Mao's Little Red Book. Bo published "red GDP" figures that focused on progress towards egalitarianism. State-owned banks were encouraged to fund the massive construction of "affordable" housing, costing US$15.8 billion. Moves to curb income disparity received publicity. Bo initiated a furious campaign to jail and execute people branded as "gangsters," a campaign spearheaded by his head of public security, Wang Lijun. The internet spread reports of Bo's "revitalisation" of Chongqing all over China. People began to compare the charismatic, colourful, good-looking Bo with the committee men who dominated national public life.

In other quarters, however, Bo was attracting criticism. Lawyers warned that his anti-crime campaign was trampling on the rights of the accused. Suspects were being convicted on trumped-up charges; lawyers were penalised and sometimes jailed and beaten for defending the accused; torture was used routinely.

Bo's brassiness and self-promotion, meanwhile, had started to embarrass the leadership, particularly other members of his "princeling" faction. His predecessor as party chief in Chongqing, Wang Yang, who had gone on to become party secretary of Guangdong province, was coming under criticism by implication and by comparison. Wang, widely viewed as the leading liberal reformer of the current generation, is a protégé of Hu Jintao and closely associated with Wen Jiabao. He told a provincial party plenum early in 2012, "Thirty years ago, reform focused on shaking off the shackles of ideology; today's reform must focus on breaking the constraints of the existing pattern of vested interests." A widely disseminated report from Qinghua University by Professor Sun Liping warned that such vested interests threatened to hold back reforms, leaving China in "a transition trap." *China Youth Daily* agreed: "In the early days of reform, 'crossing the river by feeling the stones' was a practical need. At present, the problem is that some people enjoy feeling the stones so much that they do not want to cross the river any more."

The contrast between Wang's approach to reform and Bo's was stark. But this was much more than a battle of ideas, as Beijing was discovering. Early in 2012, the top leadership became aware that Bo had been bugging their communications when they visited Chongqing. The *New York Times* revealed that an August 2011 phone call between Hu Jintao and Ma Wen, who was head of both the Ministry of Supervision and the National Bureau of Corruption Prevention, and one of the most powerful women in China, was tapped on Bo's orders. This naturally led to surreptitious enquires and stepped-up surveillance, led by the Central Commission for Discipline Inspection.

The resulting tensions suddenly burst into the public sphere on 6 February 2012, when Wang Lijun drove the 340 kilometres from Chongqing to Chengdu, the capital of Sichuan province, accompanied by two bodyguards and a driver. En route, Wang called a contact in the Sichuan government and asked to meet him for lunch. There, he asked the contact to help by making an appointment with the US consulate, which the man did. Wang was met at the consulate gate by an American official, and entered.

In the meantime, news had reached Chongqing of Wang's whereabouts. Bo deputed Mayor Huang Qifan to travel there to attempt to talk to Wang. By some accounts Huang was accompanied by as many as seventy police cars, although this is disputed. But Wang did not talk with Huang. Instead, when he left the consulate after twenty-seven hours, he was met by central security agency officials and accompanied by them to the airport. He caught a plane to the capital and disappeared. Officially, he was said to have gone on "vacation therapy." The American ambassador, Gary Locke, told *Newsweek*: "It felt like something out of a spy thriller."

Such a story could not be suppressed in the new internet world, even in China. Some commentators later suggested that this suited the central leadership, for it had already decided that Bo had to go. Speculation about Wang's flight – and whether he had sought asylum from the Americans – continued for weeks. By the time Premier Wen addressed the media at the National People's Congress in March 2012, rumours had surfaced that the Wang case would trigger Bo's downfall.

Wen said at his press conference in the Great Hall of the People, "Reform has reached a critical stage. Without successful political structural reform, it is impossible for us to fully institute economic structural reform and the gains we have made in this area may be lost." Referring to Bo's tumultuous reign in Chongqing, without mentioning Bo by name, he went on, "The new problems that have cropped up in China's society will not be fundamentally resolved, and such historical tragedies as the Cultural Revolution may happen again … Over the years, successive governments and people in Chongqing made enormous efforts to promote reform and development and have achieved remarkable progress. The current party committee and government must seriously reflect on the Wang Lijun incident and the lessons from this incident."

Bo had been expected to ride his popularity into the Politburo Standing Committee at the National Party Congress in October 2012. Instead, he was dramatically sacked as soon as the National People's Congress ended in March, from his position as party secretary of Chongqing, and later from the Politburo too. In addition to the insider information provided by Wang, he was damaged by rumours of hypocrisy and corruption, by the flamboyant lifestyle of his Oxford and Harvard-educated son, Bo Guagua, and by the troubling behaviour of his high-flying wife, Gu Kailai, a lawyer and businesswoman. Bo subverted the key requirement of top leaders: that they espouse and practise stability and consensus.

The backstory began to emerge. Neil Heywood, a 41-year-old English wheeler and dealer, who had worked closely with the Bo family, especially with Gu, had been found dead on 14 November 2011 in the Nanshan Lijing Hotel, also known as the Lucky Holiday Hotel. A three-star, six-storey hotel high in the hills to the south of the city, it had seen better days. The official cause of death was given as excess alcohol consumption, although Heywood was not known as a heavy drinker. He had helped to arrange the admission of Bo Guagua into his own alma mater, Harrow. It was later alleged that he had also helped the family to shift substantial funds overseas. Gu and Heywood had a big falling-out, according to the prosecutor's office, over money and over fears for the safety of Bo Guagua, who was by then studying at Harvard. In July Gu and a family employee, Zhang Xiaojun, were charged with murdering Heywood by getting him drunk and forcing him to swallow cyanide. Gu pleaded guilty and a one-day trial took place away from the public gaze, in the city of Hefei, capital of Anhui province. She was handed a suspended death sentence, meaning she is likely to serve about fifteen years in jail. While only the most basic facts of the melodrama could be confirmed, she was portrayed in various ways – at first as a Lady Macbeth, and then as an unstable woman driven to desperation by anxiety, provoked by unspecified threats to her son.

It emerged that Wang knew about the incident and had become increasingly concerned as the pressure tightened from central investigators. He did not wish to be implicated in a murder, and is said to have confronted Bo in mid January. Bo's response was to demote Wang, on 2 February, to vice-mayor responsible for education, science and the environment. Wang appears to have become worried that his life was now at risk (the numbers of executions and extra-judicial arrests and disappearances had soared in Chongqing under his watch) and fled to the US consulate, either to seek asylum or to obtain a degree of protection by letting the Americans know some of his secrets.

Bo defended himself from the tide of growing rumours with characteristic bravado, by holding a press conference during the National People's Congress. But it was too late. The strength of Premier Wen's words revealed that the leadership had decided to remove him. Subsequently, vast numbers of stories have swirled around, some possibly started by the party establishment after it closed ranks against Bo.

The party leadership had secured two crucial outcomes: it had seen off a threat from within by an extraordinarily popular local official, and it had reaffirmed its preferred leadership style, one based on conformity and consensus. At the same time, however, many people in China have been asking themselves: if Bo was such a dangerous and destabilising, perhaps even criminal, element, how did he become a Politburo member in the first place? The veteran *Time* and CNN correspondent in Beijing, Jaime FlorCruz, cited an old Chinese adage: "Those who win become emperors, those who lose become bandits."

What does the Bo affair mean for the party's future? Cheng Li says that following the scandal, which has revealed flaws in China's system, "there is an opportunity to reach a new consensus and seriously pursue political reforms. China must now either make changes to be on the right side of history or be left behind." Few are seriously expecting Xi or even his successors to introduce democratic structures as they are known in the West, however. The Bo surge was tackled by inner-party intrigue rather than "intra-party democracy."

The political demise of Bo also underlines the return of a tendency – which reached manic proportions under Mao but was ameliorated under Deng – to purge political opponents and their families. These days, they are often charged with corruption – although in an opaque system in which there is very little accountability for senior leaders, it is very difficult to define corruption, or to identify why one leader's mis-step is significantly more "corrupt" than another's. Essentially, it is about losing power tussles; it is about the dangers of over-reach.

This ten-year period under Xi Jinping will test, says Cheng Li, whether China can move away from secret trade-offs and towards "a more institutionalised transition to power sharing." Despite the brief popularity of the charismatic Bo Xilai, most people are content to be ruled by apparently hard-working leaders rather than flamboyant per-sonalities. But they still have scant knowledge of how those leaders have emerged on top – or who they really are.

CHAPTER 11: LIFE AT THE TOP

ONCE ELEVATED TO JOIN THE TWENTY-FIVE MEMBERS OF the Politburo, a Chinese leader and his – it is still almost invariably his – spouse will probably never again eat in a restaurant, stay in a hotel, fly in a plane or even drive on a road at the same time as any member of the public.

Even within already highly secure buildings, areas to be visited by a leader are locked down. I was once inside China Central TV, which requires considerable security clearances to enter, when a little-known Politburo member arrived for a function. It proved impossible for anyone to leave the building for some time as a result, although the TV workers I quizzed weren't sure who the VIP actually was.

It remains generally accepted that leaders are unable to live normal lives, that they are "above" normal people. Leaders don't even eat the same food as other folk in China. The country has been plagued in recent years by food scandals. The most notorious was exposed soon after the Beijing Olympics, when it was discovered that nitrogen-rich melamine was being added to milk products to increase their apparent protein content. This caused kidney failure in many babies, with at least six dying as a result.

One angry blogger asked, "What are the people in the government doing? They just want mistresses, they want cash, but out here we're dying!" Another said, "When they tell us some official is sacked, they are just giving us part of the story. The rest isn't reported. They just move on to other jobs."

Outraged netizens soon unearthed a speech made by Zhu Yonglan, the director of the State Council Party and State Organisations Special

Food Supply Centre, in which she explained proudly that there were Central Security Bureau farms and supply bases in thirteen regions of China, supplying current and veteran cadres with "high quality organic food products." It was already fairly well known that Mao Zedong had established a high-security farm in the Fragrant Hills to the west of Beijing to grow food for the exclusive consumption of the party leadership in Zhongnanhai. But it was less well understood that leaders all around the country were being fed secretly grown organic produce.

Zhu said, "There are only a handful of products that merit the label 'Special Product for Central Party and State Organs,' inspected according to rigorous national approval processes. No chemical fertilisers, pesticides, growth hormones, antibiotics, contaminated or polluted materials, chemical additives or preservatives or genetically modified products are used." This food is specially produced, transported and examined according to strict party standards, overseen by her agency, which was established in 2004. This agency also sources the leaders' drinks, including teas and alcohol, and regularly reviews the products it endorses. Zhu said, "If their standards do not remain of the highest calibre, they are excluded." Rice for the party is mainly grown in the north-east, fish and prawns are farmed in the Yangtze River city of Wuhan, tea is grown in mountainous Yunnan, and beef comes from cattle grazing the steppes of Inner Mongolia.

Zhu's speech only came to light because the company in Shandong, Ke'er, to which she was talking, had begun to use its party certification in public promotions. Such information about how the leaders live rarely spills out into the public domain. Zhang Zuhua, however, a dignified, upright figure whom I meet in a tea-house just west of Tiananmen Square, knows something of this hidden world: in the 1980s and 1990s he worked in the party HQ at Zhongnanhai, where he knew Hu Jintao personally.

A government minister has a very modest income, Zhang says, of about US$20,000 a year, a half or a third of the salary of a leading professor. But there are myriad other benefits. A leader will rarely if ever need to spend his own money. Even after retirement, most day-to-day needs are met by the party-state. A minister will have a driver, a secretary, assistants. He is entitled to a home of at least 200 square metres, according to regulations, can travel abroad several times a year, and is probably driven around in an imported black Audi. The expenditure on each minister might be about US$1 million a year, says Zhang, and the benefits don't stop there. "He can assign good jobs to family members. That's not corruption; it's what is provided for by the system. And you receive better provisions with higher rank."

The higher a leader's rank in China, the less he does for himself. This was underlined when US President Barack Obama walked down the steps of Air Force One on arrival in Shanghai, in the rain. He was holding his own umbrella – the element of his arrival that most excited Chinese viewers. Raymond Zhou, a *China Daily* columnist, reflected that it was "an iconic image." He wrote, "Few in the country he landed in would expect a president – any president of any organisation – to hold an umbrella. That is the job of underlings." To Chinese TV viewers that night, Zhou said, Obama "managed to appear to be a man of the people." A similar response echoed around China when TV viewers watched Taiwan's President Ma Ying-jeou give his victory speech after winning a second term in early 2012. It was pouring with rain in Taipei, but Ma spoke to his supporters outside, holding his own umbrella – again, inconceivable in China.

Chinese leaders must give much of their time to the party. Says Zhang, "The higher the rank, the less time they spend with their families. If they do get time, they spend weekends with families out of Zhongnanhai" in family compounds that are usually just to the west. The first-generation leaders, including Mao himself, had their families living with them inside Zhongnanhai. After Mao, leaders chose to keep their own homes elsewhere, living in Zhongnanhai on only a semi-permanent basis. There was not enough space for all the leaders and their families, and most leaders' spouses have not wished to remain so confined.

Mao liked swimming, and several pools were built within Zhongnanhai for him. There is a leisure club with a full range of recreational facilities. Underground tunnels enable leaders and their staff to attend meetings in other venues such as the Great Hall of the People and the Public Security Ministry, both nearby, without travelling by road and halting the traffic.

Elsewhere in Beijing, leaders can visit or stay at the state guest-house, Diaoyutai, which has massive grounds and is run by the foreign ministry but managed on a day-to-day basis by an upmarket hotel group. They can also visit the walled enclave in the Fragrant Hills where their organic food is grown, which includes several villas. In the summer, they can take their pick of villas at Beidaihe, the nearest beach resort to Beijing, where informal planning takes place before important party gatherings. And each city has its own state guest-house where leaders stay securely and discreetly when they are travelling, and to which key local officials can be invited for banquets.

Zhang says, "If leaders want to keep circles of friends they can, but this highly enclosed political system prevents contact with members of the wider public. If they want to see ordinary people, there must be several layers of checking first. It's very complicated." This is part of the sacrifice that a Chinese leader must be prepared to make.

Instead, leaders gain a sense of how ordinary citizens feel by scanning the results of regular for-their-eyes-only opinion surveys, Zhang says. These might come from private companies, or from big government institutions such as the Chinese Academy of Social Sciences. One assumes that the top leaders have unfettered access to the internet. In the past, they were the only people to receive – every morning and evening – *Reference News*, a collection of articles from the media around the world, collated and translated into Chinese by Xinhua. Dissidents, aware of this, would focus on having their stories relayed in the international media to which leaders were said to pay greatest attention. Today, Xinhua provides the leadership with exclusive accounts of events around the nation prepared by a huge network of reporters dedicated to the task.

While leaders enjoy state-supplied housing, living in an official residence has its anxieties, especially during factional disagreements. An acquaintance told me of his visits to the home of a distant relative who is a senior cadre and a close adviser to one of the top leaders. My acquaintance said he could not help but notice that there was a television set in nearly every room and that they were usually all switched on, with the volume turned up high. His assessment – which it would have been inadvisable to mention in the house – was that the noise was intended to disrupt anyone who might have been listening in.

Richard McGregor, a journalist with the *Financial Times*, reveals in his ground-breaking 2010 book *The Party* that the offices of about 300 senior officials – those ranked vice-minister or above, including the executive chairmen and women of China's biggest state companies – all have red phones on their desks, with encrypted four-digit numbers that connect them only with people who have similar phones. They are members of the ultimate insiders' club. McGregor describes these phones as "a powerful symbol of the party system's unparalleled reach, strict hier-archies, meticulous organisation and obsessive secrecy."

★

In May 2012, Chen Yong, writing in the *Economic Observer*, described the preparations of a businessman, Zhang Chun, for the party congress. Zhang tells Chen, "For people who are not public officials, being a national delegate to the CCP means one is very near to the highest authority in China." He scans China Central TV news bulletins closely, he reads party newspapers like *People's Daily*, he attends party courses. He also cultivates relationships with fellow party members within his own firm, where a party committee has been set up to establish that the company is "politi-cally correct."

Zhang, who began running a family business and is now president of several listed companies, tells Chen, "The chances of getting to be a national delegate are one in a thousand. I have been very nervous ever since I was recommended." Entrepreneurs like him were not eligible to join the party until 2002, when, under then general secretary Jiang Zemin, the national congress opened the doors – a move which has changed the shape of China's private sector more than it has the party itself.

Zhang has organised courses for his staff to learn party history and theory, paid for them to watch "red movies," and instructed them to read party leaders' speeches. And he sends them on "red tourism" excursions: "We regularly organise trips to Jinggang Mountain [where the Long March began] to revisit the party's history." He says that "being a party delegate will help promote my business." However, the price is eternal vig-ilance: "I can't make any mistakes. Everybody, especially party leaders, have their eye on me" – causing him so much anxiety, he is losing sleep. After attending his first congress in 2007, Zhang says, he was exhausted – because he knew that mistakes were "absolutely unacceptable."

Before he was confirmed as a delegate, inspectors from the Organisa-tion Department visited his offices. They looked over the premises and asked him why he wanted to be a delegate, what books he read, what he thought of the party's positions. He tells Chen he hadn't thought much about such matters before, but cramming the "correct" information helped him to answer appropriately.

A leadership position in the party can have other perils. Take the example of Comrade Guo Shizhong, who died in 2008 aged only forty-six

– of overwork, according to the local government body where he was a family-planning official. Xinyang City authorities in Henan announced that all local media "should make powerful propaganda from the stories of Comrade Guo's spirit, his love for his job" – which was so great, they said, that the hospital was unable to rouse him from his final, fatal fatigue. The city's party committee posthumously awarded him the title of "outstanding party member." The deputy party chief could not stop weeping at the funeral, and the eulogy was interrupted by cries of grief, reported the *Jinbao Daily*. Several truckloads of wreaths were received.

But, the state-owned newspaper continued, "while these moving events were still unfolding, what ordinary people were revealing about model worker Guo soon eclipsed them, like thunder on a sunny day."

Hospital staff revealed the true cause of his demise to the newspaper. The admission certificate reads: "0.04 a.m., February 27. Disease: drunk. Location: Jinxin Hotel." Doctor Zhang Ke said he had helped take the patient to the sixth floor, "but I could tell he was already dying by the time we reached the third floor; his body reeked of alcohol, and he was bleeding from the nose and mouth."

The *Jinbao Daily* story demonstrates the newfound freedom of the Chinese media to uncover discomforting stories on certain topics, especially if corruption is involved. The paper went on to report that Jinxin Hotel was located next to party headquarters. Customers pay 58 yuan (about US$9) for an hour's use of a karaoke room, and a further US$15 for a hostess to dance, sing and drink with them. One of the hostesses told the newspaper that Guo arrived about 10 p.m. with several others, who "said he was already drunk. He sang quite well, with a loud voice. His favourite was 'Unforgettable Tonight.' He came often, so we had got to know him. He lay down on a sofa, as usual. By midnight, the others suddenly saw how ill he was and called an ambulance."

The story of Mr Guo's death attracted national attention in China, in part because Xinyang had become the centre of a highly publicised crackdown on cadres' binge drinking, and drinking during working hours in general. Earlier in 2008 a China Central TV crew followed Li Bin – the official assigned to lead the anti-alcohol campaign – as he burst into the office of a drunk senior cadre and sacked him on the spot.

The Xinyang party chief, Wang Tie, was behind the booze ban which, he told Xinhua, had saved the city about US$7 million in banquetting expenses in six months, and was good for officials' health. But Kang

Yinzhong, a lawyer retained by Henan Alcohol Association – a liquor-industry group that appealed against the ban – said that drinking was a private matter, and that officials should not be stopped from consuming alcohol as long as it did not affect their work. The nature of "model worker" Guo's last hours highlights the extent of the challenge facing the booze-busters.

A contemporary Chinese song called "I Want to Marry a Government Official" includes the lyric: *He has power, a car and a house / He only needs to drink tea and read the newspaper during work / He never spends his own money on cigarettes and drink / He can get free food every day / He can get promoted just by kissing the boss's backside.*

Members of the party elite often appear infinitely richer than their incomes would suggest, and the statistics back up the popular impression. Wang Xiaolu, an independent-minded economist who spent eight years at the Australian National University from 1989 and is now based at the China Reform Foundation, found that in 2010, China's official statistics concealed a "grey economy" worth a breathtaking US$686 billion, then equivalent to 24 per cent of the gross domestic product.

Wang has twice conducted face-to-face surveys with thousands of households, in 2006 and 2009. The second study, which like the first was part-sponsored by Credit Suisse, covered nineteen of China's thirty-one provinces, autonomous regions and municipalities, and involved people in sixty-four cities and fourteen counties. Questionnaires were completed by 4195 households, about double the number in the first survey.

In the second survey, the average household income was 90.4 per cent higher than in the official data, which are based on government surveys conducted by the National Bureau of Statistics. In Wang's survey, the annual disposable income per capita of the top 10 per cent of households was US$23,000 – an astounding three times the amount indicated in the official surveys. Wang explains that respondents understate their income in government surveys for reasons such as "worrying that such information will be passed on to tax authorities." Wang's surveys are conducted by interviewers who know the respondents personally. Thus, he says, "the respondent will feel more comfortable and willing to disclose their true income." (In China, people tend to under-report their income even to friends, such is their inherent dislike of paying taxes.) Most of the grey income – 63 per cent of it – ends up in the hands of the wealthiest 10 per cent of households.

The total hidden income comprises 9.3 trillion renminbi (US$1.5 trillion), an extraordinary 30 per cent of China's gross domestic product. Wang says the size of this secret wealth, which disproportionately benefits people at the top, helps explain the government's push for faster wage growth and fairer income distribution. He believes that "Chinese property, European luxury goods, high-end retailing and gaming in Macau could be the biggest beneficiaries" of the hidden economy.

Other evidence corroborates Wang's findings that the official data are off-track. For instance, an average sedan costs about US$16,500 in China, with at least a further US$3300 in annual running costs. Wang says families who can afford to own a car thus need an income of at least US$33,000 per annum, taking into account hteir other basic expenses. Official figures show that almost 15 per cent of urban households own cars. Yet this data also says that the top 20 per cent of households have an average annual disposable income of just US$14,700. Where do these piles of cash come from?

Wang lists them. They include presents and gifts received at weddings. These are traditional and legal. But, he says, "some officials collect huge amounts in the name of their children and relatives," up to hundreds of thousands of dollars at a time. "We believe these are, in effect, bribes." Government agencies pay staff bonuses as well as wages. Some, including state-owned enterprises, "use public funds to gift welfare or extra income to officials, managerial staff and workers, sometimes avoiding taxes."

He lists "benefits in the property sector through insider trading and fake auctions, windfall profits in financial markets through insider information, spreading false information, market manipulation and government officials benefiting through the misuse of power for personal gain." He says "corrupt activities arising from the abuse of administrate power" lie at the heart of the grey economy. Another survey covering 4000 enterprises in China asked how much the companies paid officials of government and regulatory agencies. Only 19.8 per cent of the managers surveyed said they made no such payments.

This helps explain why university graduates rush to apparently poorly paid government jobs. The official newspaper *China Daily* says the appeal is all in the fringe benefits – housing, health cover, car, and those other "grey" taxing powers – that operate outside the formal pay structure. The newspaper quotes Allan Zhang, aged twenty-eight, who quit his job as a software engineer with a multinational firm to become a public servant. He says his allowances add up to almost triple his wage, "and as for grey income like gifts and coupons, you just name it …"

Around the turn of the millennium, people working for state and party agencies in China's cities were allowed to buy – for nominal amounts – the apartments in which they had been living, in China's version of Margaret Thatcher's at-a-stroke privatisation of Britain's council houses. Although the state retains freehold, urban titles were extended to seventy years, making these city properties eminently bankable. This has reinforced a sense of grievance in rural China, where 600 million of the 1.3 billion population live, despite other concessions in recent years including the abolition of agricultural taxes and the provision, at least in theory, of free education.

Wang says public investment is another source of grey income in China today. When the Beijing-to-Shanghai high-speed train project and the west-to-east natural gas transmission project were checked by the National Audit Office, overcharging, fake invoices and irrelevant fees were found to account for US$429 million. Land sales are a massive feature of developing China, officially worth US$250 billion in 2009. Offering exemptions from land transfer fees has become a major source of grey income for local officials, Wang says.

There is nothing grey about China's red-blooded economy. But the fact that so much of its economic activity is hidden would appear to support the case for renewed reform.

Liu Xiaobo, the jailed Nobel Peace Prize laureate, told me a few months before his arrest, "Everything is a state secret." He said that the party's leaders see themselves as "like members of the imperial family, who won the land and the sky through battles. In the past it was the emperors and their families who conquered all and thus gained the right to rule alone. Since the Communist Party of China defeated the other parties, now it believes the land and sky belong to it. And this party rule extends further than family rule ever did. The imperial family penetrated, in power terms, to county-level officials. But the Communist Party has penetrated deep into villages, deep into all administrative levels."

This includes, especially, the rising entrepreneurial and intellectual middle class. The party leadership vowed that the student protests of

1989 would be the last. Since then, it has deployed its growing economic resources to woo the middle classes, and has been spectacularly successful. In the 1980s, after the Cultural Revolution eviscerated faith in old-style communism, middle-class youth flirted with democracy and liberalism. Today, they have mostly moved on, and instead espouse nationalist and traditional – essentially Confucian – values, alongside personal material goals. Although huge numbers of university graduates must scrabble, sometimes without any success, for jobs, they have not protested in the streets. The "mass incidents" that worry the authorities today mostly happen in marginalised rural areas, where they can be more readily suppressed.

A Chinese postgraduate student studying in Melbourne described to me as a "clear mistake" a reference in the media to a soldier taking items from a store after the 2008 Sichuan earthquake. It must be wrong, he said, because the People's Liberation Army could never, thus did not, behave like that. For him, as for most young Chinese today, it is as if the events of 1989 never took place.

Many people looking in from outside at China's development search for signs of a recognisable liberalism in the middle classes, a liberalism they cannot find in the all-powerful party. David Goodman of the University of Sydney observes that China's economic transformation "is seen as hopeful by those who see an equation between industrialisation and economic development on the one hand and the emergence of a peace-ensuring liberal democracy on the other. The argument that these people are 'just like us' is very seductive, especially if it is delivered without any hint of irony."

Goodman argues convincingly, however, that the new Chinese middle class is largely the creature of the ruling party, rather than of the market. China's "entrepreneurs … are less the new middle class than a future central part of the ruling class." They are quite unlike the nineteenth-century European bourgeoisie in the extent to which they have emerged from and retain close relationships with the established political system. For this is not China's first wave of modernisation, as is often presumed by those who believe that Deng Xiaoping conjured this remarkable industrial machine from an imploded peasant nation.

The Republican era (after 1912) saw sustained attempts at modernisation, Goodman points out, in various parts of China under both warlord rule and colonial influence. Much of this economic activity was externally directed, so that parts of the economy were considerably better integrated into the world economy by the early 1920s than they would again be until the 1980s. The establishment of the People's Republic of China in 1949 saw renewed and sustained modernisation and industrialisation. Managerial and professional jobs multiplied, so that during the 1950s the people who filled them became "the backbone middle classes" of the new party-state.

Many in these classes were purged during the Cultural Revolution, but as they and their families were then restored, "so too middle-class reputations rose again." Some of this group transformed themselves into new-style entrepreneurs during the 1980s, especially as opportunities emerged to gain from their privileged access to assets.

And what of the entrepreneurs who have appeared more recently? Goodman highlights "the close associational links between the new entrepreneurs and the party-state; they are neither independent of nor excluded from the political establishment, which on the contrary seeks actively to incorporate them if there is no pre-existing relationship." This was the chief innovation of Jiang Zemin, who opened the doors for capitalists to join the party.

Goodman says that the reallocation of state assets over the last couple of decades "sometimes left less than clear distinctions between ownership and management." In Hangzhou, an entrepreneur was asked if he had paid for the state assets he now controls. His response was clear: "There's no need. These were previously the assets of all the people, and we are the people."

Goodman believes that even the massive income inequality now being officially acknowledged (the Asian Development Bank has described China as having one of the biggest wealth gaps in the world today) is understated because of the extent to which businesspeople in China, who tend to be incorporated in the party-state apparatus, enjoy "cost-less (to them personally) access to resources and effectively subsidised income not available to others."

The pattern of economic development in the People's Republic fits more closely that of Germany, Japan and Russia during the late nineteenth century than that of Britain or the USA, he says. "In those countries, the state played a central role in industrialisation, as opposed to the laissez-faire capitalism of the earlier European experience based on the protection of the individual outside the state."

Goodman says that in China today, "where new entrepreneurs did not already participate formally in the activities of the party-state, particularly at leadership levels, they have now found themselves fully incorporated; and many new entrepreneurs would appear to depend on family networks of influence grounded in the party-state," even extending to small-scale businesspeople in the private sector. Many of these new entrepreneurs have come from the ranks of the professional and managerial middle class. Others, more truly independent, are required to cooperate with the party-state "if they desire to maintain a growth trajectory." This may mean they are expected to take up a local leadership position, and perhaps to surrender some equity to a government body.

This is part of what Goodman sees as "a growing imperative for successful businesspeople to join the party." A common generational pattern is that leading cadres are recruited on intellectual merit from the peasantry, then as they retire their children become businesspeople, "building on the local relationships and networks of influence that their parents have developed." Thus in China, "ownership, management and control are intertwined in ways that cut across previous analyses of middle (or indeed any other) class behaviour." All of China's classes are increasingly portrayed as middle. It's just that some are decidedly more middle than others.

How does this new middle class live? The astounding truth about who is buying what in China sank home to Briton Paul French when he realised that the staff in his Shanghai marketing company were all wearing security passes, although they did not need them to get into the office. One of his Chinese staff took French to a store that sells passes and lanyards for about 50 US cents each. Customers pick out the pass that they think will give them the most kudos – McKinsey, say, or Ernst & Young, both of which are on sale. One of French's colleagues was wearing a pass for the Royal Bank of Scotland, which had failed during the global financial crisis. "The security pass hung on a lanyard has become a symbol of the middle-class white-collar worker," French says. "If you're male and hope to be married, you need to wear one – because there aren't enough girls for everyone." As French observes, this story "shows how hungry people are to be middle class."

In the early days after China's opening up to the world thirty years ago, many Western companies rushed in but then crashed spectacularly, French says, in part because "their margins were terrible." Since then, they have been bolder about pushing up those margins. Today, the world's most expensive iPads are on sale in Shanghai, just thirty kilometres from where they are made. Nautica-brand clothing cost 20 per cent more in China than in the USA, but sales are still growing by 28 per cent per year.

A typical middle-class family earns between US$6000 and US$15,000 per year, French estimated in 2011 – "that's dad, mum, and the little emperor or empress. That covers 70 to 80 million households in China, roughly 240 million people, fairly concentrated in a few cities. They don't have anything to do except work, sleep and shop. They're mostly not involved in politics, don't go to church, don't volunteer."

Where do these families live? "Increasingly, not downtown," says French. The people downtown in Chinese cities today are Hong Kongers, Singaporeans, Taiwanese and other foreigners, daytrippers from other parts of China, or office workers on their lunch hours. "The middle class is living in giant new suburbs." Shanghai – already a city of 12 million people – is currently building nine satellite towns of a million residents each, all living in high-rise apartments. The typical family apartment is about seventy-five square metres. "For twenty-five years since the one-child policy, no one has built anything except two-bedroom flats."

Infrastructure in these suburbs is minimal, he says: "The government provides no community facilities except, if you're lucky, a school." Retailers are often required to turn their lights on, not off, when they lock up at night, "so that it looks as if it's a community where something is happening. In a one-party state, no one is sure how to develop original social infrastructure."

These satellite suburbs are often dominated by a single Western store. There are Tesco and Ikea towns, for example. "It's a day out, a shopping theme park. No one goes to the zoo or to a real theme park, because that costs money. If you go to Ikea, you can pretend to be Swedish for a day. It's massively appealing to the Chinese." But because the customers lack any do-it-yourself experience, most pay a premium to have Ikea staff come to their homes to assemble their purchases.

These are very much commuter towns, deserted during the working week. When a Marks & Spencer store, for instance, opens in a new Shanghai suburb, "500,000 people will go there over a weekend. But during the week, there's no business. You could close the store. There's just grandparents left there during the day, and they don't go to M & S."

Come the weekend, however, the white-collar middle classes "are desperate to be clad head to toe in M & S gear. And they serve M & S ready-meals of Sichuan chicken and egg fried rice at dinner parties, and let people see the packets."

The days of the luxury shopping mall, of marble palaces full of designer stores like Prada and Versace, "which look as if they were designed by the mistresses of the property developers," are numbered, French says. "Mostly, they're ghost malls." More typically these days, a developer looks for one key tenant like Ikea, Tesco or KFC: "No one lost money selling fried chicken to the Chinese." Then two 25-storey towers will be built on top. One tower might house apartments – trading on the prestige of the foreign retailer – and the other one of China's burgeoning budget hotel chains, where rooms can be hired for one, two or twenty-four hours. One such tower can be built for about US$42 million, around the cost of a middle-sized provincial store in Britain, French says. "And you get your money back in twelve months."

Some retailers have failed, however. American electronics firm Best Buy imported its sales model to China, employing its own staff and training them to answer questions and compare alternative products. In a typical Chinese electronics store, the sales staff are employed by the brands, not by the shopkeeper, and only demonstrate their own products. Customers do their research, mostly online, beforehand. "Chinese customers will not ask questions about the products in front of other people because it's a loss of face," says French. "So we get a girl from, say, the washing-machine maker, to dress in a Barbarella suit and list its features, and the customers will nod their heads as if they already knew." "Best Buy was too early" with its more educative approach, he says.

Consumers are obsessed by luxury brands, which are bought primarily to show that the purchaser has lots of money. But a backlash is already starting to develop against some of the biggest European brands, French says, because they are being sold in tier-two and -three cities, to people who aren't considered wealthy, and who may even be dismissed as "*tou baozi*," "potato dumplings" – that is, as peasants.

One ubiquitous product in Chinese middle-class homes is the Lock & Lock range of containers, imported from Korea. The firm went to immense lengths, French says, to develop a glue for the labels that is easy to rinse off. But the brand carries such status in China that people tape the labels on to keep them from coming off in the wash.

Some global brands are staying ahead by creating sub-brands designed specifically for the Chinese market. Villa & Hut Kafes have their "Shanghai chai." ("Nothing particularly Shanghai about it," says French, "but it'll do well, it implies respect.") Burberry has introduced "Dragon" and "Silk Road" lines. "They bling it right up and price it right up," says French, who organises "private VIP parties" where some of these products are sold. "You hire a night club, have some nice Russian or Ukrainian girls hand snacks around, offer some cheap fizzy wine, get a TV newsreader to host the evening, make the customers feel special, and they'll rush to buy the gear."

French sees the consumption phenomenon as "a great success story": "From famine to gluttony in two generations." A worker on average pay in Shanghai will have doubled her or his wealth in the last seven years, yet basic costs such as taxi fares have scarcely increased. (People working in failed factories, French says, have been given taxi licences by the city government.) Both travel and food are still highly subsidised, which helps the middle class to keep consuming. "It costs just cents to travel on the subway," while petrol subsidies ensure "you don't need to worry about filling up your SUV."

In the same period, the focus of middle-class aspirations has changed. Five to ten years ago, says French, "aspirational Chinese wanted to own factories. Now, with the government saying you can never fire anyone, and the price of commodities and energy and wages up, and the Americans saying they won't pay any higher [for manufactured goods], that's changed. There's too much capacity. That's killed entrepreneurship. Middle-class people just want to work in an office now. And the other billion are all wanting to become middle class too, and get their security passes and lanyards."

It is becoming very difficult to persuade people to work in factories, he says, even if they are paid up to three times as much as back-office clerical workers. "The chances of finding a desirable husband or wife are much greater in the office." As a result, he says there's a danger that unless the education system can change fundamentally to incorporate creativity, China may, like much of Latin America, find it difficult to move beyond the US$10,000 a year earnings barrier.

So much for the aspiring middle class – but what of the really rich? By the year 2006, China already had 800,000 millionaires (measured in US dollars) and 106 billionaires. Rupert Hoogewerf, the founder and chief executive of China's leading rich list, the Hurun Report, said at the time that besides gaining hugely in wealth, the super-rich were also gaining something new: respectability.

Hoogewerf, like French an Englishman living in Shanghai, has been measuring wealth in China since 1997. The cut-off point for his rich list in 2006 was assets of US$105 million. A third of those who made the list were Communist Party members, and the average age was forty-seven. Real estate was their most common core business. They mostly lived in coastal eastern China, with 150 based in the surging southern industrial province of Guangdong. Although only 8 per cent spoke English, many of their children were educated overseas, mostly in North America or Britain. About 10 per cent had become members of one of China's two representative bodies, the National People's Congress or the Chinese People's Political Consultative Conference. "They're the ultimate clubs in China," said Hoogewerf.

Most of the top hundred have stopped giving interviews, he said, because they prefer to keep a low profile. "But they still love the luxury industry, and the mistress market." One of the list members recently boasted to Hoogewerf that he was wearing a US$25,000 tie. "They show off – but typically, only within their own circles." Only 8 per cent were women, but these included some of the richest self-made women in the world – six of the top ten globally. And a woman, Zhang Yin, the "dragon queen of waste paper," topped the Chinese rich list in 2005. Men still tend to gravitate to stable careers, Hoogewerf said, while women were more likely to pursue creative, risk-taking paths. Only a dozen of the richest women had inherited wealth; "most of them were poor people twenty-five years ago."

The audacity of the rich continues to impress him. He told me of an entrepreneur who had just made a list, published early in the 2000s, of those worth more than US$10 million. When the US firm Enron collapsed, this millionaire flew straight to its headquarters in Houston and offered US$50 million for Enron's half of a power station in Chengdu. He succeeded, and then leveraged that investment into wealth of at least US$300 million.

Not everyone with money in China welcomes such interest in their lives and lifestyles. Hoogewerf admitted that "people used to say that our list was the 'death list,' and people were afraid of becoming famous for fear of being identified and charged ... in the Chinese saying, a pig is afraid of becoming fat." In 2001, the second and third placeholders on the list were arrested. "When people tracked back through their careers, they tended to discover what they called 'original sin'" – shortcuts to wealth, made early on, that might have been illegal.

When Hoogewerf first began compiling his lists, "the general opinion was that anybody with money was corrupt." The "five colours" theory then prevailed. Red was for wealth made through party connections, blue through customs and excise scams, green through the military, black through smuggling, and white through drugs or weapons. Since then, "there has been a sea change," he said. Now the rich are "viewed as heroes, especially by young people. They give talks at universities. Students aspire to follow in their footsteps." They are giving more of their money away, especially to educational and medical charities.

The rich remain vulnerable, however – especially if they do not join the party. In 2007 Huang Guangyu, then aged thirty-eight, was the wealthiest and best-known businessperson in China. The following year, he was forced to quit as chairman and director of the company he founded – China's first nationwide white-goods retailer, Gome (meaning "beautiful country" and pronounced "go-may"). He was subsequently jailed for illegal stock trading. Not long before his arrest, his wealth was estimated at US$9.3 billion.

In contrast, Zhang Jindong, the president of Suning, Gome's chief rival, was the ultimate insider. He was vice chairman of the All-China Federation of Industry and Commerce, an influential organisation affiliated with the party, and was a delegate to the Chinese People's Political Consultative Conference, which advises the government. At the time of Huang's arrest, Suning announced 200 new stores alongside its existing 850, while Gome, then with 1399 stores, was only planning fifty new premises.

The influence the party and its leaders continue to exercise, and the solidarity that they expect, extends even to how people dress. When Hu Jintao addressed leading cadres at the Central Party School in 2008, his speech was weighty but predictable. However, the occasion was truly revolutionary in another sense – the fashion statement Hu made.

China's leaders have traditionally led the way when it comes to national fashions. Sun Yat-sen, the founder of modern China, came up with the collarless jacket that Mao Zedong adapted and made his own.

But after the Cultural Revolution, this uniform, redolent of the hated Red Guards, was abandoned. Leaders began to wear Western suits, the cloth and cut of which climbed in quality as the Chinese economy soared.

But when Hu decided it was time for a new look, everyone else who counted, or wanted to count, swiftly followed suit – meaning, in this case, no suit. He addressed the party school wearing a white shirt with the top button undone, and casual trousers. And everyone else shown on the China Central TV footage of the event that night was dressed exactly the same.

Xinhua reported that Hu's dress-down example would enable people to relax and to save energy. It said the televised scene "struck viewers with a sense of closeness and warmth." Two days after the speech, members of the parliamentary Standing Committee decided they too should meet in shirt-sleeves, and should adjust the air conditioning in the Great Hall to 26 degrees Centigrade, which the State Council had declared the correct setting throughout China. Previously, the Great Hall was chilled down to 24 in summer. (Temperature is a matter of state in China. Mao's declaration that people living north of the Yangtze could heat their homes in winter, but that those to the south should be warm enough to make do, persists.)

Such a capacity to micro-manage even the clothes people wear, and the temperature inside people's homes, must be exercised with care as the population becomes wealthier. Few citizens, however, are prepared to take such dictates on. And for those with ambitions to reach the top, whether within the party or in business or both, following such edicts is all part of the path to success. The prize for correct performance throughout a career: a life lived behind a high wall, in a forbidding city of comrades.

CHAPTER 12: DISSENT AND REFORM

THE MOST FAMOUS THORN IN THE SIDE OF THE PARTY IS THE courtly, professorial Liu Xiaobo, who was seized from his modest Beijing apartment in 2008, held incommunicado for six months, mostly in a room without windows at a secret location, and then charged with "inciting subversion of state power." His chief crime appears to be that he was a leader in drafting and circulating "Charter 08," a social-democrat style manifesto calling for human rights, democracy, an end to the dominance of the Communist Party and its separation from the structures of government and the state. This latter idea was the crucial, unacceptable line which the signatories dared to cross. The original draft was signed by 303 people including retired party officials, former newspaper editors, lawyers, academics and artists, as well as some who described themselves as "peasants" and "workers." By the time it was excised by the net police, 10,000 people had signed their support.

A former philosophy professor at Beijing Normal University, Liu was jailed for twenty months in 1989 for joining a hunger strike in support of the democracy movement, and spent three years at a re-education camp from 1996 for questioning the party's sole governance of China.

The authorities were especially concerned about the charter because its supporters extended beyond the "usual suspects" of veteran dissidents, and because it generated nationwide interest without apparent detection until the last days before its publication on the sixtieth anniversary of the Universal Declaration of Human Rights. The manifesto took its name from Charter 77, a petition written in 1977 by Czech intellectuals and artists that contributed to the eventual undermining of the Soviet Empire in Eastern Europe. One of the drafters of that charter, Vaclav Havel, led the "Velvet Revolution" and became president of Czechoslovakia and then the Czech Republic for fourteen years (he would eventually become a great admirer of Liu's). Xinhua quoted police as saying that "Liu has been engaged in agitation activities, such as spreading of rumours and defaming of the government, aimed at subversion of the state and overthrowing the socialist system."

Liu was jailed for eleven years and his wife, Liu Xia, an artist and poet, remains under house arrest. When I interviewed Liu not long before his arrest, he appeared the epitome of the classic Chinese scholar: a spare man in spectacles, with a worldview both wryly fatalistic and surprisingly optimistic. Entering a traditional Beijing tea-house near his home, he looked around, checking for paid listeners. He insisted that he had no personal enemies in the Chinese establishment, and that he was prepared for a return to jail. Although he had been advised by the authorities to take up work overseas and not return, he said, "This is my country."

He answered a call on his mobile phone from his wife, who was wondering where he was; he assured her he was meeting friends, and that she was not to worry. Later, she tells me, "All he has is a pen and some paper." And, occasionally, access to the internet, the only place where he was able to publish his writings before his 2009 jailing – although even then, publication was often followed by a visit from the police and the swift removals of his posts. He is not a member or organiser of any group or party, except for Charter 08.

Nor, technically, is Liu even a dissident. In 2010 a Foreign Ministry spokesman, Ma Zhaoxu, declared that China has no dissidents. The celebrated artist Ai Weiwei, son of one of China's best regarded poets of the twentieth century, Ai Qing, responded with a droll tweet: "Dissidents are criminals. Only criminals have dissident ideas. The distinction between criminals and non-criminals is whether they have dissident views. If you think China has dissidents, you're a criminal. The reason China has no dissidents is because they have already become criminals. Does anyone have a dissenting view about all that I've said?"

The party may parade its determination to silence its critics, Liu told me, but its control is decreasing. "It has lost its capacity to persuade people through its ideology. In Mao's time, one sentence, or one decision, from him, and all the country would know it. But now people don't believe in their ideology. No one can be persuaded to learn this or that communist dogma. And in Mao's day, all the rice bowls were distributed by the party. Today, even if I am not inside that party-state system, I can still make a living via other economic channels."

After our long talk over tea, Liu and I walked together. He appeared reluctant to say farewell and kept up his commentary until a taxi stopped. Then he smiled and gave a little wave and said, "No matter how rich a society is, as long as it is ruled by a privileged class which gains its wealth from an unbalanced and opaque system, there will be strong discontent. And any defence of this group's economic interests will evolve into a defence of its political rights."

When the party-state arrested and jailed Liu, it proved too late to contain his fame or his ideas. And Liu, as the party discovered, is not alone. There are many other thinkers in China who are strongly critical of how the country is run. Many, probably most, of them are highly individualistic, not disposed to join causes or groups, and lack outlets within their own country through which to express their views. They may not be prospering in this Age of Prosperity, but they survive, and they stay where they are.

Zhang Yaojie, who teaches at China Arts Academy, arrives at the Holiday Inn in west Beijing – where a coffee shop is set against a giant indoor waterfall – wearing a blue sweatshirt. He has a crewcut, and gazes intensely through gold-rimmed, oblong glasses. He can publish his commentaries on China in academic journals, but not in the mass media.

He says, "We should admit that most people can have a modestly good life in China today. But if you do something regarded as wrong by the party, your rights can't be guaranteed. Your rights can be invaded by the party. Your house can be demolished and your land confiscated, or traded in the stock market by more powerful people. No one will help you. Day by day some people lose their rights. And anybody is vulnerable, even people like [former party luminaries] Hu Yaobang or Liu Shaoqi."

He traces this tendency back to the party's roots. "To beat down the landlord and distribute land is the slogan of any uprising of peasants in Chinese history, aiming 'to take over the earth under the sky,'" he says. "It's not a uniquely communist slogan. In most cases where they succeeded, they beat down the old landlords and made themselves the new ones."

Such communism is not something imported from Russia, he says; it always existed in Chinese history. "In China we never really had private ownership. Possessions were always in theory in the hands of the emperors. So the CCP is a culmination of Chinese history and tradition, which never gave us law or real democracy or private ownership. And the CCP will survive, in part because most intellectuals always speak to and for the insiders, not those who are outside. They will speak up for the party as long as they're given a house and job by the party to do so." Party cadres ask him why he writes contentious articles using his real name. "I answer that to publish otherwise indicates that not telling the truth is accepted. This is one of the country's problems – that everybody is trained not to tell the truth. Everybody is telling lies, they trick themselves and others."

Most people are not especially courageous, Zhang concedes. "My grandfather didn't stand up before he starved during the Great Leap Forward" under Mao. "And I never had enough food before I was eighteen. Hunger pressed the truth out of me." There is a phenomenon in China, he says, whereby "the less you believe something, the stronger you advocate it. You think that just speaking of it will bring benefits. It rules out mistakes. Fake words become a form of exchange for profit."

Professor Wang Binglin, the deputy party secretary at Beijing Normal University, is the yin to Zhang's yang. He is both a realist and an idealist, like Zhang – but comes down on the other side, on that of the party's continued benign rule. Wang views the CCP's key ideological task as "to absorb different streams of thinking and unite them. It's difficult, but the party must do it. And new ideas are being developed because conditions are changing. China is so large a country, so divided in many ways, that we need united thinking." In this view, the party does not so much generate ideology as co-opt and conflate new values as they emerge. This makes it hard either to pin down or to oppose the party's own ideology – or to become especially enthused about it.

Over time, Wang says, the party has sought to broaden its base. Under Mao and Deng, farmers were crucial. The "Three Represents" of Jiang Zemin, the party's general secretary from 1989 to 2002, emphasised the role of intellectuals and called on the party to "absorb advanced and outstanding members from the new classes." Hu Jintao's emphasis on "harmony" and scientific development also included a broadening of the party base. But incorporating all these different interests, Wang says, is becoming harder and harder to coordinate.

To what extent is democracy one of the new ideas being embraced by the party? Wang says: "We are persisting with the experiment of village-level elections – in some areas it's been successful, in others not. There is as yet no plan to take direct election to a higher level. For instance, the heads of the town and county are still being elected indirectly by representatives, not directly. Historically, China was a feudal system and power was won through struggle, often a bloody one. As we emerge as a modern society, the elements of democracy are becoming stronger and stronger.

"Now the party system is such that one party is in power with the assistance and involvement of other parties" that have token representation in the National People's Congress, but under the supervision of the CCP. "That means the transition of power can be realised smoothly, through peaceful consultation," if it is ultimately conceded, says Wang. By having a single party in power, however, he says that China can more easily avoid the detrimental impact of power struggle, because transition of leadership happens within the party. "If we have a two or three party system, the transition might degenerate into struggle."

Professor Anne-Marie Brady, an associate professor in political science at the University of Canterbury in New Zealand, says that in China "there is an internal longing for harmony and happiness that lies deeper than ordinary fear or the desire to escape misery or physical destruction … [although] many outside commentators still assume China's current one-party political system relies on force to stay in power."

And Arthur Kroeber, a leading analyst based in Beijing, points out that "Western critics tend to assume that political legitimacy can only be conferred by elections." But in China, a regime's legitimacy comes substantially from its capacity to mobilise the country's bureaucratic tradition, he says. "The system's ability to respond to a wide range of problems, to maintain social order, to provide a steadily increasing level of public services, and to increase China's standing in the world, are all important contributors to legitimacy." Democracy naturally intrigues Chinese people, but has not become a core demand, with many giving a higher priority to another remote ideal – a rule of law independent of the party.

China's history has been one of frequent conflict and mistrust between emperors and their bureaucracies. They have also often acted as a balancing influence on one another. Today, however, without an emperor – even a Mao or a Deng – the party bureaucracy has little to constrain it, and powerful rent-seekers inside the system, such as state-owned enterprises, often enjoy free run. Xu Youyou, a researcher with the Chinese Academy of Social Science, says, "China is in a great transitional period. Some people are benefiting greatly, some losing ground. And it is the beneficiaries who are most strongly supporting the government."

There have been tentative moves towards reform, even from within the party. Those with the most to gain from the current system have the most to lose from its collapse, and so cannot afford to ignore calls for change altogether. The party has permitted various experiments in elective democracy and judicial independence, but these have largely been restricted to second-tier "intra-party" arenas. Early in 2012, the party opened itself to a limited debate about the country's economic direction. The chief underlying question was whether to focus on maintaining a stable and unchanging political and social structure, or to introduce reforms beyond the economic opening of the previous thirty years.

Any further steps towards modernisation are likely to come from within the party, rather than from outside models or advice. As Carl Walter and Fraser Howie write in their definitive 2011 book *Red Capitalism*, "party leaders believe they are better positioned than any market to value and price risk."

The Soviet Union is often held up as an example of the risks involved in allowing too little, or too much, reform. *People's Daily* published a commentary attributing the collapse of the Soviet Union to "its failure to carry out real reform" of its economy. It said China's stability had followed from Deng's economic reforms thirty years earlier. "The reform in China has cost, but it pays more," it said.

What degree of reform can the party safely allow in this new era? In his speech to the National Party Congress in 2007, Hu Jintao used the terms "democracy" sixty-one times, "socialism with Chinese characteristics" fifty-two times, "scientific development" thirty-eight times, "opening up and reform" thirty-four times, and "social harmony" thirty-three times. Five years later, in 2012, he reiterated that it was necessary to meet "the growing spiritual and cultural demands of the people."

Shortly before the 2007 congress, a collection of essays was published with the dramatic title *Storming the Fortress: A research report on China's political system reform*. Five of the authors were from the Central Party School and the vice president of the school, Li Junru, wrote the introduction. The fortress in question was not the party itself, but the administrative impediments to progress. The 366-page paperback book was published by the comparatively obscure Xinjiang Production and Construction Corps Press, indicating that although its authors were insiders, their argument was not yet being officially endorsed by the party. But it was announced that the book had been circulated to the top leaders, indicating the prospect at least that they would engage with the issues.

Storming the Fortress spoke of building a democratic, law-based modern state. It said that political reform "is essential for the long-term stability of the party and the country." It advocated moving towards the separation of powers – a huge shift in a country where all legal and political levers are ultimately pulled by the party's top leaders. Among the ideas canvassed in the book were whether China should consider "radical views" such as the introduction of general elections, of a multi-party system, of freedom of the media, and of "nationalising" the People's Liberation Army – placing it at the disposal of the nation rather than of the party.

The writers themselves recommended "intra-party democracy" of the sort Hu had promoted – encouraging more competition for positions inside the party – as well as a government focused more on service, with transparent budgetary and taxation systems. The priority, they said, echoing Deng's drive of thirty years earlier, was to reform political mechanisms that were hindering economic development, and thus to confirm the people's trust in the party.

They advocated giving the National People's Congress the greater powers the national constitution provides for, but which have remained circumscribed by the party, and reducing the number of delegates from 3000 to about 450. They wished to extend the supervisory role of the Chinese People's Political and Consultative Conference, which in theory represents diverse groups in the community. They advocated a media law to clarify the limits of party and government control. Perhaps most radically, they suggested that party and government leaders should not interfere in judges' verdicts, and that chief prosecutors be elected by People's Congresses, while the right of party committees to dismiss them should be withdrawn.

Crucially, the book insisted on the continued supremacy of the party, with parliamentary committees reporting to the relevant party committees. Change must be steady, it said, to avoid the risk of a popular "explosion" – referring to the events leading to the fall of the Iron Curtain in 1990 – as the market system continues to mature.

Five years on, virtually none of this program had been taken up, or even seriously discussed in public. Indeed, Liu Xiaobo had been jailed for state subversion for merely circulating such ideas.

There have been democratic experiments in China before, but the ruling party has always reasserted its authority. In 1911, during the Republic of China, the KMT stepped in after villages and towns organised their own elections. It might choose to let local areas nominate their own representatives, it decreed, but such processes would remain at its discretion. Although the Republic eventually began to hold national elections on the mainland – the last, in 1948, shortly before China fell to Mao's communists the following year – it was too late for democracy to take root. One of Mao's most effective moves was to remove "landlords," who were often the village leaders, and hand some sovereignty back to local "peasants" – but only provisionally. Power remained essentially his, and the party's, to give and take.

It is now over a century since Puyi, the last emperor, was removed from the throne. Claims that China cannot be expected to take significant steps towards liberal democracy because Western countries took much longer to modernise are not entirely convincing. Britain, for instance, went further and faster down the reform path in 100 years, especially during its century of industrialisation, than China has in the same timespan.

In China, progress is held back by the faith of party leaders that all sovereignty must stay under their control. It is not just that the party is safeguarding China, but that it believes it *is*, in an almost mystical sense, China. Necessity may sometimes prompt the party to consider reform, but the end is always to strengthen and maintain its grip on power. The result is a political culture that leading American sinologist Andrew Nathan has called "resilient authoritarianism," and party expert David Shambaugh has described as a mixture of "atrophy and adaptation."

One such move to retain control through adaptation took place in 2006, when then Premier Wen, in his annual state-of-the-nation address to the National People's Congress, announced a massive redirection of the government's resources to the countryside and the rustbelts, especially in the industrial north-east, in an effort to stall growing unrest among farmers and displaced workers. Their frustration at feeling locked out of the country's growing wealth had triggered 87,000 protests and demonstrations in 2005, according to official figures. Wen claimed this shift as "a new historical starting point" for China.

Premier Wen peppered his speech, which also launched the government's eleventh five-year plan, with the phrase "building a new socialist countryside." He vowed that the leadership would turn its full attention to the pressing plight of farmers, the urban poor and displaced workers. The agricultural tax, levied by Chinese governments for 2600 years and based on the size of the taxpayer's family and its farm, would be rescinded.

Without on-the-ground support for change, however, achieving this shift would be difficult. Zhang Ming, a rural expert at the People's University in Beijing, says, "Local officials are now like a bunch of wolves circling a hunk of meat. You can't expect them to act for the farmers' benefit." Xu Yong, the director of the Centre for Chinese Rural Studies in Wuhan, agrees: "The current institutional arrangements were designed to take money from farmers. They're not efficient at transferring money to them or providing services."

At the NPC in March 2012, in a dramatic farewell address after ten years as premier, Wen warned of the pressing need for further reform. He raised the spectre that "such an historical tragedy as the Cultural Revolution may happen again" unless appropriate reforms were implemented. "Without successful political structural reform, it is impossible for us to fully institute economic structural reform and the gains we have made in this area may be lost," he said.

The party and country are now being guided by Xi Jinping, who is inevitably considering whether to continue this pursuit of social and political reform, or to let it slip quietly away and find a new ideological focus. The interim goal, during the leadership transition and probably beyond, one that especially suits party conservatives and nationalists, is *wen wei*: to maintain stability.

CHAPTER 13:

IS THE FUTURE THEIRS?

"One aspect of a country's greatness is surely its capacity to attract and retain the attention of others. This capacity has been evident from the very beginnings of the West's encounter with China."

—JONATHAN SPENCE

MEET A TYPICAL MODERN CHINESE COUPLE.
Fang Hui has given birth to her first child. She has flown with her husband Zhang Yupeng – they are both aged thirty-four – back to her home in Ningxia, where she comes from a Muslim family, for the event.

They met and live in Shenzhen, the city bordering Hong Kong that Deng Xiaoping founded in 1980, when it was a mere fishing village.

Fang and Zhang are typical Shenzheners. They shifted there from northern China, they met there, they're not sure they want to stay there … but they will. Nowhere else offers them the same opportunities.

Zhang, aged thirty-four, a fitness trainer, arrived there a dozen years ago with US$650 in his pocket. He spent three months finding his first job, using up all his savings. He and Fang, an aerobics instructor, met in the gym where they each finally found work. Together, they saved US$35,000 towards starting a gym of their own.

"When I was a boy at school," says Zhang, "I had a dream of starting a business of my own. People here in Shenzhen, especially, share such dreams." They ended up borrowing a further $50,000 from relatives and friends because "no bank will give credit to people like us in China. It's almost impossible for individuals to apply for loans."

For the first few years the gym just broke even. The couple lived on Fang's commissions from online marketing for an American company that makes cosmetics in nearby Zhuhai. They also made a small profit from selling clothes. They were in debt to their landlord for some time.

"We were under big pressure," says Zhang. "We were trapped in debt and had to fight our way out. Like being pushed onto a battlefield, or at a casino, you have one last dice to throw, you have to roll it and back your good luck."

And a couple of years later, sure enough, the business turned around. They now employ thirty part-time and full-time staff.

"It's a new thing, going to a gym," says Fang. "Our parents' generation would not have imagined paying money to exercise. But income levels can now support it. People are influenced by Western and Hong Kong lifestyles, they are in a new city, they are fighting for a new life, they know they need to stay fit."

Zhang is becoming a well-known figure in the neighbourhood. He appears often on TV, as a strong man on games shows, and in a series of adverts against beating children. Their mothers are vying to be invited to live with the family and supervise the *aiyi*, the maid who will be employed full-time to look after the baby, as is usual in middle-class Chinese families.

"We have been ready for whatever happens," says Fang. "You create your own job, try to avoid failure and seek success." The American formula.

Fang still doesn't like the humid climate of Shenzhen, and living costs are high. "It does have a civilisation, but it's a modern one. You don't feel grounded here. You're still skimming on the water's surface."

This is a common feeling among the emerging generation in China today. This sensation of skimming – of having material goals but uncertain values and only a vague cultural awareness – is especially disorienting because it comes within the oldest continuous civilisation in the world. China is a country with a single political party, a single written language, a dominant Han culture, a state-controlled media that mostly speaks with one voice on the big issues that matter. But it is also a society of individuals, and strikingly so. No matter what you say about China, the opposite is likely to be equally true somewhere else.

This future as a place to seize opportunities, to raise families, to get ahead – but also to build a better quality of life – is what has attracted people like Zhang Yupeng and Fang Hui to move so far and create a new home. This is the new China that is being hailed – as much from outside as from within – as an emerging global model, the way the world will become in the twenty-first century.

A McKinsey report says that in 2025, China will have 221 million cities of more than 1 million people. Europe has thirty-five today. China's cities will by then have 50,000 skyscrapers, 170 mass-transit systems, 5 billion square metres of paved road, and overall 1 billion residents. Their average income will be about US$10,000 a year, double what it was in 2012. But what will life be like in those cities? Will the air be breathable, the water drinkable? What values will their inhabitants hold dear? What will they be learning? What will their attitudes be to their neighbours, both near and far? How much control will they have over their own and their families' futures? And will we all, then, end up living in a version of this Chinese world? Is gravity somehow pulling the world its way?

As Jonathan Spence, the dean of contemporary China historians, points out in *The Chan's Great Continent: China in Western Minds*, the fascination is not new. Marco Polo's modestly titled *The Description of the World* was the publishing sensation of its day 700 years ago, and waves of awed accounts of life in China have followed regularly since. The completeness and confidence of China's traditional culture, the magnetism of its aesthetic, the unbroken span of its civilisation until its mostly catastrophic twentieth century, not to mention China's size and population, command the attention of any educated person.

Faced with such a vast nation, and such an epic history, generalisations are not only inevitable, but they can even be right. The written language from centuries ago remains comprehensible to virtually all Chinese. There are remarkable threads of continuity. At the same time, people in China speak many dialects, some mutually incomprehensible. This is a country with a vast range of cuisines; the food in the north is wheat-based, in the south rice-based; some is incredibly spicy, some comparatively bland. Its wealth gap is far greater than the USA's – the wealthiest 10 per cent earn on average fifty-five times the poorest 10 per cent, and most of that wealth comes from the "grey economy": perks, side-deals, rent-seeking on a vast scale. Shanghai, an icon of early twentieth-century cosmopolitan chic, is today an icon of early 21st-century cosmopolitan chic, while in Western China people scrape a living with wooden tools, sleeping in bare houses with earthen floors. Almost half of Chinese people say they cannot afford a visit to the doctor. Look on this China as a continent of many countries. Think, say, Europe, east and west. What is true about Sweden is probably not also true of Rumania. Sichuan, the mountainous province with the peppery diet and the pandas, has a population of 5 million more than Germany, the biggest country in Europe.

Its critics can seem small from this perspective. Xinhua ran an article responding to Western critics of the country's role in the 2009 Copenhagen climate-change conference under the headline: "Verdant mountains cannot stop water flowing; eastward the water keeps on going." Just as the rivers that flow east across China's plains from the Himalayas are unblockable, so the world's attention, its power and its wealth, will keep shifting eastward too.

Two Americans, John and Doris Naisbitt, are preaching the strength of the China Model in the West. They have found considerable success through their series of "Megatrend" books, highlighting China's success and its promise. They write, "China is creating an entirely new social and economic system. It is creating a political counter model to western modern democracy fitting to Chinese history and society, just as America created a model fitting to its history, society and values more than 200 years ago. Economically and politically, China has left the path of imitation, determined to become the innovation country of the world. In the next decades China will not only change the global economy, it will challenge Western democracy with its own model."

This sense of inevitability about China's brisk march is not new. The Naisbitts are modern variants on a theme that reached an earlier apogee just when China was at its cruellest, lowest ebb. The American Maoist Scott Nearing wrote admiringly during the Cultural Revolution of China's "attempt to lift the entire human race to a higher plane of social consciousness and take a long step towards the brotherhood of all mankind." Another admirer of Mao, Arthur Galston, said that "no one seems to have to tell anyone else what to do in this harmonious world." The Australian Labor Party minister Tom Uren said during this era, "China has undertaken a process in which material incentives are being steadily abandoned in favour of moral incentives. The people do not work for material gain for themselves or out of insecurity. I have observed at first hand many examples of the Chinese people taking joy in their work for the benefit of the whole society. The thoughts of Mao … will be a guide to the future shaping of all human society."

The great sinologist, art historian, diplomat and writer Pierre Ryckmans – originally from Belgium, eventually moving to Australia – writing as Simon Leys, was scathing about such propagators of the China model in his influential book *Chinese Shadows* (first published in French in 1974). He wrote, "Western ideologues now use Maoist China just as the eighteenth-century philosophers used Confucian China: as a myth, an abstract ideal projection, a utopia which allows them to denounce everything that is bad in the West without taking the trouble to think for themselves. We stifle in the miasma of industrial civilisation, our cities rot, our roads are blocked by the insane proliferation of cars, et cetera. So they hurry to celebrate the People's Republic, where pollution, delinquency, and traffic problems are non-existent. One might as well praise an amputee because his feet aren't dirty."

He argued that "the Maoist fashions that prevail in the West today in some intellectual circles are remarkably similar in their dynamic to the passion for all chinoiserie in the eighteenth century. It is a new exoticism based, like the earlier ones, on ignorance and imagination. With the best intention in the world it shows, unconsciously, an immense contempt for the Chinese, for their humanity, their real life, their language, their culture, their past and their present."

Mao has now gone, for the most part. The model has changed. The China that the world encounters today is thoroughly internationally engaged. It is, especially in its grasp of changing technologies, a modern – some would say *the* modern – society. And yet its core institutions, as we have seen, have scarcely changed since 1949, while the rest of the East Asian neighbourhood has changed in so many respects.

This China – strikingly successful in bringing large numbers of people out of poverty, while the elite and their families retain control – offers a seductive model that is being eagerly taken up by the leaders of countries that have not yet settled into democratic structures: Vietnam, Laos, even to a tiny degree the hereditary cult that is North Korea; the Central Asian dictatorships; a growing part of the Middle East starting with the Gulf; Cuba; much of Africa. Myanmar has begun to shift, however, towards a more liberal-democratic path. Beijing sometimes gives more than it receives to cement its developing world leadership, for instance by according most-favoured-nation status to Vietnam, Laos and Cambodia before they even join the World Trade Organization. The Chinese model is awkwardly attractive to the leaders of some countries that had already become democratic, such as Venezuela. It is inspiring India to compete with its own adaptive path towards rapid development, one that depends on increased domestic rather than international inputs.

The model is praised in the West, too, especially by business leaders, for instance at Forbes 500 conferences and the World Economic Forum, which has instituted an annual summer session in China. Such praise provides great reinforcement for Chinese leaders. The World Bank is just one of the international institutions that champion China – its greatest client and success story – as a model. Perhaps most interesting is the appeal of the model to Russia, which as Azar Gat, professor of national security at Tel Aviv University, writes in *Foreign Affairs*, "is retreating from its post-communist liberalism and assuming an increasingly authoritarian character as its economic clout grows."

Randall Peerenboom, in his 2007 book *China Modernizes: Threat to the West or Model for the Rest?*, catalogues the "ample evidence" that "other countries are looking to China for inspiration." They are attracted by China's pragmatic approach to reform. The official newspaper *China Daily* hosted an online discussion of the topic "China is a role model to all developing nations. After centuries of oppression and domination by Western nations, most developing nations are trying to pull themselves up from poverty. They look at China's rapid progress as an example. China also gives aid and technical help to these nations." Unsurprisingly, it attracted a torrent of supportive responses, such as "China has shown that you can be successful by expanding through commerce and diplomacy, not by the imperialism demonstrated by the US and UK," and "China as a role model focuses more on business development."

Many formerly believed that the USA was destined to be the prime beneficiary not only of the "end of history" following the collapse of the Soviet Union, but of economic globalisation. Now China, too, is sharing in those benefits – perhaps leading the way – as the new engine-room of global growth. Once, many commentators anticipated that as China grew wealthier and more enmeshed with the global economy, it would not only become, in the words of former World Bank president Robert Zoellick, a "responsible stakeholder" in the international system, but would also become more politically "normal" in a Western sense.

But China is demonstrating that it can dictate the terms by which it engages with the world. This may have been true for some time, but it is only since it surged ahead through the economic crisis – that is, the American-European downturn, not strictly a global event – that it has realised it has this capacity, and has started to act on it.

For instance, the deal eventually cobbled together at the 2009 Copenhagen climate summit, although dismissed by disappointed critics in Europe, was essentially forged by Barack Obama and Wen Jiabao, representing the two biggest greenhouse-gas emitters. Premier Wen led a powerful group of four that included India, Brazil and South Africa. (As Obama walked into the room where the deal was done, he called out to the Chinese leader, who was already sitting at the table with India's prime minister, Manmohan Singh, and Brazil's president, Lula da Silva, "Mr Premier, are you ready to see me?")

Another example was the 2010 meeting of the World Economic Forum in Davos, Switzerland. These days the organisers of such events are eager to attract prominent Chinese participants. And increasingly, they turn up – but on their own terms. In this case, it was then vice premier – now premier – Li Keqiang. The chief executive of Deutsche Bank, Josef Ackermann, a co-chairman at Davos, revealed in an interview with Bloomberg after the event that "China didn't want to discuss Google." Google had caused a furore with its threat to quit China over censorship and cyber-warfare. To oblige, the issue was promptly taken off the agenda at Davos, where business leaders explained that Li had told them during a private session that they – and by implication Google too, of course – had to follow China's rules. "People have their commercial interests," said Ackermann bluntly. Among those who accepted the need to remove the Google issue from discussion was Eckhard Cordes, the chief executive of Metro, Germany's largest retailer, which has a growing presence in China. He told journalists at Davos, "From a business perspective, China is doing well, and at this point of time here, I should refrain from making political comments."

The West has long been aware, and wary, of China's potential economic clout. Robert Kapp, a historian and former president of the US-China Business Council, has written, "Has the West been waiting for China to 'get back' at 'us' for a century and a half, in ways that somehow make it easier to diagnose today's Chinese demeanour in those terms? Are we somehow now 'getting' what we have been 'waiting for'?" He notes that as early as 1911, the American sociologist Edward Ross said, "Jealousy of the foreigner, dearth of capital, ignorant labour, official squeeze, graft, nepotism, lack of experts, and inefficient management will long delay the harnessing of the cheap labour power of China to the machine. Not we, nor our children, but our grandchildren will need to lie awake nights ..." when China's "economic competition will begin to mould with giant hands the politics of the planet."

This capacity to mould international politics was demonstrated in 2012, when Beijing persuaded Cambodia, the chair of the 2012 ASEAN summit, to block a proposed move to pursue a multilateral agreement on oil and gas in the South China Sea. The USA, as well as China's chief rivals for these resources, especially Vietnam and the Philippines, were lobbying for such an agreement. The dispute prevented the summit from issuing a concluding statement, the first time ASEAN had failed to do so in its forty-year history.

The conventions of international diplomacy tend to suit the party: long negotiations, slow consensus-building, fluid alliances rather than clear-cut factions. The inclination of the Chinese leadership is to postpone awkward decisions at home, and it would prefer to do the same in the international arena: keep everyone talking for as long as possible, avoiding any radical action that might alienate one side or the other. This is Beijing's preferred approach to a host of issues: North Korea, Iran, adjusting the Chinese currency. China's new status as a global player, however, exposes it to pressure to act more decisively. China's leadership worries that because the country's development remains a work in progress, and because its own legitimacy is fragile, becoming a global "model" exposes it to awkward scrutiny. Wen Jiabao thus explicitly ruled out any desire to export the "China model."

Wang Yuzhu, the director of regional cooperation at the Chinese Academy of Social Sciences in Beijing, told me that far from being the new master of the universe, China is both misunderstood by other nations and misunderstands them. It is burdened by nationalism and needs space and time to become a team player. He views the South China Sea issue as "very, very important," not so much because of the sea's economic or military value, but because if handled correctly, it will demonstrate China's capacity to maintain good relations with ASEAN countries. "The real challenge aroused by the South China Sea controversy is not to China's claim to territory but to its development of good relations with its neighbours and the wider world."

This goes to the heart of China's foreign policy, he says. China may now be the second biggest economy in the world in annual output, having overtaken Japan in 2011. But it remains a developing country. And the party's legitimacy continues to rest on economic growth – which in turn requires a stable, cooperative global framework. "To tackle our internal problems such as the uneven distribution of wealth, and corruption, step by step, we need stable international relations," says Wang. He is concerned by the rise of Chinese nationalism, and fears what might happen if this spirit infects China's foreign policy. "Are we really so strong? ... Do we really want to try and conquer the world? First we should look at the US, and see the tears that its overseas wars have brought it, its economic crisis, too." This call for a more modest economic and diplomatic strategy recalls Deng Xiaoping's advice: "Maintain a low profile, keep a cool head and never take the lead."

At home, overreaching can be similarly dangerous. The cost of renovating Beijing for the 2008 Olympics was a heavy one. The city's "conservation plan for twenty-five historic areas" meant, essentially, knocking the buildings down, removing the occupants to more remote parts of the city, and creating in a couple of neighbourhoods an ersatz version of Olde Worlde Beijing, designed to attract retailers. The plan was announced in 2002 by the city government, without prior public consultation.

The most controversial of the conservation areas was Qianmen (or "front gate"), the ancient trading, artistic and hospitality heart of Beijing, whose history dates back 600 years through the Qing and Ming dynasties. Qianmen is the district immediately south of Tiananmen Square, just outside the massive walls that protected the Forbidden City and its surrounding imperial zone. The emperors paraded down the "heavenly route" through Qianmen to make their annual sacrifice for good harvests and prosperity at Tian Tan, the Temple of Heaven. Sitting astride Beijing's north-south axis, the district was unique for its curved *hutongs* – four-sided courtyard homes surrounded by alleys. They were arranged in curves because a river ran through Qianmen, from which fresh fish were once caught and sold on the banks. The oldest and most famous shopping street in Beijing, Dazhalan, was here. Beijing Opera, Chinese acrobatics and Peking duck emerged from these alleyways.

The area used to contain famous "guild halls" run by China's many provinces, where visitors from the regions – perhaps coming to sit the famous exams, or to bring petitions to the government – could stay while visiting the capital. Most of these buildings were demolished. One has been "restored" as a poorly built modern copy. In the "protected" areas all buildings were razed, except for those rated "grade one" or "grade two" for exceptional historic significance. These could still be demolished if the district government assessed them as lacking the strength to survive. Leaking roofs and cracks in walls were enough to condemn them.

Compensation was set at US$1250 per square metre, about half the market value. Once residents had signed to accept this payment, they had to move out within three days. He Fengnian, then aged fifty-six, had lived in the area since 1959. With his wife and adult son he was living on a US$200 a month pension, having retired from an engine manufacturer when it went bankrupt. Their home was tiny and shabby, just eight square metres. Although the compensation payment would contribute towards a flat elsewhere, He would have to pay the rest – about US$20,000, which he did not have and had no hope of raising. "Why do they want to pull down our houses?" he asked. "So they can make money out of the demolition and reconstruction. Will they demolish our home by force? Who knows, the party will do whatever it wants."

The developer, Soho, was founded and is run by a fashionable married couple, Pan Shiyi and Zhang Xin, rich-list regulars frequently profiled in international lifestyle magazines. Their signature projects, with integrated high-end flats and expensive restaurants, are tall and glossy, with sleek lines enlivened by metallic and neon effects. There could be few greater contrasts than between the lifestyle of Pan and Zhang and that of the He family.

Sui Zhenjiang, director of the Beijing Municipal Construction Committee, said that the relocated people "can now enjoy the advantages of modernisation." He said, "The commercial value of the land is not very high." Most relocated residents could look forward to improved living standards. But they were losing their community. Many worked in the city but could only afford to move to remote high-rise suburbs, requiring a costly and time-consuming commute. A placard erected in Qianmen read, as the razing of the area reached its peak: "We will continue to oppose the people who come to *chai* (demolish) until the last day."

A neighbourhood can be demolished and rebuilt in today's China. For individuals, a fresh start is not so easy. China is mostly free of ugly graffiti. But walls all over the country are daubed with mobile phone numbers. Drug dealers? Prostitutes? No. In almost every case, they are offering the documentation people need to survive, transition or even thrive in this challenging new world.

Amongst the forged documents for sale are *hukous*, the papers that allow people to live in particular places. A Chinese friend, for instance, was brought up in a city several hours' flight away from Beijing, where he now lives. Although he arrived in the capital fifteen years ago and has held good jobs since, he has not been able to obtain a *hukou*. He says that if he had worked for a state-owned company or a foreign company with a big investment in China, he might have been able to claim a *hukou*. Without one, if he wants to leave China, even on a business trip, he has to fly back to his hometown to obtain approval, a process which could take many days. If he and his girlfriend were to have a child, they would have to pay several thousand US dollars every year to send the child to a normal state school, because they don't have a *hukou*.

The anonymous forgers also sell passports, foreign visas and educational qualifications, probably the hottest selling item. Why don't the police close them down? Simply, it seems, because the police have other priorities and the forgers are too fast-moving (they can of course reinvent themselves swiftly).

Sometimes, of course, China's seemingly relentless march towards modernity and global domination is derailed. In July 2011, two of China's much-vaunted new high-speed trains crashed on a viaduct in the suburbs of Wenzhou, killing forty and injuring 192. The railways minister, Liu Zhijun, had been sacked a few months earlier over corruption claims. China's state auditor reported that corrupt building companies and officials had received US$27 million from construction of the US$30 billion Beijing to Shanghai rail link. This crash halted the country's ambitious strategy to market its system internationally and to become the world's leading provider of high-speed rail systems.

Three weeks before the crash, a spokesman for the railways ministry had claimed that China's new high-speed system was so superior to Japan's that the two "cannot be mentioned in the same breath." After the collision, Japan Rail stressed that its bullet trains had never had an accident and stepped up its bid to develop a high-speed rail service in

Thailand between Bangkok, Chiang Mai and Rangoon, a route that China had expected to build and operate.

Just as China's trains have been forced to slow down, so have scandals such as the Bo Xilai affair forced the new leadership team to focus on steadying and consolidating, rather than experimenting.

These days the party is not elevating reformers into leading positions anyway; its priorities are consensus and continuity, goals best suited for committee-men. An editorial in the *Economist* in May 2012 compared the two personalities who had attracted most interest in China that year – Bo Xilai and the blind human rights lawyer Chen Guangcheng. The editorial observed, "Inherent tensions are starting to throw the inevitability of China's rise into question. For all their success in building an increasingly modern country, China's leaders have no broader vision for what they want their country and its people to be. It is no small irony that, when it comes to defining a society in which the government obeys the laws and individuals' lives are to be respected, it is the blind man who has the clearest vision."

A widely repeated anecdote from an earlier era has Mao's urbane premier, Zhou Enlai, responding to a question during a visit in 1971 by US Secretary of State Henry Kissinger. Asked what he thought of the French Revolution, Zho replied, "It's too soon to tell," demonstrating the awesomely long-term nature of Chinese thinking.

Unfortunately, the evidence indicates that this story is apocryphal, inspired by a misunderstanding. Zhou was in fact answering a question about the wave of "revolutionary" student protests in Paris in 1968. As a veteran diplomat, naturally circumspect about pronouncing on recent events, he withheld his verdict.

As, perhaps, it would be wise to do about China's own chances of pursuing its revolution to a successful conclusion.

CONCLUSION:
CHINA BEYOND THE PARTY

MOST OF CHENGDU'S 4 MILLION PEOPLE HAD TAKEN bedding from their flats and were camping out, in parks and along the banks of the city's two rivers, after being warned of a fierce aftershock. A few days before – on 12 May 2008 – a terrible earthquake had killed 68,000 in the nearby mountains. They were cosseting their dogs, playing cards or Chinese chess or the two-stringed *erhu*, chatting to neighbours, eating peppery kebabs from roadside stalls.

Suddenly two young men emerged, marching at a fierce pace along the riverside path. The figure in front shouted out (in Chinese), "People of China! You have been sinful and selfish. And now even the earth is shaking in grief. Repent!" Behind him, his comrade swiftly followed: "Jesus Christ is the answer! Call on him and he will save you." And again, over and over, first one voice and then the other. In the disaster zone of Sichuan, of which Chengdu is the capital, there was a whiff of the apocalypse around.

In China more generally these days, there is change in the air, a sense of new and surprising possibilities, even of salvation. The artist and writer Zhang Yihe said after the quake, "The disaster is providing redemption to the government and the people: those in power are learning to be humane, and the Chinese people are learning to be compassionate." China's response to the quake attracted worldwide admiration for its openness and humanity. The contrast with Burma's handling of Cyclone Nargis, and even with the USA's response to Hurricane Katrina, was marked. Could compassion and generosity become integral features of China's public face?

When the quake happened, Premier Wen Jiabao – a former geologist – had just arrived back in Beijing from a visit to Henan. Before he reached home, he turned around and flew right back to take personal charge of the rescue operations, becoming so ubiquitous that he was widely dubbed "China's grandpa." People could relate to this human face of government, weeping, stumbling, kissing children, in the thick of it.

The barriers usually so carefully erected to media access were never put in place. Instead of simply reprinting stories from Xinhua or rebroadcasting from China Central TV, China's domestic media could and did plunge in themselves, filing extraordinary stories of heroism and harrowing tragedy. The foreign media, often treated with suspicion and circumscribed, were free to go everywhere and tell the world what was happening.

Unprecedented numbers of volunteers joined in the relief effort alongside the soldiers and fire fighters. About 100,000 travelled from all over the country to Sichuan, many of them young people. And another first: in responding to the Sichuan quake, China officially mourned the loss of *laobaixing* – ordinary people. The entire nation stopped for three minutes' silence a week after the quake. The event opened the door to the public expression of personal emotion, as did Princess Diana's death for many Britons. It showed the nation and the wider world what could be achieved when government and people worked together.

Yet the party remains a jealous institution, reluctant to operate in genuine partnership with individuals or organisations it does not control. After sixty years in power, the CCP's impact on the national culture has been immense. It pervades public space, both physically and virtually. But private life, family life, meetings between friends – these are distinctly different: they are warmer, freer, more argumentative. This final chapter presents a China beyond the party, reminding us that China is bigger than the People's Republic.

In 2011 in Foshan, southern China, a two-year-old girl was hit by two vans while walking alone in a market. Eighteen people walked past without helping and she eventually bled to death. Within days, CCTV footage of the incident was watched by more than a million people.

Liu Shinan, the assistant editor-in-chief of *China Daily*, said, "Everybody in China knows why" people don't help strangers in the street. "It is the result of the many cases in the past where the helper has been accused by the beneficiary, or the beneficiary's family, of being responsible for the accident." In another notorious case, a young man, Peng Yu, helped an elderly woman who had fallen down in Nanjing. She later said Peng had pushed her over. The court found for the woman and ordered Peng to pay some of her costs, arguing that he would not have stopped to help her if he had not been to blame. In Rugao, a bus driver pulled over when he saw an 81-year-old woman lying on the ground near her overturned tricycle. With his help, she recovered sufficiently to tell police that the man's bus had knocked her over. Fortunately for the driver, the bus was fitted with a camera and the police released him after viewing the film. When this case hit the national news, sales of such cameras went through the roof.

Kindness is still common in China. But people are extraordinarily wary of how they behave in public spaces, for they are accountable to the authorities to an extreme degree. There are signs, however, that society may be moving in a new direction.

Take He Xiao-ying, a waitress in a Chengdu tea-house.

"I don't have much education," she says. But after the 2008 Sichuan earthquake, she was determined to do something to help and volunteered to be an aide at the West China Hospital. When I met her in the days after the quake, she was wearing an "I [heart] China" T-shirt and a bright yellow smiley face badge, to which she clipped her identification card. She helped survivors to go to the bathroom; she propped them up in bed and hung up their drips; she listened to their stories.

Her husband stayed at home, looking after their four-year-old daughter. She comes from Mianyang county, to the north of Chengdu, the scene of much devastation. But her relatives all survived. She had never volunteered like this before, she says, "But our home place is suffering so much, I had to do something. And my time in this hospital will leave me a beautiful memory."

Over 100,000 volunteers joined the relief effort. In the mountainous Sichuan countryside I encountered half a dozen friends from Beijing. Steering their three brand-new four-wheel-drives to the side of the rock-strewn road to allow a PLA mobile generator and a fire brigade rescue truck to chug past, they waved cheerfully at their new comrades. Unlikely as it would have sounded a few days before, they were working side by side, engaged together in public service. Members of the Beijing SUV Club, these volunteers had raised funds to pack their vehicles with supplies (medicine, clothing, food), taken leave from their jobs and driven the 1600 kilometres to the quake area in just twenty-three hours. They carried red and yellow banners to show their solidarity with the victims; Chinese flags covered their clothing and fluttered from their cars. They were edging their way, as dusk approached, through the worst hit town of all, the ground zero city of Beichuan, heading for more remote villages in the mountains beyond.

The response to the Sichuan quake – the flood of volunteers, a New People's Army – took everyone by surprise: the government, the NGOs, the volunteers themselves. No one coordinated it. It was a spontaneous response, especially by twenty-somethings, members of a generation that has been widely criticised for caring only about making money and having fun. A generation in the USA still weighs its worth, to a degree, by whether it attended the Woodstock festival in 1969, or joined demonstrations against the war in Vietnam. In 2048, older Chinese will be comparing notes about what they did during the great quake of '08.

The roads from Chengdu up to the mountainous areas near the epi-centre of the quake were full of volunteers' vehicles, decked out with bright banners declaring solidarity: "Sichuan people, hold on"; "China, let's go." These cars were waved through the toll gates. The Jiuzhou stadium on the edge of Mianyang became the biggest refugee camp in the region, housing about 30,000 people. It was a heartbreaking scene. People of all ages slept on concrete under the stands. Volunteers who had driven 2500 kilometres from Guangdong handed out bread they had bought on the way. Workers from a local fast-food chicken shop distributed free rice and chicken soup. Health workers dressed injuries and dispensed medicines. Hairdressers from a local beauty salon offered haircuts. And staff from the psychology department of the South-West China University in Chongqing provided counselling.

Dr Liu Yan-ling had been there for a week, listening to harrowing stories. She and her team of volunteers set up a wall on which people could stick messages of sympathy or hope. The aim was to help people articulate their feelings and come to terms with them. There were thousands of notes and drawings, many on the heart-shaped paper provided by Liu's team: "My darling brother Gan, I hope you have a smooth ride to heaven"; "Teacher, I miss you"; "All this will pass, tomorrow will be better"; "I'm feeling happy, I have a book to read now."

At one of the few late-night restaurants in Chengdu, a carload of young men arrived in uniforms bearing the logo of the China Red Cross.

It was midnight and these volunteers had clearly just returned, grimy and hungry, from a long day at the quake zone. The other diners burst into spontaneous applause. The New People's Army was taking its bow.

★

The generous response to the 2008 earthquake was not a one-off. As the country has prospered and a new wealthy class has emerged, private groups and individuals have started to fill the yawning gaps in public welfare. The country now has thousands of non-government organisations. They are reluctantly tolerated by a ruling party that remains intensely suspicious of potential rivals. It is possible to gain government approval for philanthropic activities – but only if the government knows pretty well what the group is doing, and agrees with it. There is no right of free association in China.

The government, however, is starting to make more use of local NGOs – provided they have no suspect links with overseas counterparts or foreign governments. NGOs are increasingly receiving state funding to help provide social services. In many areas there is no government machinery to deliver, say, meals to elderly people living alone. Local governments are turning to NGOs to fill the gap. All over China, private philanthropists are stepping in where the party-state has failed.

When Gao Feng was nine, he came home from his village school in Sha'anxi, in China's heartland, to discover his mother was gone. He cooked himself some rice, cried himself to sleep and went back to school the next day. After a week, a distant relative arrived and told him his mother had been arrested in a fight over land and jailed for six years. Gao had never known his father. He was taken to a remote mountain village and set to work looking after livestock, carrying water and scavenging lumps of coal. He ate only leftovers.

Can this be the same country where millions of millionaires now live? Charles Dickens provides more insight into Gao's world than any of the "how to make money in China" tomes that cram the business sections of bookstores. Dickens's England was undergoing a similar wrenching transformation, experiencing – like contemporary China – the best of times and the worst of times. His novels capture the opportunity, the pain, the excitement and the dislocations of such rapid social and economic change. And like Britain 150 years ago, China today is racing from rural to urban, from farm to factory, from extended family to nuclear family, from a pristine environment to palls of pollution. Oliver Twist, meet Gao Feng.

I meet Gao in a children's home in the countryside in Sha'anxi province, not far from where the terracotta warriors were discovered. A photograph is stuck to the canteen wall. It shows two girls clinging tearfully to their father, who is about to go on a long journey – the longest – to his execution by a bullet to the head. His crime: murdering his wife. The girls were left to their own devices, to beg, to find compassionate relatives, or to starve.

Zhang Shuqin, fifty-eight, is the home's founder and director. She was sent to work in the countryside during the Cultural Revolution, then became a "barefoot doctor" before joining the police. She was seconded to work with the prison service, editing its magazine. In her interviews with prisoners, one theme dominated: what would become of their children? A mother herself, Zhang felt particular empathy for the female prisoners. "Many of them had given up on their own lives, but still had hope for their children," she says.

Zhang visited the city government's legal and social departments and found that no one was responsible for doing anything for the children of inmates. When the police arrested a parent, they simply left the child or children (in rural areas, where more than one child is allowed) home alone. "Many children walked a very long way on their own to wait outside the prison where their parent, usually their mother, was held," says Zhang. "Some stole money or food or clothes to give to their mothers." On arrival outside the jail, they were usually ignored. "Some died of disease or even starvation" while waiting forlornly to be reunited with their parent.

When Zhang proposed helping them, a common response was: why help the children of bad people, when the children of good people are also in need? But in 1996 she set up China's first home for the children of prisoners and executed criminals in a run-down house behind a market in Xi'an, the capital of Sha'anxi. She has received no financial support from the central government and only modest help from local governments. But local taxi drivers collect unsold food from restaurants and drop it round late at night. Police volunteer in their spare time. Judges have donated generously. Her first home so swiftly filled with children – brought by the police or by relatives, or arriving on their own – that Zhang planned a bigger one, in the countryside. She persuaded an entrepreneur to buy the land

and to help build houses and a canteen. He was a former prisoner himself – another Dickensian touch. Today, the homes are mostly kept afloat by donations and by selling crops the children grow themselves.

At the Sha'anxi home, children of twelve or thirteen receive a formal education for the first time, attending local schools alongside local children. "I think this is their right. We want them to melt into the mainstream of society and receive a normal education," says Zhang. Some have spent years as virtual slaves of distant relatives, cutting grass for pigs to eat or herding goats, says Zhang's deputy, Jin Chang. Some have survived on food scavenged from rubbish bins. One boy, nicknamed Black Bean, who came from a mountain village, had been brutally attacked, his wrist broken, when he arrived. He was four. "He didn't even know how to cry," says Jin, a retired teacher.

When the home first opened, local villagers donated supplies. "They soon understood that the children are not to blame for their parents' crimes," says Jin. "These children demand more compassion and patience. They've all had zigzag lives. They call many of us 'mama.'" The two girls who clung to their father in the photo are among them. So is Gao Feng, who has grown into a lanky fourteen-year-old when I meet him. Three years earlier – two years after his mother went to prison – the police came for him and delivered him to Zheng's centre; his mother had heard about the home and asked Zheng to track him down. "I felt quite strange at first," Gao says. "I only played by myself. But now everything's familiar." He visits his mother regularly. She will soon be out of prison. He is set on becoming an archaeologist. "I like old things. I found some ancient coins in a field once." He is in the right place, only a couple of hours' drive from the greatest unexcavated tomb in the world, that of the first emperor, Qin, who surrounded it with the famous terracotta warriors.

Zhang believes there are 600,000 children like Gao in China. Even now that she has opened five homes – two in Sha'anxi and others in Henan, Jiangxi and Beijing – she can only care for 700 children at a time. Her aim is to set up homes in all of China's thirty-one provinces, as a model for others to follow. But she fears that this will take too long, given the desperate present need. She has therefore developed a second set of aims, for broader, nationwide reform. She has allied with the All China Women's Federation, a powerful, party-controlled organisation, to campaign. She has conducted research and provided the results to the relevant government departments. She now wants, above all, to influence party policy, and has started to receive the media coverage and official recognition that might make such lobbying possible.

Zhang is not alone. China is full of gutsy individuals – often women – who refuse to accept that some of their country's 1.3 billion people can simply be left behind. China has had commendable success in hauling hundreds of millions out of abject poverty. But the party, ever insecure, is reluctant to cede authority to others to operate charities, even in the face of enormous need and of its own failure to provide for those on the margins. Individuals such as Zhang have broken through this institutional anxiety, however, chiefly by working so transparently and with such evident love that they have won public and official approval.

Another is Han Rufen, a retired teacher known to her pupils as "Granny Han." When her seven-year-old grandson was due to start school, the headmaster of the only local school (where Han had herself been a teacher) refused to enroll the boy, whose IQ had been measured at just 39. Although the school ran a class for mentally challenged children, it was "meaningless to educate such a child," the headmaster said. When Han's daughter-in-law persisted, the headmaster responded testily, "Why should you give birth to such a fool in the first place? If your mother-in-law is so capable, let her teach him." Han resolved to do just that. But she got nowhere with the boy.

A friend, a psychologist, visited from Beijing and recommended an expert in the field. Han used her savings to take a correspondence course with him. She then consulted a nearby children's hospital, which gave her a list of thirty local children with a similar disability. Han visited their homes. In several cases, she found the front door unlocked and the child inside, tied to a table or chair while the parents were at work. With the support of half a dozen or so of these families, Han set up a tiny special school, funded by the parents themselves.

When the number of students began to outgrow her modest resources, somebody suggested Han contact a local church-based charity. Through the church, contact was made with UNESCO and with a larger church in Beijing. Funding was found to train some teachers in Hong Kong. The school was extended, new classrooms built and equipment purchased. When a local official came to inspect it, he pronounced it too good for such children and threatened to redesignate it to the city's regular school system.

A supporter of Han, an American-Chinese woman who had lived in China for many years, witnessed this row. On the train home to Beijing, she expressed her chagrin to a fellow passenger. "I can do something about that," he said, and picked up his mobile phone. He was the deputy mayor. The school was saved and is now a model for others, attracting visitors from other parts of China. Today, Han's "fool" of a grandson is working in a factory and living in his own flat.

The party's unwritten contract with the Chinese people is based on its ability to provide rising living standards. But as the country grows and inequality deepens, are the party's core institutions up to the job? Will it need either to allow a greater role for non-state actors, or to revive the old cradle-to-grave dependence on the state, with the vast costs such a system involves? For now, most Chinese people seem content that life is – or holds out the promise of being – better. They have never enjoyed any capacity to influence governments, and few expect to do so. But still, there is that distant thunder, the rumble of dissent and dislocation. Are the party's institutions ready to deal with demands for change?

Such calls are not yet being voiced loudly. But the rapid support received by Charter '08, the emergence of private philanthropists in response to the yawning welfare gaps, the popular enthusiasm for volunteering – all suggest that the new leadership group will one day have to decide whether, and if so how far, the party is willing to concede civic space, just as an earlier generation did with business space. As the party has permitted more commercial liberties, this freedom has come to be seen not so much as a favour as a right. This is new ground in China; although the constitution guarantees many rights in theory, in practice they have been so circum-scribed by regulations and caveats that – especially in the absence of independent courts – they have tended to seem like gifts handed down from on high, readily withdrawn again. But the freedom to conduct busi-ness, exercised daily by many millions of people, is now all but impossible to take back. And the bounds of this freedom have gradually expanded, from the right to own private property, to the right to start a small busi-ness, to the right to private personal expression – although still not to disseminate those personal views widely.

Since the Sichuan quake, the right to engage in private charity work has also begun to be reclaimed. Without putting them into words, the volunteers articulated their demands with their actions: we no longer view the party and its People's Liberation Army as sufficient proxies for us – we want to be actors too.

★

In the cultural sphere, too, there is activity beyond the party. Just a few years ago, the only people nationally known in China were a handful of politicians and "model workers" relentlessly feted by the state media. How times have changed. Today, thanks to television and the internet, celebrities are emerging who have not been carefully screened and promoted by the party.

The Paris Hilton of China, Yang Erche Namu, was born in 1966 in the foothills of the Himalayas in Yunnan province. She is a member of the Mosuo, a matrilineal society of 40,000 whose women can and often do take multiple male partners. Reinventing herself every few months, she has been a singer, a writer of fourteen autobiographical books, a producer of live stage shows, a notoriously controversial judge on the *Super Boys* TV talent quest, a model, a fashion designer and a confessional blogger. She travelled with Michael Palin as his on-camera guide in his TV series *Himalaya*.

She is disarmingly egotistical: "I am half Mother Teresa, half Madonna," she says in a practised manner as she tucks into a plate of *gong bao* chicken in a Taiwanese café in Beijing, her personal assistant hovering anxiously nearby. Growing up, she tells me, her family had no mirror. The first time she saw herself was in her reflection in Lake Lugu. She was so stunned by her own beauty that, like Narcissus, she fell into the water and nearly drowned. She has recently built a house in her home village. "Since I'm the princess, I call it Namu Palace."

"I always wanted to be famous, to be a celebrity," she says. "It's convenient. I get lots of beautiful things. I get a better discount in stores. I go to the front of the line in banks. I get the best table in restaurants. Some celebrities say they hate to have their photos taken, just to make themselves seem cool. That's bullshit. The people who take your photo make you famous. But you do also pay a price." She once dozed off waiting for a flight in the first-class lounge at an airport – she constantly flies between her homes in Beijing, Shanghai, Chengdu and Yunnan – and opened her eyes to find "twenty mobile phones almost in my face, waiting to photograph me the moment I awoke. They have absolutely no shame," she says delightedly.

Cheng Li, a former lifestyle magazine editor and now China's leading food photographer, says that "even with a tight censorship system, the internet still gives everyone the possibility of becoming a journalist. Everyone can be the source of tabloid news about celebrities, and this really heightens interest. But because the threshold is quite low, people disappear from the celebrity ranks very quickly too." This world of instant, often short-lived fame might seem far removed from the political sphere. Pop singers and movie stars are regularly invited to the White House and to 10 Downing Street; the same cannot be said of the Great Hall of the People. (Celebrity business people are another matter. They are often depicted as heroic figures and invited to announce big investments or philanthropic efforts alongside politicians.) But as these celebrities gain national and international attention, the world is encountering Chinese people who are neither politicians nor officials. Chinese and foreign audiences are seeing more of life beyond the dictates of the party.

One figure who has managed to live beyond the establishment while maintaining a devoted fanbase for many years is the iconic rock star Cui Jian. In 1989 he stood in Tiananmen Square, tied a red bandana over his eyes, gripped his guitar and sang a song that remains the great anthem of Chinese rock music. "*I keep asking endlessly,*" he sang – in Chinese of course – "*when you will go with me / but you just laugh at me / I've nothing to my name. / I'll give you my dreams, / and give you my freedom. / But you just laugh at me. / I've nothing to my name.*"

Cui was then aged twenty-seven. Since then, official tolerance of him has waxed and waned; relations have mostly stayed on the frosty side. However, his status as China's pre-eminent charismatic rocker has not wavered, nor has his capacity to draw crowds when he is permitted to perform. His father was a professional jazz trumpeter and his mother was a member of a dance troupe; Cui himself joined the Beijing Philharmonic Orchestra as a trumpeter at age twenty. Although he does not see himself as strongly influenced by the West – he had no rock 'n' roll education, for instance – he shares what he sees as the questioning disposition of Western culture. He describes his music as China's "third sound," the first being officially produced music ("unchanging for sixty years, very political") and the second mainstream Canto-pop, in which "looking good and making money are what counts." The "third sound" is more individual, Cui says. "It doesn't matter too much whether the market likes it or not."

Rock music is at a low ebb in China today, he says. "Not so many people trust it or believe it can really change their lives, especially students. They believe in education and in jobs for the future. They don't feel they need fresh ideas any more." When he is invited to perform on college campuses, the authorities are often nervous. They "think it's hard to control rock 'n' roll, that the music makes trouble, so they have often banned it."

The relationship between high-profile Chinese artists and the authorities is often complicated. Ai Weiwei, bearded and bear-like, is both unique and one of a Chinese type: laconically witty; unbowed despite being famously spirited away and held without charge for eighty-one days in 2011; curious about everything and impeccably polite. He has worked in many artistic media, perhaps most famously collaborating with the Swiss architects Herzog & de Meuron to design the "Bird's Nest" Olympic stadium. How does he describe himself, I asked him on a visit to his extraordinary blank-walled compound in north-east Beijing. He casts around in English: "Maybe a confused man. Sometimes withdrawn. Sometimes angry ... I've been called many, many titles, and I practise in many fields. But I've not grown used to any of them. If you're asking about my profession, yes, I'm an artist. That's best, it leaves little to explain. Art today is about attitude and lifestyle. The rest follows."

Ai inherited his quiet curiosity from his father, Ai Qing, one of China's most famous poets. Ai Qing's poetry is widely read in China today, but he died before his son had ever heard his poems read aloud. "He was an enemy of the state. His poetry was forbidden and burned by the whole nation." Ai Weiwei's favourite poem of his father's starts: "Snow falls on China's land / Cold blockades China ..." Former Premier Wen Jiabao also liked to quote from Ai Qing, especially the couplet: "Why are my eyes always brimming with tears? / It is because my love for this land is so deep ..."

Ai says: "We knew our father was famous and influential, but anti-revolutionary. He had to do hard labour and admit his crime. They accused him and beat him and forced him to say what he had done wrong. So there's no glamour for me" in dissidence. Life improved for the family under Deng Xiaoping, and Ai attended the film academy in Beijing alongside superstar directors Chen Kaige and Zhang Yimou. Ai was himself catapulted into public life when he joined the "Stars" group of avant-garde artists who exhibited their work in 1979, just as economic – but not political or artistic – freedom was increasing. This group believed every artist was a star, emphasising individuality over group identity. Deng's government, however, was unresponsive to calls for greater freedom of expression; its focus was firmly on economic development, "just repeating that we needed a richer, more modern nation," Ai recalls. "I was completely disillusioned and just wanted to escape to any place possible."

He went to the USA, first to Philadelphia and then to New York, where he attended the Parsons School for Design. He didn't have much contact with American artists, however. "I was just one of the people going to galleries, hanging around." And working just to survive. He did house cleaning, babysitting, carpentry, framing and printing. "But I never had a steady job." When Ai's father became ill, he returned to Beijing. "I was disappointed in China. People had told me it was changing so much. To me, it wasn't. Just some surface change. The system was still there."

Ai is saddened by the official neglect of contemporary culture. The US$20 billion makeover of Beijing incorporated almost no new art. "The new airport," he says disappointedly, "has so many walls ..." The cadres who commission such buildings have no interest in art, he says. "And they have total power. They can spend money like emperors." It is hard to say what will emerge from the bustling Chinese art scene in the long-term, he says. "There's a lot of energy and passion. What is going to come out of this boom? A new message? We still don't know."

His mobile phone proves too insistent to ignore. Ai nods dutifully, and nods again. It's his mother. Look after your health. And don't get into any more trouble by speaking to foreign journalists. He sighs and continues talking.

Artists like Ai and Cui have found ways to express themselves while living alongside the party, albeit uneasily at times. Today, many people are carving out a space beyond the party online. Humour plays an important role here; the Chinese web is a very funny place to visit, full of satire despite the efforts of the stentorian net police. When the pop star Michael Jackson died, Chinese internet users assembled a brilliantly funny montage of Cultural Revolution-era People's Liberation Army films to the soundtrack of his song "Beat It." Another video shows Adolf Hitler fulminating against the sins of Chinese microbloggers. An especially crazy stream of inventive mockery followed the discovery, in 2011, of something fishy on the official website of Huili county in Sichuan province. The netizen who spotted the blunder explained: "I had nothing to do today so I visited the website for our county government. The headline story was about the upgrade for the road to the countryside. I looked at the photo and I almost coughed out half a litre of blood! Even a rank amateur like myself can tell that this was a Photoshop job, and they had the nerve to put this on the home page!"

The photo showed three officials pointing at a new road in apparent pride. Only they appeared to be floating above the road as if arriving from space. It seemed they hadn't really left their comfortable offices, preferring to have an image mocked up. Within hours the net was flooded with images of the same officials: in Africa admiring lions and giraffes; on the moon; leering at scantily clad women; watching the operation to kill Osama bin Laden alongside Barack Obama; and greeting the recently deceased North Korean leader Kim Jong-il, who may indeed now be hovering, like them, in some workers' party nirvana.

Foreigners often assume that China is a single entity. They speak of "eating Chinese" as if Chinese food comprised a few famous dishes, usually all from the south. In fact, the phrase "Chinese food" makes sense only in the way that "European food" does. Even China's languages are spectacularly disparate. English has more in common with Italian than Mandarin (with its four tones) has with Cantonese (with its superhuman nine). China has maintained the longest uninterrupted civilisation in the world, but it is also a country of great variation and fierce individualism.

On a recent visit to Beijing, I met, on the far outskirts of the city, Zhou Duo, a famous figure from the 1989 demonstrations. Before Tiananmen, he was well known as a pioneering success story, one of the first to reap the rewards of the opening-up of the economy. He was a founder of China's first big successful IT firm, Stone. Since 1989, however, he has not been able to obtain regular paid work; he has been put into an official deep-freeze. He refuses to go into exile, preferring to live in a starkly stylish home on the rural fringe, funded by his wife's work in Beijing TV and by gifts from supporters. These days, he mostly keeps his thoughts to himself.

In their basement, Zhou and his wife have installed a substantial home theatre, where Zhou insisted on showing me Tim Burton's typically eccentric adaptation of *Alice in Wonderland*.

"That is China," Zhou said enigmatically when it ended. Curiouser and curiouser.

ACKNOWLEDGEMENTS

I AM WELL AWARE THAT FOR ALMOST EVERYTHING THAT IS TRUE about China in one place at one time, the opposite holds true at another time, another place, and I must concede that on such a vast topic others hold different and contrasting views. But the core of my book comes from boundlessly interesting and sincere – and often extraordinarily brave – Chinese people I have met. Their understanding of how their nation is ruled – often reflected in the choices that have determined their life paths – contains an unmistakable kernel of truth. My interviewees merit my deepest thanks.

I must also acknowledge the immense debts I owe to my guides over many years into the entrancing and sometimes troubling world that is China. They include – although I cannot list them all – Geremie Barmé, Tom Bartlett, Jean-Pierre Cabestan, Chia Yen-on, David Chu, Antonia Finnane, John Fitzgerald, Graham Fletcher, Paul French, Paul Glasson, David Goodman, He Baogang, Bruce Jacobs, Philippa Jones, Stephen Joske, David Kelly, David Lague, Martin Mertz, Paul Mooney, Alistair Nicholas, Jane Pan, Richard Rigby, Ted Rule, Ed Smith, Harry Sung, Richard Tsiang, Tony Voutas, Michael Wadley, Shelley Warner, Steve Waters, Verna Yu, and last but far from least Zhang Yufei, without whom this book would not have been conceivable.

I wish to thank my editor in chief at the *Australian*, Chris Mitchell, for his constant support, my friend Peter Browne for expert advice at a crucial stage, and especially the team at Black Inc. – including publisher Chris Feik and editor Denise O'Dea – for their extraordinary patience and professionalism.

And I thank my family: my wife Jan McCallum and my children Rose and Christian, for tolerating the constraints and the chaos that have come with living not only with me, but also with this book for the last few years.

ENDNOTES

INTRODUCTION

xxii: "the first Darwinian-Leninist party in history …" N. Bequelin, "The Limits of the Party's Adaptation," *Far Eastern Economic Review,* Vol. 172, Iss. 10, December 2009.

xxii: "The East Is Rich …" G.R. Barmé, "Olympic Art and Artifice," *The American Interest*, July/August 2008.

CHAPTER 2: CADRE SCHOOL

19:     "Terry Woronov …" T.E. Woronov, "Performing the Nation: China's Children as Little Red Pioneers," *Anthropological Quarterly*, Vol. 80, No. 3, Summer 2007.

20:     "Antonia Finnane …" A. Finnane, "'Asianising' Education: The China Option?" *Inside Story*, 26 March 2012.

20:     "'Today's Communist Party is a highly developed bureaucracy …'" A. Nathan quoted by E. Bumiller, "Sometimes a Book Is Indeed Just a Book. But When?", *New York Times*, 23 January 2006.

29:     "The notes were spotted by *China Digital Times* …" "Developing a New Understanding of the Communist Party at a Party School," *China Digital Times*, 17 January 2011. Translated by D. Weinland.

CHAPTER 3: HOW THE PARTY RULES

39:     "Cheng Li …" See for example Cheng L., "The Powerful Factions among China's Rulers," *BBC News*, 6 November 2012.

CHAPTER 4: THE ENFORCERS

48:     "Jerome Cohen … " Conversation with the author, 14 July 2009. See also J. Cohen, *The Criminal Process in the People's Republic of China, 1949–1963: An Introduction* (Cambridge, Massachusetts: Harvard University Press, 1968).

49:     "Klaus Mülhahn …" K. Mülhahn, *Criminal Justice in China: A History* (Cambridge, Massachusetts: Harvard University Press, 2009), p. 40.

51: "Randall Peerenboom writes ..." R. Peerenboom, *China's Long March Toward Rule of Law* (Cambridge, UK: Cambridge University Press, 2002), p. 6.

52: "Willy Lam ..." W. Lam, "The Politicisation of China's Law Enforcement and Judicial Apparatus," *China Perspectives*, No. 2, 2009.

57: "A century ago, writes Mülhahn..." Mülhahn, *Criminal Justice in China*, pp. 68–69.

57: "Jerome Cohen commented ..." Conversation with the author, 31 August 2011.

CHAPTER 5: THE MEDIA AND THE MESSAGE

67: "He writes under the pen name Shinjankancai ..." Excerpt from his blog, published 18 October 2008. Translated by Fan L. of *China Digital Times* at the University of California, Berkeley.

70: "In early 2010 the International Federation of Journalists published a report ..." *China Clings to Control: Press Freedom in 2009* (International Federation of Journalists, 2009).

74: "In 2010, Google was only expected ..." Note issued by I. Khan of JP Morgan, 12 January 2010. See D. Frommer, "Google's China Exposure," *Business Insider*, 12 January 2010.

CHAPTER 6: ART AND CULTURE

81: "They are avid consumers of mass media ..." Nielsen estimated that the US television audience in 2008–09 reached about 290 million. CCTV's own research states that more than 90 per cent of Chinese families watch the Spring Festival Gala every year on television.

CHAPTER 7: CONTROLLING LEGENDS

101: "The historian Jonathan Spence explains ..." J.D. Spence, *The Search for Modern China* (New York: W.W. Norton, 1990), p. 263.

103: "Frank Dikötter ..." F. Dikotter, *The Age of Openness: China Before Mao* (Berkeley and Los Angeles: University of California Press, 2008).

104: "Sheila Melvin ..." S. Melvin, *The Little Red Book of China Business* (Naperville: Sourcebooks, 2007), p. 5.

CHAPTER 8: CONFUCIUS'S COMEBACK

117: "Pierre Ryckmans ..." *The Analects of Confucius*, translation and notes by S. Leys (New York: W.W. Norton, 1997), p. xvi.

118: "An official broadcast from Beijing in 1974 ..." First cited in English by the Hong Kong-based journalist L. Mathews in the *Pittsburgh Press*, 22 January 1978.

121: "writes David Kelly ..." D. Kelly, "How China Stands Up: The Critique of Chinese Historicism," paper presented to the Association of Asian Studies annual conference, Honolulu, April 2011.

121: "Belief in universal values has faded ..." Xu J., "Universal Civilization or Chinese Values?", *Kaifang*, 4 June 2010.

122: "Richard Komaiko, writing in the *Asia Times* ..." R. Komaiko, "Hitler and the Chinese Internet Generation," *Asia Times*, 25 May 2011.

122: "In 2008 Song Hongbing's book ..." S. Hongbing, *The Currency War* (Beijing: Citic Publishing House, 2007). Transated by R. Callick.

122: "Mark Lilla, a professor of the humanities ..." M. Lilla, "Reading Strauss in Beijing: China's Strange Taste in Western Philosophers," *New Republic*, 17 December 2010.

CHAPTER 9: DOING BUSINESS

126: "Yasheng Huang, professor of political economy ..." Y. Huang, *Capitalism with Chinese Characteristics* (Cambridge, UK: Cambridge University Press, 2008).

139: "Xia himself has a cameo in Friedman's book ..." T. Friedman, *The World Is Flat* (New York: Farrar, Straus & Giroux, 2005), p. 34.

143: "Carl Walter and Fraser Howie ...": C. Walter and F. Howie, *Red Capitalism: The Fragile Financial Foundation of China's Extraordinary Rise* (Chichester: Wiley, 2011).

147: "in a report produced jointly in 2012 ...": *China 2030: Building a Modern, Harmonious, and Creative High-Income Society* (Washington, DC: The World Bank, 2012).

CHAPTER 10: MEET THE LEADERS

152: "It remains the only dedicated biography of Hu ..." Ma L., *Hu Jintao xin zhuan* (Hong Kong: Ming Pao Press, 2006).

154: "At Chinese New Year in 2010 ..." W. Clem, "Xi Sends SMS to 'Dear Comrades,'" *South China Morning Post*, 7 January 2010.

154: "Kerry Brown ..." K. Brown, "The Insider," *Foreign Policy*, 13 February 2012.

159: "Cheng Li writes in *Asia Policy* ..." Cheng L., "China's Fifth Generation: Is Diversity a Source of Strength or of Weakness?", *Asia Policy*, No. 6, July 2008.

159: "David Barboza ..." D. Barboza, "Billions in Hidden Riches for Family of Chinese Leader," *New York Times*, 25 October 2012.

160: "Willy Lam, a leading expert ..." W. Lam, *Changing of the Guard: Beijing Grooms Sixth-Generation Cadres for 2020s* (Washington, DC: Jamestown Foundation, 1 September 2010).

161: "Cheng Li has written in *Asia Policy* ..." Cheng L., "China's Fifth Generation ..."

163: "A widely disseminated report ..." *A Research Report on Social Progress for 2011* from the Social Development Task Group of the Sociology Department at Qinghua University, 9 January 2012.

CHAPTER 11: LIFE AT THE TOP

170: "Richard McGregor ..." R. McGregor, *The Party: The Secret World of China's Communist Rulers* (London: Allen Lane, 2010), pp. 8–10.

174: "Wang says the size of this secret wealth ..." Wang X., *Analysing Chinese Grey Income*, a report for Credit Suisse, 6 August 2010.

176: "David Goodman ..." D. Goodman, *The New Rich in China: Future Rulers, Present Lives* (London: Routledge, 2008), p. 37.

177: "The Asian Development Bank has described China as having one of the biggest wealth gaps in the world today ..." "China's Income Gap Asia's Fastest Growing, ADB Says," *Caixing Online*, 29 October 2012.

CHAPTER 12: DISSENT AND REFORM

189: "Anne-Marie Brady ..." A. Brady, "The Velvet Fist in the Velvet Glove: New Approaches to Social and Political Control in China," lecture presented at the University of Technology, Sydney, 18 April 2012. See also A. Brady, *China's Thought Management* (London: Routledge, 2011) and A. Brady, *Marketing Dictatorship: Propaganda and Thought Work in Contemporary China* (Lanham: Rowan and Littlefield, 2008).

190: "As Carl Walter and Fraser Howie write ..." C. Walter and F. Howie, *Red Capitalism*, p. 86.

193: "resilient authoritarianism ..." A. Nathan, "Authoritarian Resilience," *Journal of Democracy*, Vol. 14, No. 1, January 2003.

193: "atrophy and adaptation ..." D. Shambaugh, *China's Communist Party: Atrophy and Adaptation* (Berkeley and Los Angeles: University of California Press, 2008).

CHAPTER 13: IS THE FUTURE THEIRS?

197: "A McKinsey report says that in 2025 ..." J. Woetzel et. al., *Preparing for China's Urban Billion* (McKinsey Global Institute, February 2009).

197: "the fascination is not new ..." J. Spence, *The Chan's Great Continent: China in Western Minds* (New York: W.W. Norton, 1988).

198: "Almost half of Chinese people say they cannot afford a visit to the doctor." The Chinese Red Cross Foundation stated on its website in December 2012 that "There are 450 million farmers in China who cannot afford to get hospital medical treatment. Disease has become one of the most significant reasons for poverty among Chinese farmers in the countryside." See http://en.crcf.org.cn.

198: "Two Americans, John and Doris Naisbitt ..." See their website http://www.naisbitt.com/bibliography/chinas-megatrends.html.

198: "The American Maoist Scott Nearing wrote admiringly ..." Cited by D. Caute, *Fellow Travellers: Intellectual Friends of Communism* (New Haven, Connecticut: Yale University Press, 1973; revised edition 1988), p. 378.

198: "Another admirer of Mao, Arthur Galston ..." A. Galston, *Daily Life in People's China* (New York: Thomas Y. Crowell Co., 1973), p. 164.

199: "'Western ideologues now use Maoist China ...'" S. Leys, *Chinese Shadows* (New York: Viking Press, 1977), p. 201.

200: "The World Bank is just one of the international institutions ..." A. Gat, "The Return of Authoritarian Great Powers," *Foreign Affairs*, July/August 2007.

200: "Randall Peerenboom, in his 2007 book ..." R. Peerenboom, *China Modernizes: Threat to the West or Model for the Rest?* (Oxford: Oxford University Press, 2007), p. 9.

FURTHER READING

Confucius. *The Analects of Confucius*. Translation and notes by Simon Leys. New York: W.W. Norton, 1997.

Dikötter, Frank. *The Age of Openness: China before Mao*. Berkeley: University of California Press, 2008.

Garnaut, John. *The Rise and Fall of the House of Bo*. Melbourne: Penguin, 2012.

Jenner, W.J.F. *The Tyranny of History: The Roots of China's Crisis*. London: Penguin, 1994.

Leys, Simon. *Chinese Shadows*. London: Penguin, 1978.

Li Zhisui *The Private Life of Chairman Mao*. New York: Random House, 1996.

Lieberthal, Kenneth. *Governing China: From Revolution through Reform*. New York: W.W. Norton, 2004.

McGregor, Richard. *The Party: The Secret World of China's Communist Rulers*. London: Allen Lane, 2010.

Rittenberg, Sidney and Amanda Bennett. *The Man Who Stayed Behind*. Durham, NC: Duke University Press, 2004.

Shambaugh, David. *China's Communist Party: Atrophy and Adaptation*. Washington, DC: Woodrow Wilson Center Press, 2008.

Spence, Jonathan. *The Search for Modern China*. New York: W.W. Norton, 2001.

Walter, Carl and Fraser Howie. *Red Capitalism: The Fragile Financial Foundation of China's Extraordinary Rise*. New York: Wiley, 2011.

Wasserstrom, Jeffrey N. *China in the 21st Century: What Everyone Needs to Know*. Oxford: Oxford University Press, 2010.

INDEX